PRIMROSE

Reaktion's Botanical series is the first of its kind, integrating horticultural and botanical writing with a broader account of the cultural and social impact of trees, plants and flowers.

Published

Apple Marcia Reiss
Bamboo Susanne Lucas
Birch Anna Lewington
Cactus Dan Torre
Cannabis Chris Duvall
Carnation Twigs Way
Geranium Kasia Boddy
Grasses Stephen A. Harris
Lily Marcia Reiss
Oak Peter Young
Palm Fred Gray
Pine Laura Mason
Poppy Andrew Lack
Primrose Elizabeth Lawson
Rhododendron Richard Milne
Rose Catherine Horwood
Snowdrop Gail Harland
Sunflowers Stephen A. Harris
Tulip Celia Fisher
Weeds Nina Edwards
Willow Alison Syme
Yew Fred Hageneder

PRIMROSE

Elizabeth Lawson

REAKTION BOOKS

For primroses, primrose lovers and
the Lawson-Whalen-Fernandez-Hillman-Shelbred-Slattery family

Published by
REAKTION BOOKS LTD
Unit 32, Waterside
44–48 Wharf Road
London N1 7UX, UK

www.reaktionbooks.co.uk

First published 2019

Printed and bound in China by 1010 Printing International Ltd

A catalogue record for this book is available from the British Library

ISBN 978 1 78914 077 4

Contents

The common primrose (*Primula vulgaris*) growing wild in Cornwall.

Introduction:
The Primrose Path

> Do not, as some ungracious pastors do,
> Show me the steep and thorny way to heaven,
> Whiles, like a puffed and reckless libertine,
> Himself the primrose path of dalliance treads,
> And recks not his own rede.
>
> WILLIAM SHAKESPEARE, Hamlet

Shakespeare's phrase 'the primrose path' has been repeated often, and in a wide variety of contexts, in the 400 years since *Hamlet* appeared.[1] In some ways it has defined our relationship with primroses, both literally and figuratively, suggesting as it does the complications of love. We see a mossy bank, perhaps above a meandering stream, where compact, earth-hugging plants, their wrinkled leaves a vibrant green, their flowers a haunting pale yellow, announce the fragile balancing point of the end of winter and the beginning of spring. It is a place where young couples might tryst when the weather improves. In the language of flowers, the primrose denotes lovers' fears and uncertainties.

Shakespeare's alliterative metaphor sprang from a long history of human connection with the common primrose (*Primula vulgaris*), and its relatives the cowslip (*P. veris*) and the oxlip (*P. elatior*), wild flowers distributed throughout Europe, Russia, Asia Minor, North Africa and the Middle East. In northern European mythology, the primrose was 'Freya's flower', Freya being the pagan virgin goddess of love, beauty, sex, fertility and spring. Later, when the Virgin Mary replaced her, the primrose received names such as the 'keys to Heaven' and 'password'. Spring is a potent time, and primroses carry in their many names and biology the attributes of that potency.

The name primrose had many variants in medieval Latin and Old French, from prima rosa to primerose, primerole, prymrose and prymerolle. *Primus* is the Latin for first, and *ros* or *rosa* was used generically to mean flower. The botanical name *Primula* literally means 'little first one'. Before the concept of species developed in the seventeenth century, the common primrose, the cowslip and the oxlip were treated as near-identical triplets with a wide array of folk names applied interchangeably. However, Shakespeare is said to have anchored the name primrose to what became known botanically as *Primula vulgaris*, the common or English primrose. Charles Darwin would finally clarify the various species' unique biological positions: the common primrose with its open-faced, pale yellow-green flowers, lacking a flowering scape, attached singly to the basal rosette of leaves by slender pedicels; the cowslip with its small, bright-yellow, red-spotted belled flowers dangling in umbels from tallish scapes; the oxlip with dainty, lemon-yellow flowers, neither flat nor tubular, drooping slightly in elegant umbels from delicate scapes of intermediate height.[2]

These flowers dominated lore and legend from the days of Dioscorides (*c.* AD 60) until the nineteenth century, when undaunted plant hunters started trekking to the East and opened the treasure box of primrose species found in the Sino-Himalayas of China, Tibet, Myanmar (Burma) and India. Eventually botanists would place between 450 and 500 species in the genus *Primula*, in the family Primulaceae. The hundreds of hybrids of horticultural renown that have been found in the field or fashioned by human intervention multiply this number many times over. While many of the species described by horticulturalists as 'shy', 'recalcitrant' or even 'impossible' resist cultivation, the hybrids are more amenable, lending themselves to garden settings.

Heron landing among cowslips in Reg's Meadow in Andover, Hampshire,
a property of the Hawk Conservancy Trust.

The title of this book uses 'primrose' as a collective name encompassing all species and hybrids belonging to the genus *Primula*. This has been common usage in North America. Europeans tend to reserve 'primrose' for one species, the common primrose (*P. vulgaris*), and use 'primula' (unitalicized) as the non-technical, collective name for all *Primula* species and hybrids. In this book I will follow both conventions for designating the collective grouping, that is, primroses and primulas, depending on the context and the sources from which I draw quotations. I will use 'common primrose', somewhat repetitively for clarity, for the uncommonly beautiful *Primula vulgaris*.

The fluidity with which botanical, common and horticultural names and terms are interchanged or used with different meanings confuses even the experts. The well-known 'evening primrose' is not, botanically, a primrose. It belongs to the genus *Oenothera* in the Onagraceae family. The primrose, botanically, is not a rose, which belongs to the genus *Rosa* in the Rosaceae family, although the many-petalled, ruffled blossoms of double primroses look like the old

Primula vulgaris. ssp. *sibthorpii*, a subspecies of the common primrose found wild in Greece and Turkey, and named after Oxford professor of botany Humphry Waldo Sibthorp (1713–1797). It is shown here in plantsman David Stuart's Scottish Borders garden.

centifolia or cabbage roses. There is a wild rose, a true rose, which is known botanically as *Rosa primula* and in common usage as the 'primrose rose', because of its translucent yellow flowers. Delicate fern-like leaves waft a lovely perfume into the air, giving it yet another name, the incense rose. The Bedlam cowslip is not a cowslip, but rather belongs to the genus *Pulmonaria* and is most often called the lungwort. And then there is the American cowslip, also known as the shooting star, which botanists have recently renamed *Primula meadia* from *Dodecatheon meadia*. The primrose historian faces many pitfalls in tracing lineages and sorting out identities among primroses.

Further, there are a number of groups of primroses that go by names that do not reveal their membership in the genus *Primula*. The auricula (*Primula* × *pubescens*) – an ancient hybrid of two European alpine species, *P. auricula* and *P. hirsuta* – first appeared in a garden in Vienna in the sixteenth century. The former has clear yellow flowers, and the latter rosy-pink flowers. This seemingly straightforward union of pink and yellow opened an extravagant Pandora's box of colour effects found nowhere else in any floral palette. Fortunately the hybrid was fertile, and breeders still produce novel tints and tones by cross-pollinating between progeny. Names such as 'Leathercoat', 'Green Jacket', 'Mustard Sauce', 'Toffee Crisp', 'Cinnamon', 'Tawny Port' and 'Trouble' hint at the unusual combinations of greens, browns, auburns, maroons and murreys shown in their flowers, along with the usual floral tones of delicate to strong pinks, yellows and blues. In addition, a farina or powder often coats the leaves and flowers of the auricula in decorative patterns, creating other-worldly effects. Auriculas have inspired profound awe in the general public and enslaved numerous horticulturalists.

The polyanthus (*Primula* × *polyantha*) is currently considered a complex hybrid of the common primrose, the cowslip, the oxlip and a juliana-type hybrid primrose.[3] It originated in England in the seventeenth century, but by the mid-twentieth century was grown commercially from California to Australia. Its progress from wild flower to pot plant, the 'polychrome princess of the petrol pump', reflects the burgeoning enterprise of plant breeding and the intent to improve plants.[4] The early stages are a matter of conjecture.[5] In 1629 the herbalist John Parkinson described 'the Primrose Cowslip' in his

Overleaf: Primrose Belarina' 'Pink Ice', a double primrose developed by Cambridgeshire plant breeder David Kerley.

A drawing of Auricula 'Sir John Moore' (1876) that appeared in Shirley Hibberd's
The Floral World and Garden Guide (vol. 11).

masterpiece *Paradisi in sole paradisus terrestris* (Park-in-Sun's Terrestrial Paradise). Historians believe this represents recognition of the naturally occurring hybrid between the common primrose and the cowslip, later called the 'false oxlip'. It is larger than each of its parents and, like the cowslip, its flowers are grouped in umbels on tallish stalks. Another early name was the 'polyanthos primrose', polyanthus being a corruption of *polyanthos*, the Greek word for many-flowered.[6] At some point the false oxlip hybridized with the true oxlip, either in its species form (*P. elatior*) or as a hybrid of the common primrose and the oxlip (*Primula × digena*), and either with human help or by chance proximity and with the help of a pollinator – in 1922 the Quaker naturalist William Miller Christy recorded the visit of a brimstone butterfly to a common primrose, a cowslip and an oxlip on a single flying trip.[7] Polyanthus hybrids that have stout-stalked umbels have also been called bunch-flowering primroses.

Some time in the late seventeenth century the red-flowered polyanthus gave rise to a bewitching new form, the gold-laced polyanthus. The flowers possessed a rich golden eye and petals strikingly laced with gold. The red yielded to deep brown, mahogany and tortoiseshell shades that seemed especially designed for enhancement by the golden edging. Varieties multiplied, some with silver lacing, as each sowing of seeds produced specimens with slight variations that were collected with the same kind of mania as that which surrounded the tulip in early seventeenth-century Holland. James Justice, a wealthy Scottish plant enthusiast who is known as the introducer of the pineapple, spent so lavishly on the hundreds of varieties of gold-laced polyanthus that he went bankrupt. He had the largest collection of auriculas in Europe at the time of his untimely death in 1763.

Primroses are harbingers of spring, their flowers rising snow-covered from beds of soggy leaves, winter-burned grass and mud. Even the exotic-looking auriculas are extremely hardy, able to withstand temperatures as low as −40°C (−40°F). Perhaps one of their greatest feats has been surviving the move from mossy bank to supermarket,

Gold-laced polyanthus in window box of shop
on Brick Lane in Spitalfields, London.

where, constrained in small pots under artificial lights, they flower fragrantly next to coffee and pastries. Many people today know primroses only from such a context. One of the major producers of the supermarket primrose, Sakata Ornamentals in Japan, calls its offering Primula acaulis (unitalicized), which is a discarded synonym for the common primrose. The Latin *acaulis* means 'without a stem' and refers to the common primrose's lack of flowering stalk or scape. Sakata's Primula acaulis is actually a hybrid of the common primrose (*P. vulgaris*) and the polyanthus (*Primula* × *polyantha*).[8] The names 'poly-anthus' and 'acaulis' are sometimes used to describe these two basic types of hybrid primrose, those with flowers in umbels on tall, strong stalks (good for window boxes) and those with flowers arranged singly on short, slender stalklets (easier for supermarket packaging), respectively.

At 31,000 seeds to about 28 g (1 oz), supermarket primroses can be grown economically. They easily accommodate breeders' demands – compactness and 'unbeatable impact for impact sales'.[9] Although the iconic pallor of the common primrose (*P. vulgaris*) has given way to the bright hybrid colours necessary to attract attention in the hyper-intense display of goods in the modern supermarket, the symbolic significance remains. An American editorial writer recently explained why she bought a supermarket primrose: 'The burst of color reminded me that hope lay ahead. That the season of renewal, regeneration and restoration was nearly upon us and that we'd soon be flourishing. Oh, yes there is power even in a solitary primrose plant.'[10] Bringing spring home in a small pot on a bleak late winter day appeals to people worldwide.

'I threw the pearl of my soul into a cup of wine. I went down the primrose path to the sound of flutes. I lived on honeycomb.' So wrote Oscar Wilde in *De Profundis* (1905), the letter he wrote from prison to his friend and lover Lord Alfred Douglas. Perhaps Wilde should have cultivated a primrose path of the literal kind, as did Alfred, Lord Tennyson at his home in Farringford on the Isle of Wight. Tennyson's path was captured forever by the prominent Victorian watercolourist Helen Allingham (1848–1926). Tennyson was able to buy Farringford because of the success of his poem 'In Memoriam' (1850), a requiem for a friend who died young. Canto LXXXV ends with the lines

Ah, take the imperfect gift I bring,
Knowing the primrose yet is dear,
The primrose of the later year,
As not unlike to that of Spring.

In other words, the end-of-season primrose, like the poem, hovers in imperfection. Tennyson reclaimed paths through a part of his property he called the wilderness, and placed his writing hut nearby. His wife, Emily, recorded in her diary that they both gathered and planted primroses, in between entertaining countless distinguished visitors, such as the primrose lover Charles Darwin (see Chapter Two).[11] Queen Victoria's rural retreat Osborne House was also on the island. When Prince Albert visited Farringford, he left with a bouquet of cowslips for her.

A primrose path in Japan appeared in an issue of the British magazine *Gardens Illustrated* in 2016.[12] The Japanese woodland primrose, *P. jesoana*, lines the border of a path in a private forest known as Tashiro's Forest on Hokkaido, Japan's northernmost island. It is

Primula vulgaris 'Blue Zebra' for sale at Trebah Garden, Cornwall.

The Primrose Path at Farringford by Helen Allingham (1848–1926), a watercolour painted at Tennyson's home on the Isle of Wight, *c.* 1880–95.

a 6-ha (15-acre) refuge reclaimed over a period of 22 years from a clear-cut forest (one that has been logged) by a horticulturalist named Izumi. As the forest regenerated, he created woodland paths bordered with native wild flowers and built a traditional-style thatched house and contemplation hut in his isolated sanctuary.

Although primroses were brought into gardens and domesticated hundreds of years ago, they began their evolution in the wildest of sceneries. High peaks and ferocious weather shaped their genetics. The primrose path began in the Sino-Himalayas, where extreme geographical and climatic conditions vigorously rocked what ecologists call a 'cradle' of species diversification. The primroses that migrated into the benign woodland and meadow habitats of Britain and Europe would eventually number in the millions, but many of their Asian relatives struggled to survive in small populations on remote scree and crags. Shaped by the Earth's variable geography and climate, and by the diverse humans who collected and tended them, primroses have developed a compelling character. From the minute to the willowy, their biology personifies 'tenacity and fecundity'.[13] Their flowers attract human pollinators, as well as the winged kind, and have inspired artists, scientists, plant-breeders, amateur gardeners and writers to devote lifetimes of work to them. The noted horticulturalist and broadcaster Geoffrey Smith wrote: 'A love of primroses is almost instinctive.'[14] A naturalist's tour of their far-flung habitats in the first chapter of this book reveals some of the 'extraordinary details' of their life histories.[15]

one

The Naturalist's Primrose

There are a million sanctuaries for harassed plant life. And they in turn protect it as they can from the ravages of Nature.

FRANK KINGDON-WARD, *In the Land of the Blue Poppies* (1924)[1]

The 'ancestral' primrose or 'archaeprimula' solidified its genetics about 25 million years ago in the towering mountain ranges of the eastern Sino-Himalayas that surround the Qinghai-Tibet Plateau, an area that has been called the Third Pole.[2] Biologists describe the landscape, which is now divided among Nepal, Bhutan, northern India, China and Burma (Myanmar), as a 'cradle of diversity'. Here, a climate of extremes and a complex topography, which includes high peaks, cliffs, scree, bogs, meadows and forests, acted as a 'species pump', leading to the intense speciation (formation of species) characteristic of the genus *Primula*. Of the 450–500 primrose species, roughly 78 per cent (about 334 species) occur in this region. These are relatively 'recent' mountains, geologically speaking, and uplift continues today as the Indian tectonic plate advances north underneath the Tibetan Plateau.

Biologists point to immigration, climate change and niche evolution as key processes that foster speciation in a volatile geography. Habitats in these lofty mountains range from 1,300 to 6,000 m (4,300–19,700 ft). Minute primroses anchored themselves in the narrowest crevices, their roots many times longer than their

Bhutanese stamp
honouring the
country's native
P. reidii.

above-ground rosettes, enduring intense sunlight, extreme cold, deep snow and even monsoon conditions. As sister species went their separate ways on neighbouring peaks, new evolutionary pathways emerged courtesy of busy genes. 'Hotspots' of biodiversity abounded. Larger primroses developed in the milder conditions of bogs and meadows. The archaeprimula is thought to have been one of the candelabra types, like *P. japonica*, in which the flowers are arranged in tiers of whorled inflorescences.[3]

The Hengduan Mountains, some 780,000 sq. km (300,000 sq. miles) of north–south peaks covering western Sichuan province and northwestern Yunnan province of China, and eastern Tibet, constitute a hotspot. The Arnold Arboretum in Boston, Massachusetts, has been collaborating since 1997 with the U.S. Government agency the National Science Foundation to inventory plant and fungal species there, and has documented 113 species of *Primula*, many of them narrow endemics, a term that describes species that inhabit restricted localities.[4] Even as primroses migrated into Eurasia, Europe, Scandinavia, North America and Africa, adapting to some extent to flattened landscapes, many maintained their status as endemics, holding their own in relatively small populations in remote places.

Japanese primrose (*Primula japonica*), a candelabra type thought to be an ancestral form, growing along a stream at Cornell Botanic Garden, Ithaca, New York.

Distinctive habitats can occur just metres from one another. Researchers studying the alpine area (above 3,000 m/9,800 ft) of a single mountain, Sherjila, in Tibet, found four distinct primrose habitats that contained twelve species.[5] The descriptive names for these habitats – forest shade, sparse woods, forest-edge wetland and alpine cold – indicate the nuanced conditions that lead to specialization. Slight differences in light, temperature, humidity and moisture, when combined, create distinct micro-habitats for distinctive species.

One of the species found on Sherjila is the famed *P. cawdoriana*, a striking high-alpine species with velvety leaves and downward-facing,

Primula klattii photographed in Tibet (Xizang), Shuri Tsho, 5,180 m (16,995 ft), by alpinist Harry Jans.

The Earl of Cawdor's primula (*Primula cawdoriana*).

lavender-blue, lacerate flowers. It is named after the Fourth Earl of Cawdor, Scotland, who in 1924 accompanied the plant hunter Frank Kingdon-Ward on an expedition to the Tsangpo Gorge (see Kingdon-Ward's photograph of the gorge in Chapter Three). The young earl, John Duncan Vaughan Campbell (1900–1970), who was more of a sportsman than a plant hunter, found the pace of Kingdon-Ward's botanizing maddeningly slow. He wrote in his journal: 'If ever I travel again I'll make damned sure it's not with a botanist. They are always stopping to gape at weeds.'[6] This species, which has languished since its first introduction in cultivation in Europe, recently surprised David and Sheila Rankin, the owners of Kevock Garden Plants in Midlothian, Scotland. The specimen they presented at the RHS Chelsea Flower Show in 2016 was grown from seed that had been stored for decades in a freezer; it flowered just four days before the show. Even the earl might have been impressed.

Included in the Sherjila study is *P. florindae*, which was also introduced to Europe by Kingdon-Ward as a result of that trip to the

Tsangpo Gorge. It readily earns its many common names, which include giant cowslip, Tibetan cowslip, Florinda primrose and giant fragrant cowslip. Classified as one of the bog primulas, it is the largest primrose, reaching a robust, even massive 1.2 m (4 ft) tall, with fragrant, nodding sulphur-yellow flowers. Now naturalized in wet fens of the Scottish Highlands, it has a striking impact on the landscape. Kingdon-Ward named it after his first wife, Florinda.

Eventually some of these alpine primroses came down from the Sino-Himalayan mountains and migrated east and south, colonizing Eurasia, Europe, Scandinavia, North America, Arabia and Africa. All this occurred relatively recently, during the Ice Ages. Migration occurred as land bridges formed; speciation increased when populations were sequestered in habitats that functioned as 'islands'. Some migration routes remain a mystery. When populations of a genus or species are widely separated geographically, they are said to be disjunct, and a reason is sought. The question of how *P. prolifera* got to Sumatra and Java from the Himalayas, for example, has caused fractious debate among plant geographers, the detectives of

Many primula species grow in the complex topography around Omta Tso, a lake in central Bhutan, photographed by plant explorer Martin Walsh.

Colour variations seen in a hybrid swarm of primroses (*P. calderiana* × *P. strumosa*) found near Omta Tso, photographed by Pete Boardman.

the plant kingdom. The pioneering phytogeographer Léon Croizat (1894–1982) fretted over the problem, arguing that 'ancient conditions of land and sea' must have permitted its migration, rather than any natural means of dispersal (bird or wind), which others had proposed.[7] The only South American primrose, *P. magellanica*, also presents a migration conundrum and a remarkable journey. Some speculate that it could have reached southern Patagonia during the Ice Ages, about a million years ago, when land bridges formed after a drop in sea level. However, bird dispersal cannot be ruled out, since their migrations can cover thousands of kilometres. In any event, one seed is enough to start a population (see Chapter Eight for Walter Hood Fitch's illustration).

The story of the primrose is connected with some of the world's most extraordinary geography. For example, the steep, mountainous ravines of Omta Tso (also written as Omta Tsho, Om Tsho and Om Tsho), a lake considered sacred in Bhutan – originally explored by the plant hunters Frank Ludlow and George Sherriff in 1937, and recently re-explored by Martin Walsh, Tim Lever and others – protect 'a swarm of primulas of at least eight shades of colours including yellow, white, purple and blue'.[8]

Primula species from around the world

There are about 21 primula species in North America, and one in Mexico (*P. rusbyi*). The weeping-wall primrose (*P. specuicola*) is endemic to the Colorado Plateau on 'vertical, weeping seepage cliffs' in hanging gardens between 1,100 and 2,200 m (3,500–7,200 ft) above sea level.[9] Linnaeus himself named the species in 1735. 'Specuicola' means 'cave inhabiting'. Because it is endangered, some websites carry this line: 'Blooming information withheld to protect the plants.' Its roughened seeds lodge in algal mats on alcove walls or on the sand deposits at the bottom of the walls in Entrada or Navajo sandstone formations.[10] In cultivation it has been found to 'abhor overhead watering'.[11] A disjunct population in the Grand Canyon occurs on seeps of Kaibab and Redwall limestone.[12] Pam Eveleigh has made a video tour of its habitat in Utah, available on her website, *Primula World: A Visual Reference for the Genus Primula*.[13]

Much more common in Colorado is the long-stemmed, magenta-flowered Parry's primrose (*P. parryi*), named after the 'king of Colorado botany' Charles C. Parry (1823–1890), a surgeon-turned-botanical explorer originally from Gloucestershire, England. In addition to dedicated botanizing, he climbed and measured many Colorado peaks (including Parry's Peak). This primrose occurs in high country, between 2,700 and 4,200 m (8,800–13,800 ft), where melting snows inundate streams, springs and wet meadows. Its vibrant beauty is somewhat marred by a persistent skunky ('disgustingly sickly resinous') smell, an unusual attribute in a primrose.[14] This robust species shares habitat with a dwarf relative, Colorado's fairy primrose, *P. angustifolia*.

The mealy or hoary primrose (*P. incana*), a wetland species, is found in only eleven populations in Montana on public, state, federal and private land. Described as 'vulnerable', it has found a protected home in Red Rock Lakes National Wildlife Refuge in the extreme southwestern corner of the state, where there are extensive wetlands. It has lavender flowers with yellow eyes and gets its common name

Colorado fairy primrose (*P. angustifolia*), photographed by Tony Frates.

from the plentiful farina, a mealy powder produced by glands, on its floral parts.[15]

The Mistassini primrose (*P. mistassinica*) thrives in the company of the carnivorous bladderwort (*Pinguicula vulgaris*) on gravelly, wave-splashed lake shores in Minnesota and northwards to Canada, and also finds congenial perches on rocky cliffs. The 'eye' includes a yellow ring around the mouth of the floral tube. Some see it as a North American twin to the European bird's-eye primrose (*P. farinosa*), although lovers of one or the other do not see a great similarity. The wide geographical separation deters botanists from combining the two as one species. The strict primrose (*P. stricta*), known in Inuktitut as *aupartuapitt*, inhabits the arctic zones of North America and Europe. The Inuit of

Nunavik made a dish using its 'exceptionally' fragrant flowers, fish roe, seal oil and berries.[16] The Laurentian primrose (*P. laurentiana*) is a lover of limestone and rivers in northeastern Maine and further north, in the Gaspé Peninsula and Newfoundland.

The natural history of the rare Maguire primrose (*P. cusickiana* var. *maguirei*) has been extensively studied.[17] Its pollinators – bees, moths and hummingbirds – must find their way along a narrow corridor (just 20 km/12½ miles) of the one canyon in northern Utah where a population of 3,000 individuals remains.[18] The primrose's survival depends on their visits.[19] The alkali primrose (*P. alcalina*) is known from one location in Beaverhead County, Montana, and four others

Hoary primrose (*P. incana*).

in central Idaho, where it prefers wet alkaline meadows near spring heads, often on the inside of meander loops and on the tops and sides of hummocks. Some populations are described as 'extirpated', dire wording that emphasizes the vulnerability of these endemic species.

Primroses are represented well in Alaska, including *P. borealis* and tiny *P. egaliksensis*, the Greenland primrose, and new species are being found as roads and explorers reach previously inaccessible areas. The anvil primula, *P. anvilensis*, discovered in 1987, is endemic to the Seward Peninsula in the northwest of the state. There is also the small primula with the big name, *P. tschuktschorum*, the chukchi ('island') primrose. Of delicate stature and lacking the farina that is usually present in northern species, it is found on Primrose Ridge (Mount Margaret) in Denali National Park, and on the Aleutian Islands, a chain of islands containing 41 volcanoes.

The European Alps became home to a number of primroses that are limestone crag specialists. In *Among the Hills: A Book of Joy in High Places* (1910), the plant hunter and 'father of rock gardening' Reginald Farrer describes his foray to the Maritime Alps above the Italian Riviera, where he happened not only on many primroses but also on the eccentric English botanist Clarence Bicknell.[20] Farrer devotes pages and pages to such species as *P. marginata*, 'the loveliest blue Primula of our Alps', which 'sheeted' boulders 'in the wide glade of La Maddalena' near the Miniera Valley, and even more pages to Allioni's primrose, *P. allionii*, which botanists call a chasmophyte – a dweller in crevices of cliffs, in this case tumaceous limestone. Often entirely inaccessible, it grows vertically and even upside down. Named after the eighteenth-century Italian physician-botanist Carlo Allioni, it is much loved among alpine plant enthusiasts for the pink profusion of outsized flowers, which open flat like a plate, sitting on dwarf cushions of old leaves. 'Rosette' is the botanical term for the morphology (form or structure) in which leaves circle a compressed, almost non-existent stem like the petals of a rose. The garden writer Noel Kingsbury calls 'the perfect hemisphere' of a *P. allionii* on the show table 'a surreal sight'.[21] Its extraordinary natural variation – in the

The Scottish primrose (*P. scotica*), photographed by Lorne Gill.

wild every plant may show variation in flower shape, size and colour – and ease of hybridization have led to many beautiful hybrids.[22] Cushion-form primroses can live for many years. Some individuals of *P. allionii* have lived for 30 years or more, with clones of the species remaining free of the viruses that tend to plague hybrids.[23]

Both *P. marginata* and *P. allionii* have become model systems in the study of polyploidy, a driving force in the evolution of plant species. Plants, unlike animals, frequently develop several sets of identical, heritable chromosomes. *P. allionii* has populations containing hexaploid (six sets) individuals, while *P. marginata* has populations of both hexaploid and dodecaploid (twelve sets) individuals. The molecular biologist Elena Conti and her colleagues at the University of Zurich continue to pose new questions about the effect of polyploidization on speciation in *Primula*. It is thought that a hexaploid *P. marginata* ancestor and a hexaploid *P. allionii* ancestor may have hybridized to produce the dodecaploid *P. marginata*.[24] Speciation of the alpine European primroses was further encouraged by the complex topography of the Maritime Alps and the Pleistocene glacial cycles. Populations with different ploidy levels became isolated when glaciers were at their peak, but reconnected when the glaciers retreated.

The many micro-habitats of the Italian/French border north of Menton, a hotspot of diversity, allowed *P. allionii* to persist throughout the Ice Ages.[25] Conti and her colleagues have mapped the populations of many of these alpine primroses, and have used modelling to predict future distribution. The exacting habitat preferences of *P. marginata* (it prefers high, rocky calcareous sites with frequent rain but well-drained soil, and a marked temperature difference between winter and summer) indicate that climate change poses a threat to its survival.[26]

Many people make pilgrimages, on bended knee, to a slightly more accessible but very small endemic, the 'well-faured Scots floorie', *P. scotica*, the Scots or Scottish primrose, one of the UK's few endemic plants, which ekes out an existence in northern Scotland and the Orkney Islands. The Scottish Wildlife Trust invites volunteers to become Flora Guardians of the wee floorie as its populations disappear and its biology falters. Some individuals never flower, and biologists puzzle over why pollinators rarely visit; fortunately, it is capable of self-fertilization. It is protected at the Hill of White Hamars Wildlife Reserve on Hoy, one of the Orkney Islands, a dramatic setting with haunting 'walls', cliffs, arches, stacks and a blowhole. The impressive stack known as the Old Man of Hoy guards this inhospitable landscape, where more than 180 wild-flower species hide in the sheep-grazed turf. *P. scotica* thrives in maritime turf, short-grazed swards misted with ocean spray. One rock gardener went so far as to transplant such turf to his garden to encourage this primrose to germinate.[27]

On the small Orkney island of Papa Westray, volunteers from the Royal Society for the Protection of Birds (RSPB) gather every three years to take a census of a population of *P. scotica* on the North Hill Nature Reserve. The largest colony in the reserve is on the cliffs of Fowl Craig, where in 2012 staff, islanders and volunteers counted 8,134 individuals, a decrease from 2009 but not the lowest number recorded. Populations are disappearing, but at least one mainstream catalogue offers seeds.[28] The problem is maintaining the plant and persuading it to thrive and reproduce.[29] Genetic analysis has shown that it has extremely low genetic diversity, which often foretells a lack of ability to respond to environmental change, and that it is an allopolyploid, which means that it carries three or more sets of chromosomes, one from a different species. The Scots primrose may have reached an evolutionary dead end, surviving only with human help, but as the botanical artist Roger Banks intimates, it is a worthwhile cause:

> The Scots primrose is the exemplar of everything a garden plant can never be however hard horticulturalists strive; brilliant magenta flowers with primrose eyes held in a crisp rosette of lettuce-green leaves[,] yet the whole plant, so delicate that jewellery is the only possible analogy, will fit into a small coffee cup.[30]

The bird's-eye primrose (*P. farinosa*) inspired the renowned naturalist Richard Mabey to a make a primrose pilgrimage. As a young man, Mabey had fallen in love with a drawing of this species by Louisa, Countess of Aylesford (1760–1832), given to him by a girlfriend. The remarkable countess bore twelve children, became an ardent botanist and made more than 2,830 watercolour drawings of wild flowers, fungi, mosses, algae and the odd dragonfly. Later, when he was working with the photographer Tony Evans on a book project

Herbarium sheet of Scottish primrose (*P. scotica*) specimens
found on the Orkney Islands in the 1850s.

that became *The Flowering of Britain* (1980), Mabey had a reason to seek
out the real plant:

> For a few weeks every spring and summer between 1972
> and 1978 we went on the road, following the primrose path
> across Britain . . . The daily round involved these essentials:
> Moments of soft light: nothing made soft petals crinkle or
> leaves take on the shine of overheated skin like fierce sun.
> Long breaks for a formal picnic spread out on a tablecloth,
> wherever possible next to a stream, so that a bottle of
> Sauvignon could be cooling in the shallows, and we could
> review the morning's work.[31]

Valentine Green's mezzotint engraving of Sir Joshua Reynolds's portrait of
Louisa (née Thynne). Countess of Aylesford. 1783.

The countess painted her specimen at the family home,
Packington Hall in Warwickshire. Her presentation is ethereal and
dainty, and to Mabey's delight it matched perfectly the plants he
and Evans found on Shap Fell in the Lake District. He captures the
limestone-loving affinity of the bird's-eye primrose:

They seemed to have been formed out of the very stuff of the rock, the calcareous farina of the limestone, the pink fragments of metamorphic rocks. I was so seduced by this conceit of stone suffusing tissue (thinking perhaps of the way a vineyard's terroir flavours its grapes) that I never even noticed the nominative bird's eye, the same colour as a forget-me-not's, which sits at the centre of the flower and perpetuates its kind.[32]

A lover of damp grassland, mires and flushes (areas inundated by sudden water flows) in limestone country, it is considered a glacial relict in Britain. It inhabits the Pyrenees and Alps and the flatlands of Scandinavia, as well as the Western Himalayas, which is termed a disjunct distribution. Its woolly coat, the epidermal farina or meal, contains flavonoids that are thought to protect against ultraviolet radiation in high-altitude areas and pathogens. It is a lover of light, its umbels tracking the Sun throughout the day, the warm flowers more attractive to the hoverflies, bee flies and day-flying moths on which it depends for pollination. In the great cast of primrose characters, it is a star.

Slovenia has named its Carniolan primrose (*P. carniolica*) the national flower. It is another 'recent' endemic, having emerged during the last Ice Age. Like other endemics, it seeks inaccessible perches on the sides of damp gorges, where it anchors long roots into rocky fissures in the mountains near Idria. A doctor found the first specimen some 200 years ago, and eventually it achieved 'new species' status in Vienna.[33] A delicate white dust decorates soft red-violet flowers, inspiring the Carniolan Primrose Dress designed by Daughters of the Liberation and offered for sale by the upscale clothing store Anthropologie.

Many of the primroses that populate the high elevations are described as reduced: their flowers may be large and their roots long, but their vegetative body is compact, even minute. The European alpine Auriculastrum primula (*P. minima*, fairy primrose, snow rosette) is only 2.5 cm (1 in.) high, dwarfed by large, deeply notched rose-pink flowers; and then there's the littlest of the little: *P. minutissima* of India and Pakistan, with yellow farina on the underside of its leaves. The Scandinavian primrose (*P. scandinavica*) of Norway and Sweden, although small above ground, has an outsize root system for anchoring it into alpine grasslands and rocky limestone ground. It is on the International Union for Conservation of Nature's Red List of Threatened Species for both countries.[34] The Siberian primrose (*P. nutans*) is considered 'delicate and insubstantial', but, for all that, is the most widespread species in the genus *Primula*, occurring widely in the European Arctic through to the mountains of central Asia, claiming for its own 'frozen arctic shores and mountain wastes'.[35]

Human beings have intruded upon some of the primrose's previously inaccessible sanctuaries. Consider the Sinai primrose (*P. boveana*), described by the International Union for Conservation of Nature (IUCN) in 2014 as Critically Endangered.[36] Although it was abundant when the botanist Nicolas Bové found it in 1832, it has recently been reported as 'one of the rarest species worldwide', and its area of occupancy is just 6 sq. km (2 1/3 sq. miles).[37] Ecologists call it 'a high-elevation specialist'.[38] About 200 mature individuals remain in the St Katherine Protectorate (SKP) in southern Sinai, Egypt, clinging to the gorge walls of Shaq El Mousa and Shaq El Garaginiah. Although it is remote, tourists now find their way to the SKP, trampling flora, leaving rubbish, degrading the habitat and reducing the flower's population. A species in a specialized micro-habitat may disappear under a few footsteps.

Species with marginal lifestyles supply geneticists with ready-made experiments. Another dwarf perennial, *P. interjacens* in China, is described as narrowly endemic to limestone crevices in south-central Yunnan, occupying an area just 25 by 3 km (15½ by 1¾ mi.). Long roots anchor it deep into the nooks and crannies of precipices and crags. 'Endemic' is for the most part synonymous with 'endangered', because species with small populations are subject to loss of genetic variation through genetic drift (for instance, the earthquake or rockslide that wipes out a portion of a species' genetic storehouse through loss of individuals). But scientists have found high genetic diversity in this particular 'narrow' endemic species. The rocky habitat and a low investment in pollen transfer and seed production have favoured its local persistence.[39]

While it is possible that all the primrose's hiding places will never be found, new species from previously inaccessible areas are still being documented. In the 1990s three new Italian primroses made botanical headlines. One, *P. albenensis*, is found in the western,

Primula minutissima photographed in 2010 by ecologist Miroslav Dvorský in S. Zanskar, Ladakh, a high-altitude region of the northwest Himalayas.

eastern and southeastern areas of Monte Alben in the Bergamesque Prealps of Lombardy, Italy.[40] It seeks out shady fissures, and is aromatic throughout, like its home country. Pam Eveleigh's first blog post of 2016 on *Primula World* was a listing of six new primula species, five from China and one from the Iberian Peninsula.

As travellers, botanists, plant hunters and horticulturalists explored Earth, they found primroses. Attracted to their beauty, they secured seeds and sought to bring them home. Now national collections are held in many countries, including the Jensen-Olson Arboretum in Juneau, Alaska, which maintains the U.S. National Collection. Meanwhile, horticulturalists continue to try to coax far-flung species into cultivation. The Kevock Garden display at the RHS Chelsea Flower Show in 2014 combined primrose species and hybrids to portray the lure of the species primrose amid the beauty of showy, amenable garden hybrids. The garden writer Stephen Lacey wrote:

> My favourite pavilion exhibit this year was Kevock Garden Plants, with its little mountain of tumbling white alpine saxifrages, some dashing blue Himalayan poppies, and a miniature bog of multicoloured candelabra primulas. Heaven. And in its mini-dell, a lonely plant of a pale and retiring primula called *P. ambita* from China is, they told me, the only specimen of its kind in cultivation.[41]

The display beautifully illustrated the range of form in *Primula*. Candelabra primulas, introduced by plant hunters more than 100 years ago, are tall and showy, a staple of modern gardens, in contrast with the 'pale and retiring' *P. ambita*. Native to central Yunnan at 2,000–2,700 m (6,500–8,800 ft), this primrose likes wet areas near streams and ditches. It was found in 1915 by the 'botanical pioneer' Heinrich Handel-Mazzetti, whose precise description of the spot guided the plant hunter Jens Nielsen to find it again in 2014.

Cliff-face habitat of *P. albenensis* on Monte Alben, Bergamo, Italy.

A closer view of *P. albenensis*.

Kevock Gardens managed to germinate one seed. The plant is softly hairy, the eye pale yellow, the throat pale green.

The primrose path takes turns through many of Earth's habitats, from woodlands to high limestone scree, cliffs, caves, seeps, hanging gardens, wetlands and boggy meadows. It is no wonder that these primroses from the rooftop of the world – 'endless forms most beautiful', to use Charles Darwin's wording about species diversity – challenge horticulturalists to cultivate them at home, conservationists to protect them in the wild and scientists to study their strategies for survival.

two

Mr Darwin's Primroses

Who is there that does not know the Primrose, the
Cowslip, and the Oxlip? The differences between
which even a child would be ashamed to be told that
it was unacquainted with: and yet to this hour it is a
question among the most learned Botanists if they
are really distinct species.

WILLIAM CURTIS, *Flora Londinensis* (1777)[1]

The three yellow-flowered primroses native to Britain, the
common primrose (*P. vulgaris*), the cowslip (*P. veris*) and
the oxlip (*P. elatior*), were both muse and guinea pig for
Charles Darwin for almost 30 years as he engaged with one of the
most fundamental questions in biology: what is a species? Darwin
was fascinated by variation, and speciation, nature's way of containing unending variation. Near the beginning of *On the Origin of Species*
(1859), he writes:

When a young Naturalist commences the study of a group
of organisms quite unknown to him, he is at first much per-
plexed to determine what differences to consider as specific,
and what as varieties; for he knows nothing of the amount
and kind of variation to which the group is subject; and this
shows, at least, how very generally there is some variation.[2]

Some people are by temperament lumpers, glossing over variation, and others splitters, refining variation through the eye of a needle. Joseph Dalton Hooker, the famous nineteenth-century explorer, botanist and herbarium-builder at the Kew Royal Botanic Gardens, was a lumper, writing that 'it is my fate to destroy species as I go.'[3] A close friend of Hooker, but neither lumper nor splitter, Darwin wanted to understand the biological rationale of a species concept. When Swedish botanist Carl Linnaeus had grouped the cowslip, the common primrose and the oxlip under the one name, *Primula veris*, in his *Systema Naturae* in 1735, consternation had simmered in the populace.[4] Linnaeus, with so many plants, animals and minerals to classify, wasn't too worried about the details, but Darwin was. He declared that, with regard to speciation, 'the most interesting case on record is that of the Primrose, common oxlip, Bardfield oxlip and cowslip.'[5]

Darwin had begun researching primroses in the 1850s, while writing *Natural Selection*, a manuscript that he abandoned and cannibalized for *On the Origin of Species*, which he rushed to publication when his fellow evolutionist Alfred Russel Wallace appeared on the scene. This unpublished manuscript is available online and contains some of his earliest comments on the problematical primroses. He writes that 'it is universally acknowledged that in England there are so many intermediate forms found wild that it is most difficult to draw any strict line of demarcation between the two extremes of the primrose & cowslip.'[6] At one extreme, the common primrose (*P. vulgaris*) presents itself as a compact rosette of crinkled green leaves and pale-yellow flowers close to the ground, and at the other extreme, the cowslip (*P. veris*) presents a taller, more billowy rosette with many red-freckled, butter-yellow flowers clustered in umbels on long stalks. In between lay a confusion of oxlips, some thought to be 'false' or 'spurious' (a hybrid) and some thought to be 'true' (a species). The 'true' oxlip was also called the Bardfield oxlip.

Darwin's voluminous correspondence documents his struggles to gather his own data on primroses and to understand the assertions of his colleagues. On 2 July 1855 Darwin wrote to his mentor Professor

John Stevens Henslow: 'I have already had for some months primroses & cowslips, strongly manured with guano, & with flowers picked off, & one cowslip made to grow in shade, & next spring I shall collect seed.'[7] On 11 October 1859 he wrote to the eminent geologist and theorist Charles Lyell, regarding 'Primrose & Cowslip', that 'It took me some trouble to collect evidence. I began experimentising; but my confounded health & so many irons in the fire stopped them.'[8] Among the many gentlemen with whom he corresponded about primroses were Messrs Herbert, Henslow, Watson, and Sidebotham, most of whom presented evidence he could not believe. Even Mr H. C. Watson, whom he had considered a 'most critical observer', presented him with the confounding 'conclusion that seeds of a cowslip can produce cowslips & oxlips; & that seeds of an oxlip can produce cowslips, oxlips & primroses'.[9] This must have seemed the epitome of mayhem from Darwin's point of view. The problem was that the garden was a hotspot of hybridization; unconstant observers could not know the full story. For instance, his mentor Professor Henslow wrote that he had 'raised from seeds of a cowslip growing in his garden, various kinds of oxlips and one perfect primrose'. Darwin was not convinced:

> From what I have myself observed with oxlips, I cannot doubt that this plant was an oxlip in a highly variable condition . . . This presumed oxlip was propagated by offsets, which were planted in different parts of the garden; and if Prof. Henslow took by mistake seeds from one of these plants, especially if it had been crossed by a primrose, the result would be quite intelligible.[10]

Analysing the data from his correspondents and creating reasonable scenarios for obvious misinformation clearly stimulated his thinking. By the early 1860s he was mounting large-scale experiments in his greenhouse and garden at Down House in Kent. He also enlisted his Wedgwood nieces and other family members to collect seed and make observations in the field.

Charles Darwin, aged six, with his sister Catherine;
a chalk drawing by Ellen Sharples, 1816.

A host of careful naturalists were studying the primrose problem at that time. In fact, in the nineteenth century there seems to have been as many naturalists as primroses. They were abundant near places that nurtured an intense enthusiasm for the natural world, such as Epping Forest, east of London. The Quaker naturalists of Essex included Edward Forster, Edward Newman, William Borrer, several Henry Doubledays and one Edward Doubleday. In his book *The Naturalist in Britain* (1976), David Elliston Allen describes how many of these amateur naturalists owed their achievements to early rising: 'Edward Newman regularly rose in summer at five, four or

Henry Doubleday,
Quaker naturalist of
Epping, Essex, c. 1863.

even three in the morning to do his natural history work, and much of his ceaseless flow of books and articles was written (like Trollope's novels) before sitting down to breakfast.'[11] Allen categorizes the work of the naturalists as 'a compulsive discharge of effort', their love of natural history energized by 'an utter abhorrence of sloth', 'extreme physical doggedness' and 'astonishing displays of intellectual stamina'.[12] Although eclipsing them in sheer volume of work, Darwin relied on their efforts.

It was Henry Doubleday (1808–1875) whose name would forever be joined with the Bardfield oxlip. On 3 May 1860 he wrote to Darwin:

My dear Sir,
I have read with real pleasure your very interesting work 'On the Origen [*sic*] of Species' and I may, some day, send you a few remarks upon portions of it –

My object in now writing is to say that I have tried a great many experiments upon the Primrose, Oxlip and Cowslip[,] all of which tended to confirm my opinion that these three plants are distinct species – or what are called species in all our Botanical works – I never could raise a primrose from the seed of the Cowslip nor a Cowslip from the seed of the Primrose.[13]

Doubleday experimented with and watched over his Bardfield oxlips for almost 25 years. As early as 1842 he sent plants grown from Bardfield oxlip seed to Edward Newman, the editor of the *Phytologist*, as evidence to support his side in the debate that was going on in the journal. Near the end of his life Doubleday had a nervous breakdown. Torn between the job of running his father's grocery and his work as a naturalist, he foundered. Newman had him taken to a nursing home, where he partly recovered, enough to come back to his cottage in Epping and continue to the end of his days working on natural history projects, financially secure through an annuity from his friends.

The only way to prove that the 'common' or 'false' oxlip was a hybrid as opposed to the 'true or Bardfield oxlip' was to test fertility after crossing experiments. In the course of these crosses, Darwin transplanted specimens of the four primroses into different kinds of soil ('highly manured land', 'highly rich soil', 'stiff poor clay' and 'old peat') and bagged flowers with gauze to exclude pollinators, while he himself acted as pollinator using a camel-tip paintbrush (as a pollinator Darwin was precise, but even he had to admit that it was almost impossible to exclude thrips). He studied pollen under the microscope and sketched specimens, collected, weighed and sowed seed, nurtured seedlings and studied the progeny for fertility. After performing hundreds of crosses over a number of years, he was able to say that 'the cowslip and primrose, when intercrossed, behave like distinct species, for they are far from being mutually fertile.'[14] Darwin summed up his many years of exacting research with this matter-of-fact statement:

Finally, although we may freely admit that Primula veris, vulgaris, and elatior, as well as all the other species of the genus, are descended from a common primordial form, yet from the facts above given, we must conclude that these three forms are now as fixed in character as are many others which are universally ranked as true species.[15]

It would turn out that the false oxlip was definitely a hybrid between the common primrose and the cowslip (*P. vulgaris* × *P. veris*), and unusually abundant, 'for hardly any other instance is known of a hybrid spontaneously arising in such large numbers over so wide an extent of country.'[16] This hybrid, *Primula* × *polyantha*, is the basis of the garden polyanthus. Other kinds of hybrid combinations occur, such as *P. veris* × *P. elatior* and *P. elatior* × *P. vulgaris*, and hybrids can hybridize with hybrids of different parentage. Further, abnormal individuals, such as a common primrose with flowers in umbels on tall stalks like a cowslip or oxlips that have flowers without stalks like a common primrose, sometimes spontaneously appear.[17] In other words, the casual wild-flower lover may be confused by finding highly variable specimens of *P. veris*, *vulgaris* and *elatior* in the field and garden.

Miller Christy and the Oxlip

It was left to other naturalists to solve the mystery of why the true or Bardfield oxlip (*P. elatior*), so widespread in Europe and Asia, had such a limited range in Britain. Miller Christy, another Quaker naturalist of Essex with 'Renaissance' interests, took on the task.[18] He spent eighteen years tracking the extent of the Bardfield oxlip:

> I have personally, and with considerable precision, traced the boundaries of this Area, which lies mainly in the adjacent portions of the counties of Essex, Suffolk, and Cambridge, but extends also just beyond the county boundaries of Hertfordshire and Huntingdonshire, while there is at least

one outlying locality in the northern part of Suffolk, and another in the southern part of Norfolk.[19]

He determined the 'Area' to be 1,230 sq. km (475 sq. miles). He then 'laid down with care' the boundaries of his 'Oxlip-Area' on the drift maps of the Geological Survey, and made a discovery: the true oxlip was clearly showing a preference for chalky boulder clay, a kind of glacial deposit often described as 'stiff'.[20]

Christy observed specific populations year after year. In a fully grown wood, under deep shade, oxlips put on a modest show. After

Oxlips (*P. elatior*) growing in Ithaca, New York.

the woods have been thinned, the stimulation of greater light causes an 'extraordinary change'. He writes:

> At such a time, a wood within the Oxlip-Area presents a very striking and beautiful sight, the ground appearing yellow all around. On one occasion, by counting the number of plants growing on a typical space measuring four yards square and the number of umbels those plants bore, I was able to estimate that each acre bore about 70,000 plants having between them 220,000 umbels – an estimate I have reason to believe was very much below the mark.[21]

Oxlips clearly enthralled Christy, who praised their 'elegant droop'. Modern oxlip-lovers say the same thing: the nodding flowers pass a message to observers. Christy worried that the 'modest and retiring' oxlip was 'being gradually hybridized out of existence by the more aggressive Primrose'. He saw it as a war, or at least a battle, the oxlip 'half-vanquished' and the common primrose 'advancing on all sides and even, to some extent, gaining access to its interior by means of river-valleys'.[22] In 1999 the noted woodland ecologist Oliver Rackham presented the results of his 30 years of research into this problem in a study entitled 'The Woods 30 Years On: Where Have the Primroses Gone?'[23] Through intensive mapping he was able to follow the fate of individual plants. Describing the oxlip as an indicator of ancient woodlands thriving under coppicing, he found that many of Christy's 'pioneer conclusions have stood the test of a century', but there has been no war in fact. The battle lines never moved. The hybrid swarms of Christy's day are unchanged. Climate change (dry springs and hot summers) and deer browsing have eradicated and reduced populations of the common primrose even more than the oxlip in the 100 years since Christy's observations.

The work of the nineteenth-century naturalists eventually led to a grand conservation effort for the Bardfield oxlip. In 2005 it was reported that there were only twelve oxlips left in the Great Bardfield area, and so a group of local organizations funded a project to grow 5,000 oxlips in the Writtle College glasshouse.[24] In 2007 children from the local primary school planted the first group of seedlings.[25] It is now possible to take the primrose path around Great Bardfield, a walk of about 5.5 km (3½ mi.), to see the Bardfield oxlip.[26]

The Ecology of the Primrose, Cowslip and Oxlip

In hundreds of studies, ecologists continue the work of the nineteenth-century naturalists as they probe the lives of the common primrose, cowslip and oxlip and their patterns of adaptation to increased human activity.[27] Although it retains strongholds in the country, the formerly ubiquitous primrose has all but disappeared from conurbations (extended urban areas), finding refuge in railway embankments, grave-yards and private estates; the cowslip, having been added to wild-flower seed mixes, is finding new niches on motorway verges; and the oxlip is finding protection in the remnants of ancient woodlands. Even as they dwindle in numbers, their biology becomes more fully known.

They are classified as rosette hemicryptophytes, literally 'half-hidden plants'. The overwintering buds are positioned at the surface of the soil, although they are often invisible in leaf litter and muck. The term 'rosette' refers to the circular arrangement of leaves around a compressed stem (rhizome), achieving a shape like a rose. Viewed from above, a primrose is a compact sphere hugging the ground. Perennial, a word that is well known to gardeners, refers to the cap-acity to overwinter in a dormant condition, emerging in the spring year after year. Some primroses 'aestivate' in the summer, their above-ground parts disappearing during heat and drought, and arising from underground roots in the spring. The average lifespan of cowslips in a Scandinavian population was measured at 52.3 years; the life expect-ancy of the common primrose is slightly less, about 48.3 years, and an oxlip can persist for 50 years in a favourable environment. They are all 'variable' species, exhibiting different phenotypes (appearances) based on their immediate environmental conditions.

The Cowslip Fairy.

Cicely Mary Barker, 'The Cowslip Fairy', from *Flower Fairies of the Spring* (1923).

'Vernation' is a term that is used to describe the arrangement of leaves in the bud. The vernation of this group of primroses is revolute, meaning that the leaves are tightly curled back to the midrib on the underside of the leaf while in bud. Even after unfolding, they have a characteristic wrinkled surface, the 'crimped and curdled leaf' described so aptly by the poet John Clare.[28] It has been suggested that the bumps and corrugations of the leaf funnel moisture down to the crown of the plant. The cowslip leaf has a prominent, narrow stalk that enlarges as the seeds mature, while the leaf of the primrose narrows gradually to the base and remains much smaller. The cowslip flower, which is bright yellow with an orange-red spot at the base of each petal, is apricot-scented, and the oxlip, buff yellow with a light orange ring at the throat, is peach-scented.[29] Seeds of the cowslip and the oxlip are shaken from the mother plant by means of a censer (salt shaker) mechanism, so dispersal is limited. Seeds of the common primrose, which have oil-rich structures known as elaiosomes attached, are dispersed by ants and voles slightly farther afield.

The common primrose can colonize a wide variety of habitats, but it prefers calcareous (calcium-rich) soils and woodlands, grasslands and hedgerows. It is recorded in most 10-km (6¼-mi.) squares in the British Isles, and while all three primroses make it north to Norway, it is the only one to land as far south as North Africa. It is shade-tolerant but needs gaps in the canopy if it is to flower well and set seed. Climate change, indicated by hot summers since 1970 in the UK, the fragmentation of its habitat and eutrophication (over-fertilized soil) have caused populations to decline, and small populations to show reduced fertility. Darwin noticed the scarcity of pollinators of the

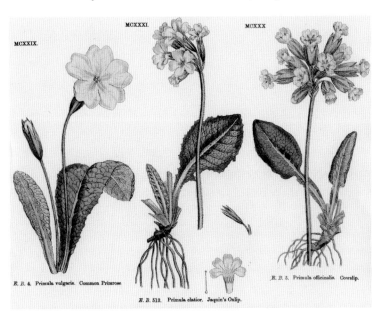

A composite of William Sowerby's illustrations highlighting morphological differences between the three yellow-flowered primroses native to the UK.

common primrose in woodlands and speculated that nocturnal moths might be attracted to the pale yellow and the scent, which is stronger in the late afternoon and evening, but he was never able to substantiate this idea with direct observation.

Cowslips prefer south-facing slopes of herb-rich meadows and grasslands in the UK, but are capable of colonizing dunes, cliffs and other marginal sites and oak-hornbeam forests in Central Europe. They occur widely throughout northern and central Europe and east through Russia on nutrient-poor habitats with calcareous, often skeletal soils. The cowslip's preferred habitat has decreased through changes in agriculture and land-use practices: formerly, cattle grazing and mowing maintained meadow grasses at just the right height. The cowslip is intolerant of shade and survives relatively well in dry conditions. Its intrinsic fertility is low. One study found that thrum plants produce more flowers than pins and another that cowslip flowering has remarkably good years (1999, 2005 and 2007) and remarkably bad (2001 and 2002). Loss of habitat, fertilizer run-off and increased ploughing have reduced numbers. Records of the *New Atlas of British and Irish Flora* indicate a decline in distribution of 13.7 per cent before 1987.

Primula vulgaris, the common primrose, by botanical illustrator and textile designer William Kilburn (1745–1818).

However, the addition of cowslip seeds to wild-flower seed mixes in the 1980s has helped them colonize new habitats.[30]

The oxlip of East Anglia is described as 'a highly sedentary perennial', which means that it is very slow to colonize an area. Introduced populations, usually begun by garden escapees, provide helpful data. One small population found at Hedgeley in south Northumberland has shown no change in number for 50 years. Common in Europe, it is found as far north as Denmark, with one population in Sweden. Although it has declined in the UK, its distribution remains constant. The oxlip colonizes spring-waterlogged soils with high levels of ferrous ions. Fallow deer (*Dama dama*) seek out and eat entire plants; muntjac deer (*Muntiacus reevesi*) are only a little less destructive. Although it also grows in calcareous soil, 40 years of hot summers and droughty springs in Cambridgeshire have caused a decline. The Hayley Wood and Buff Wood populations in that county have been studied extensively and are monitored continuously. In 1987 a brilliant display of oxlip flowering occurred in Hayley Wood after the local Wildlife Trust put up fencing to exclude deer, and undertook coppicing.[31] There were an estimated 600,000 flowers in a 0.4-ha (1-acre) plot. Rackham reports that in 1948 roughly four million oxlips grew in Hayley Wood, but by 1975 there were half that number.[32] Their 'sedentary' habit has helped ecologists to reconstruct woodland history: when a railway destroyed a corner of Hayley Wood, the oxlips that remained outlined the former boundary.[33]

Pin and Thrum: Darwin's Work with Heterostyly in Primroses

Primroses presented Darwin with another research question. Why do primrose flowers have two different kinds of 'eyes'? This phenomenon is known as heterostyly, and the two kinds of flower are known as pin-eye and thrum-eye. In a given population roughly half the individuals will have one form of the flower, and the other half a different form; they never appear on the same plant together. Darwin wrote near the end of his life in his *Autobiographies* that 'no little discovery of mine ever gave me so much pleasure as the making out of the meaning of heterostyled flowers.'[34] He had gone on a voyage of discovery around the world, but found one of the great biological mysteries in an abundant wild flower in his own back garden.

Philip M. Gilmartin, professor of Plant Molecular Genetics at the University of East Anglia and a collector and student of botanical art, provides evidence that herbalists and engravers had pictured the pin-eye and thrum-eye of primroses over a period of almost 300 years before Darwin began his research.[35] He documents through illustrations that at least seven botanists noticed the two kinds of primrose flower. The Flemish doctor and botanist Charles de l'Écluse, also known as Carolus Clusius, first illustrated the pin- and thrum-eyes of various primroses in 1583.

Carl Linnaeus's taxonomic plan was based on the number, arrangement and morphology of the reproductive organs in flowers. Much to the dismay of many people in the late eighteenth and nineteenth century, it was called a 'Sexual System'. Linnaeus's explanation of the system in *Philosophia botanica* (1751) combined the language of decorous human reproduction, such as husband, wife, nuptial bed, with inflammatory vocabulary describing plant reproduction as immodest and disorderly, for instance stamens 'gaping wantonly'.[36] This language was upsetting to people who had believed in parallels between idealized versions of their lives and those of flowers. Darwin's grandfather Erasmus Darwin, a physician and naturalist, popularized Linnaeus's sexualized language in *The Loves of the Plants*, the second part of his long poem *The Botanic Garden* (1791); his grandson would make primrose sexual behaviour literal rather than anthropomorphized.

Darwin knew he was not the first to notice pin-and-thrum primrose flowers. In the book in which he compiled much of his work on primroses, *The Different Forms of Flowers on Plants of the Same Species* (1877), he footnoted the mycologist Christiaan Hendrik Persoon, an impecunious orphaned immigrant from South Africa, as one of the first to describe the phenomenon in writing, in 1794. Persoon worked

Gold-laced
primrose
flowers
showing
pin eyes.

in near isolation. He lived most of his life in a rented room in a poor section of Paris, devoting his time to mycological discoveries and creating a herbarium. Darwin also mentioned that 'florists who cultivate the Polyanthus and Auricula have long been aware of the two kinds of flowers.'[37]

While 'pin' is a perfect way to describe primrose flowers that have long styles and carry the stigmas visible in the centre of the flowers, like the head of a sewing pin, the origin of 'thrum' is more obscure. Darwin, who in early letters had used 'thumb', offered this explanation: 'In Johnson's Dictionary, thrum is said to be the ends of weavers' threads; and I suppose that some weaver who cultivated the polyanthus invented this name, from being struck with some degree of resemblance between the cluster of anthers in the mouth of the corolla and the ends of his threads.'[38] This explanation has been

Overleaf: A thrum-eyed primrose flower.

thought plausible because many weavers were also 'florists', specialist growers of the auricula and the gold-laced polyanthus in the seventeenth century. The earliest mention of pin and thrum in text occurs in William Curtis's *Flora Londinensis* (1777).[39]

Darwin diagrammed heterostyly in a letter to American botanist Asa Gray. His names for 'pin' and 'thrum' were precise: long-styled and short-styled. The long style (the slender stalk that connects stigma and ovary) is twice as long as the short style, and the stamens have reciprocal positions in the two forms, one high and one low. There are no transitional states, and the two kinds are never found on the same plant. In the long-styled form the stigma is visible at the mouth of the floral tube, surrounded by the corolla, and the anthers are hidden halfway down. In the short-styled form the situation is reversed, the stigma being halfway down the floral tube and the group of stamens visible at the top.

Walter Crane,
'The Bold Oxlip',
1906.

Because of the difference in the placement of the male and female organs, there are differences in the shape of the floral tube and of the corolla. Darwin noted that village children preferred making cowslip necklaces from the long-styled form because they knew the corolla and floral tube lent themselves to chaining the flowers together more easily. Other differences that he measured carefully were the size of the papillae (projections) on the stigmas, differences in the morphology of the pollen grains and the number of seeds produced. He also observed that thrum plants tend to flower earlier than pin plants.[40]

Darwin wrote to Joseph Dalton Hooker: 'I never will believe that these differences are without some meaning.'[41] He went into his experiments with a theory – that heterostyly was a step towards eventual dioecy, a situation in which there are entirely separate male and female plants, as in the willow, but his work with pollinators led him to a different conclusion. Darwin was able to show that 'the visits of insects are absolutely necessary for the fertilization of *Primula veris*.'[42] The pollinators included a mullein moth (*Cucullia verbasci*) 'caught . . . in the act' by one of his sons.[43] Of the placement of primrose pollen on pollinators, he wrote:

> I found that the two kinds of pollen, which could easily be recognized under the microscope, adhered in this manner to the proboscides of the two species of humble-bees and of the moth, which were caught visiting the flowers; but some small grains were mingled with the larger grains round the base of the proboscis and conversely some large grains with the small grains near the extremity of the proboscis.[44]

From his scrupulous study of seed set, he was able to prove that heterostyly was a mechanism for ensuring heightened fertility through cross-fertilization. He defined 'legitimate' and 'illegitimate' fertilizations based on the number of viable seeds produced from the 'unions' of pollen and ovule resulting from cross-fertilization rather than

Colourized scanning electron micrograph (SEM) of pollen grains (pink)
of the common primrose (*Primula vulgaris*).

self-fertilization.[45] Walter Hood Fitch's 'Fig. 2' illustrating cross-
versus self-fertilization has become well known. Darwin's words
'nature abhors perpetual self-fertilization' became an aphorism.

The story of Darwin and the pin-and-thrum primroses soon
became well known. In 1880 the educator Arabella B. Buckley wrote
about 'The Life of a Primrose' in *The Fairy-land of Science*. Buckley, who
had been secretary to Darwin's friend Charles Lyell, began to write
about science for children after her employer's death. Her account
is detailed:

> Look at the two primrose flowers, 1 [pin] and 2 [thrum],
> p. 181, and tell me how you think the dust gets on to the top
> of the sticky knob or stigma. No. 2 seems easy enough to
> explain, for it looks as if the pollen could fall down easily
> from the stamens on to the knob, but it cannot fall up, as it
> would have to do in No. 1. Now the curious truth is, as Mr
> Darwin has shown, that neither of these flowers can get the
> dust easily for themselves, but of the two No. 1 has the least
> difficulty. The seeds are much stronger and better if the dust

or pollen of one flower is carried away and left on the knob or stigma of another flower; and the only way this can be done is by insects flying from one flower to another and carrying the dust on their legs and bodies.[46]

In attempting to avoid botanical vocabulary, she has become long-winded. However, her style may suit a volume with the title *The Fairy-land of Science*, and it is more readable than many modern versions in the scientific literature.

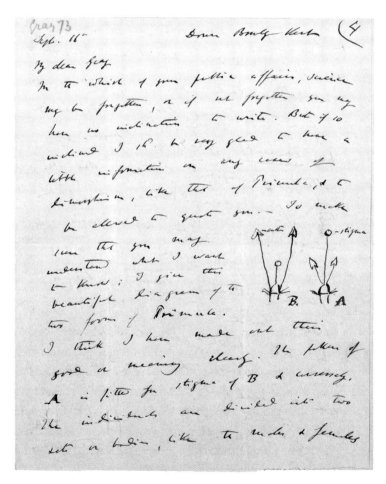

Darwin's hand-drawn sketch of pin and thrum, 1861.

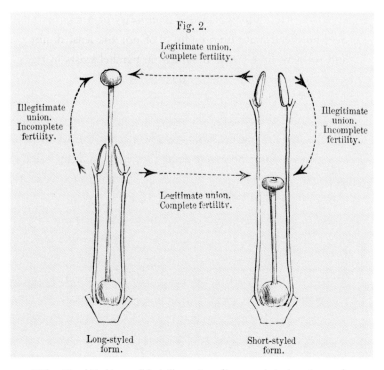

Fig. 2.

Legitimate union.
Complete fertility.

Illegitimate
union.
Incomplete
fertility.

Illegitimate
union.
Incomplete
fertility.

Legitimate union.
Complete fertility.

Long-styled
form.

Short-styled
form.

Walter Hood Fitch's woodblock illustration of heterostyly in the primrose for
Darwin's book *The Different Forms of Flowers on Plants of the Same Species* (1877).

Even easier to understand were depictions of the common primrose and cowslip in the Jung-Koch-Quentell pull-down educational
wall charts developed in Germany in the 1890s that told stories
without words. A collection of these charts found in the attic of the
science building at Randolph College in Virginia became the subject
of an exhibition, *Nature Perfected: The Art of Botanical Illustration*, at the
Maier Museum of Art in 2011 and led to their re-evaluation as artistic and educational icons of the nineteenth century.[47] Commissioned
in Germany in the 1840s when the increase in students (108 per
cent) outmatched the increase in professors (40 per cent), they were
intended to show a complete story about the life history of an organ-
ism without text: a perfect vehicle for explaining pin and thrum.[48]

The elegant breeding system of primroses went beyond Darwin's
imagining:

From the facts now given the superiority of a legitimate over an illegitimate union admits of not the least doubt; and we have here a case to which no parallel exists in the vegetable or, indeed, in the animal kingdom.[49]

His work has led to hundreds of scientific papers on primroses in the 140 years since the publication of *Different Forms*.[50] Darwin never knew of genes and the incredible detail they entail and control. If he had done, he would have learned that an archetypal supergene, the *S* locus, determines its various characteristics.[51] In the journal *Nature Plants* in December 2016 Gilmartin announced the isolation and characterization of the entire *S* locus gene cluster, which revealed that about 51.7 million years ago a primula petal gene underwent a duplication event and became part of the *S* locus in thrum plants. This gene then acquired an adaptive mutation that permitted a new function: the elevation of anther position. This occurred before speciation in the Primulaceae. Gilmartin has said that the study answers questions he has had 'since I bought my first packet of Primula seeds twenty years ago'.[52] That packet of seeds was a variety of the common

Primula vulgaris flowers dissected to demonstrate pin (left) and thrum (right).

A Jung-Koch-Quentell
wall chart (c. 1890s) tells
the 'story' of the cowslip
(*P. veris*) without words.

primrose called 'Blue Jeans', offered by the seed company Thompson
& Morgan in 1995.[53] Margaret Webster, primrose breeder (see
Chapter Four) and a member of Gilmartin's research team for many
years, played an important role in the isolation of the supergene.[54]
Recently Elena Conti and her colleagues at the University of Zurich
have sequenced 63 per cent of the genome of the cowslip (*P. veris*) in
research on the evolution of heterostyly.[55]

Virtual primroses have figured in the work of scientists like
Ben Haller, who model complex evolutionary problems.[56] He asks
whether heterostyly may promote speciation, noting that pin and
thrum occurs in 91 per cent of the genus *Primula*, which contains
about 530 species, while its sister genus, non-heterostylous *Soldanella*,
contains only 25 species. Haller and his colleagues also work with
new terms in the study of eco-evolutionary dynamics: 'magic environ-
ments' and 'magic traits'.[57] The Sino-Himalayas were just such an

environment. Darwin's observation about the shape of the corolla being different in pin-and-thrum flowers takes on a certain significance in this context. Haller suggests that 'perhaps *Primula* is an example of a case where a magic modifier, the corolla shape, evolved to allow it [to diversify]', that is to say to produce variation that solidifies into a reproductive unit called a species.[58] Another recent study, based on Darwin's model, proposes that heterostyly enhances speciation by reducing the rate of extinction.[59]

Pin and Thrum as an Aesthetic Problem

An entry on the John Innes Historical Blog offers background on the apparent lack of interest in the two kinds of primrose flower.[60] Florists, dedicated amateur horticulturalists who began raising plants for the show table in the seventeenth century, favoured the thrum-eye for aesthetic reasons. One explanation for this preference by a critic was that 'the pin-eyed flower shows a chasm or vacancy very unpleasant to the eye of the curious florist.[61] Florists gathered in pubs to exchange knowledge while socializing, an entirely different social context from that of the amateur naturalists who submitted accounts of their activities to journals such as the *Phytologist*. The scholar Anne Secord documents how vocabulary and class separated the social worlds of the Florists and the 'philosophic botanists', hampering an egalitarian approach to taking each other's concerns seriously:

> Rules established for judging flower perfection at competitions were adhered to rigidly. Points that were of fundamental importance to the florists, however, were of no interest to botanical science. Botanists prided themselves (in rhetoric at least) on not making aesthetic judgments about flowers, and the attention to variations in individual plants (so important a skill in genetics) was part of the 'noise' from which the botanist had to avoid being distracted, rather than the

'signal' (which in their world view was the essential character of the species).[62]

Florists were disapproved of as superficial observers, although in fact they looked at their primrose flowers exceedingly closely. However, their interest in cultivating 'the perfect flower' for prizes was anathema to the botanist, who favoured a wild plant thriving in a natural setting – or pressed on a herbarium sheet. The Florists grew their auriculas by hand, nurturing them with special soil preparations and protecting them from rain and soot, while naturalists and botanists visited species in the field, collected specimens in vascula and prepared them for observation in herbaria, although some cultivated living collections as well.[63]

Like the artisan Florists and the naturalist botanists, commercial horticulturalists also looked with different eyes and developed their own vocabulary. One, F. Douglas of Loxford Hall in Ilford, east of London, writes in the *Gardeners' Chronicle* of 29 March 1879 about visiting the best growers of the gold-laced polyanthus in the north of England to glean secrets about raising show-quality plants. He is a proponent of the thrum: 'However fine a flower may be as regards the lacing and ground colour, it would be worthless as a show flower if the stigmas protruded, or could be seen with the anthers down in the throat under it.'[64] (The stigma is the receptive globe for pollen at the top of the style. To the modern eye, its glistening, moon-like appearance might be even more appealing than the thrum.) Douglas continues:

> The mouth of the tube should be filled up with the anthers, forming what the old florists 'styled' a moss eye. Now if we want to obtain seeds that are likely to produce flowers of the best form and colours, such a flower must be selected as the pollen-parent. The cottagers in the North have well-marked pin flowers, which they designate 'mothers'.[65]

Mother-eyed and moss-eyed were thus names used by growers for pin and thrum, respectively. Douglas continues: 'I saw one of these "mothers" in the hands of a grower in the North last year with the flowers perfect in every respect; the ground colour was black, with the edge, centre, and radiating lines of a clear lemon.'[66]

The influential garden designer and horticulturalist Gertrude Jekyll (1843–1932), known for her forceful opinions, had something to say about pin and thrum, and about an additional feature in primroses called the 'rose eye':

> The old florists' distinction of pin-eye and thrum-eye also alters the character of the flower, for . . . when the individual bloom is observed, the single flower and the whole truss gain by the thrum-eye . . . especially when this is further enhanced by a raised fretted ridge at the edge of the tube, forming a kind of crown and giving the flower what is called a rose-eye. In the pin-eye the . . . more ornamental detail is wanting.[67]

Jekyll had no liking for the show table, but for many horticulturalists the distinction between pin- and thrum-eye has held into the twenty-first century, especially in the auricula, whose long history has not been forgotten: one of the most famous auricula growers of the nineteenth century, James Douglas, wrote that a pin-eye is 'fatal'.[68]

Darwin kept to the primrose path throughout his life. Twice a day he strolled a sandy walk that he had made at Down House. The path, which had a 'light' side and a 'dark' side, wound through deep forest and along hedgerows with views of the countryside. He called it his 'thinking path', and kicked a flint for each lap he made of it; a pile of four flints meant he was deep into a problem.[69] In 1874, eight years before his death, he wrote a letter to the editor of *Nature* with his thoughts about why birds attacked the flowers of the common primrose and short-stalked cowslips and polyanthus, a problem he had been observing for twenty years but now feared 'extermination' because

The Sand Walk, Darwin's 'thinking path' near Down House, 1909.

he was seeing hundreds of flowers destroyed.[70] Close observation revealed that small pieces of the calyx, measuring 2.5–5 mm ($^2/_{16}$–$^3/_{16}$ in.), had been snipped away, releasing nectar from the cut ends. The purpose of the letter was to ask the journal's readers to send their observations from other parts of Britain. Darwin was interested in the biology of the birds' behaviour, whether it was instinctive or learned. Although he could countenance birds feeding on nectar in the New and Old Worlds, 'with the primrose it is an unmitigated evil' and not welcome 'in this primrose-decked land' – an unusual outburst of bias from the even-handed naturalist.[71] The bestselling Victorian garden writer James Shirley Hibberd wrote of the common primrose in *Field Flowers: A Handy-book for the Rambling Botanist* (1870):

> A most versatile plant is this, and one that may be studied for a lifetime without being completely understood, as Mr Darwin would tell you.[72]

three

The Plant Hunter's Primrose

Flowers are, perhaps, the most trying of all things to collect, for they wait for no man either in flowering time or at the harvest.

E.H.M. COX, *Farrer's Last Journey* (1926)[1]

In 1858 the writer and adventurer Captain Thomas Mayne Reid, who was admired by Arthur Conan Doyle, Robert Louis Stevenson and Theodore Roosevelt, published *The Plant Hunters; or, Adventures among the Himalaya Mountains*. The novel begins with the line 'A plant-hunter! What is that?'[2] Reid, who makes the claim that 'the humblest of their class has done more service to the human race than even the great Linnaeus himself', points out that it is a 'profession' with enormous stress.[3] Botanic gardens, horticultural societies, wealthy enthusiasts and commercial nurseries sent collectors far from home with very little pay to fierce landscapes and jealously guarded hunting grounds. The weekly *Gardeners' Chronicle* carried their personal accounts, written from the field in vivid prose inspired by the first-hand experience of seeing flowers in their native habitat against immense, awesome landscapes, but the reports did not mention homesickness, depression, malnutrition, constant financial worries and medical problems. Those fell away before the romance of bringing primroses from the 'roof of the world' to ordinary European gardens.

The first plant collectors were missionaries, mainly French Catholics. In *A History of Plant Hunting in China* (1945), E.H.M. Cox

Tsangpo Gorge, photographed by Frank Kingdon-Ward in 1924.

shows his horticultural bias when he writes: 'In fact we have to wait until about 1700 until we find a missionary worthy of being called a botanist.'[4] Botanizing was dangerous as the Opium Wars of 1839–42 and 1850–60 had created tension between the British and the Chinese, and there was ongoing conflict between China and Tibet. When the Englishman Francis Younghusband led an expedition to invade Lhasa in 1904, Christian missionaries faced horrifying reprisals. The historian and garden writer Jane Kilpatrick has brought the contributions and ordeals of these plant hunters into the twenty-first century in her book *Fathers of Botany: The Discovery of Chinese Plants by European Missionaries* (2014). Père Étienne-Jules Dubernard, who is remembered for his collection of *P. dubernardiana*, suffered unprintable horrors at the hands of 'yellow lamas' during three days of torture. Père Jean André Soulié, who left his name in *P. souliei*, was so fluent in native dialects that he could pass as a native. Despite service as a physician and healer, in 1905, in the words of Cox, he was 'caught by the Tibetan monks of Batang, tortured for 15 days, and finally shot, a tragic end to a fine man and a brilliant plant collector'.[5]

George Forrest

Forrest made seven trips to Yunnan over many years. Born the youngest of fourteen in Paisley, Scotland, in 1873, he had trained with an apothecary as a teenager, before embarking for Australia to tend sheep and prospect for gold. Back home, penniless, he gained an entrée to the Royal Botanic Garden Edinburgh (RBGE) after making an archaeological find, an old stone coffin, while botanizing. His sponsors traded comments in their letters about his 'grit', proven on his first trip when he hid for days, ragged and starving, his foot impaled by a knife-sharp bamboo stalk, to escape the fury of the warring lamas and the rampage of the White Wolf, whose exploits received worldwide attention.[6]

Forrest's work ethic was legendary.[7] He sent pounds and pounds of primrose seeds back to his sponsors, more seeds than anyone in Europe had time to sow.[8] In addition to collecting seeds, he prepared 31,000 herbarium specimens, now housed at the RBGE Herbarium, and would in the end have 192 genera bearing his name, including *P. forrestii*. New digital data taken from his collections show that 87 per cent of the primulas he collected were new species. Forrest invented the practice of sending out teams of local collectors whom he had trained, while he stayed at their base to attend to the vast paperwork involved in the process. The paper used for herbarium sheets at that time came from Rangoon, Myanmar (then Burma), by rail, barge and ox cart to a frontier town called Bhamo, and then by mule to a small trading town, Tengyue.[9] Both the carrying and the transportation of this special paper were expensive and burdensome for the collectors.

The advent of the camera made collecting even more stressful. Glass plates were heavy, and development took place in a tent in the field after dark, sometimes all night. Flies mistook the camera lens for a human eye, and besieged both. Forrest was required to photograph each species in its natural habitat, develop the negatives in the field and attach handwritten notes to the resulting prints. He describes the rigours of securing photographs of the lovely *P. pinnatifida* amid torrential rain and blowing gales.[10] The photographs, many of which appeared in the *Gardeners' Chronicle*, were part of the job of a 'plant introducer' (another term Cox used for plant hunter) to heighten public interest as well as that of the patrons of the expeditions. He tried colour photography, but found it too difficult to develop in the field. In 1930 he made a film showing the long convoy of bearers needed for a plant-hunting trip.[11]

Although Forrest's centre of operations was his 'garret' at a rented house in Nvlvk'ö, he still explored intensively on foot, especially the Yulong and Cangshan ranges, looking for primulas. He was at the epicentre of primula diversity, and the staggering variation of shades bewildered him. His training at RBGE, where he internalized lessons about the nature of species, had not prepared him for such diversity. Primula species abounded, some as hybrid swarms in vast meadows, others on high peaks under snow. He was supposed to find new species and prepare a 'type' specimen, one that displays typical characteristics of the species, but it was hard to find a true 'type' in a sea of colour. He wrote home about finding primroses

from the richest and deepest crimson scarlet, through flame reds, and the richest of oranges and buffs, to every conceivable

George Forrest in China with a favourite dog.

shade of rose and pink-salmon, geranium and the bright pinks one finds in aniline dyes, back to the soft crushed strawberry and buff rose, if you can imagine such a shade!¹²

In a letter to the Regius Keeper of RBGE, the primula expert William Wright Smith, Forrest wrote about his hunt for the progenitor of all this colour, which he felt must be a yellow primula: 'Now

I feel equally certain that there must be a yellow Primula somewhere. So sure am I of this that I and all my men are on the lookout for it and there is a reward proclaimed for its capture!'[13] He did find one, but it had little seed, and its progeny never flourished in Edinburgh. In one foray Forrest set his camp at 2,700 m (9,000 ft) in the Lijiang Mountains north of the Yangtze River. There *P. dryadifolia* was waiting for him. In a letter written that evening to Sir Isaac Bayley Balfour, Regius Professor of Botany at RBGE, he describes the setting:

> Its habitat is a cup-shaped, boulder-strewn basin about a mile in extent, almost at the limit of the vegetation at an altitude of approximately 15,500 feet [4,700 m]. Snow and barren limestone peaks all around, a cutting wind, and moisture everywhere. The centre of the basin was occupied by a small lake of crystal clearness, formed of the melting snows, every depression of any size filled with heavy snowdrifts, but on the bare intervening prominences, and in every crevice of all the larger boulders capable of retaining a sufficiency of loam and moisture, was P. dryadifolia.[14]

Later, when staying in a village near Jade Dragon Snow Mountain, the southernmost glacier in the northern hemisphere, just north of the Lijiang Range, Forrest collected more *P. dryadifolia*. He wrote to J. C. Williams, the owner of Caerhays Castle in Cornwall and a member of a seed-collecting syndicate, 'I have seed enough to sow all Cornwall!'[15] Despite that, however, the species proved nearly impossible to cultivate.

Another site in the Jade Dragon Snow Mountain (Yulong Xueshan) yielded more *P. dryadifolia* in the company of its sisters, *P. pinnatifida*, *P. secundiflora* and *P. pseudo-sikkimensis*. Forrest frequented this area often, for, he wrote, 'the range in its fully fifty miles [80 km] is one huge flower garden.'[16] The mountains rise to 5,800 m (19,000 ft) in places. One plant that Forrest found in the Chung-tien district of Yunnan, named and sent back to Europe, and which has made it into cultivation, is the anise primrose, *P. anisodora*, one of the candelabra primroses, whose deep-maroon flowers with their yellow-green eyes appear in whorls on a tall flowering scape.[17]

At home in Edinburgh before his last expedition, Forrest would walk each day into RBGE and ask the propagators exuberantly, 'What's germinated this morning?'[18] In China he was often photographed with his arms fondly wrapped around a dog. He spent years and years away from his beloved wife, Clementina, and their three sons; one of his letters to her was 50 pages long on A5 paper.[19] Plant hunting was his livelihood, and he fought for respect and remuneration. RBGE sustains his memory through talks, articles and tweets releasing photos from their archive. On his birthday, 13 March, in 2016 a long row of his field notebooks appeared on Twitter.

Reginald Farrer

Born in North Yorkshire with a cleft lip and palate, and of gnome-like stature as an adult, Reginald Farrer suffered physical hardship early. The treatment for a cleft palate involved hot tongs, sulphuric acid and metal bridles. His speech was difficult to understand except by his mother until he was fifteen, his voice 'a shallow screech, like wind through cracked metal'.[20] He was educated at home in Clapham, North Yorkshire, and found solace botanizing in the limestone cliffs nearby. By the age of eight he had memorized a botany textbook, and by thirteen he had had an article published in the *Journal of Botany* on an obscure botanical point.[21]

In the first paragraph of his epic plant-hunting narrative *On the Eaves of the World* (1917), Farrer explained the impetus for his departure for Tibet. Just hearing the name of an unusual primula at the Primula Conference of 1916 inspired an obsessive search entailing months of physical deprivation and psychological stress. Some of his made-up, derogatory descriptors for plants he disliked, such as 'squinny' or 'mimp', provoked ridicule, but most often he hit the high notes. Farrer travelled with a plump pony named Spotted Fat;

an enigmatic Chinese-speaking Englishman, William Purdom, who dressed as a local when necessary to foil bandits; and his Chinese helpers Mafu and Go-go. He carried a complete set of Jane Austen, as well as plenty of whisky and rum. Despite his unathletic build, he was a tireless and enthusiastic climber:

> One must never neglect chances in the field. The one thing that you don't go after in a day's hunt will surely prove ultimately to be the one thing you ought to have gone after, just as the one gully you don't visit will surely be the one gully that holds the treasure . . . And, indeed, now that my eye was agog for it, I could discern the luminous blue sparks of the Grand Violet Primula occasionally dotting the dank ledges up and up the shady walls of the cliff, and here and there was able to wriggle my way into reach of a specimen or two.[22]

The plentiful primulas lured him on and on into a dramatic limestone landscape:

> Embalmed in bliss, I climbed about on the ledges of Primula, savouring the charm of it at leisure. And then pressed forward through the dark narrows of the chine, to where, beyond, it widened into a sort of cauldron, with cliffs of topless vastness impending everywhere.[23]

A rich vocabulary of landscape words flowed from his pen:

> Into the cool obscurity of the chine I turned, up the course of the beck, where it darkly gurgled among the grimy crusts of lingering snow-pats. And in the cool shade a new pinkness at once illuminated the sombre ledges of moss and moisture. Instinctively the flower-trained eye detects a fresh note of colour, be it near or far. There is no possibility of mistake

Wood engraver Abigail Rorer's portrait of Reginald Farrer
from *On the Hunt for the King of the Alps* (2011).

and I gasped for a minute in the delight of a Primula that was not P. stenocalyx.[24]

Rather, it was *P. urticifolia*. Farrer proceeds to rhapsodize over its beauty and lament that it has been 'atrociously wronged' in its species name, which means 'nettle-leaved'. He compares it to *P. bella*, which lies in 'cushions of loveliness' on the high summits of Tsang Chan, and to *P. minima*, which 'runs riot in carpets of colour' in the Dolomites. Soon he found the one that would become his – *P. farreriana*:

On a stout white stem of six inches they unfold above the leaves, half-hanging in a bunch of half-a-dozen or so. And they are of a loveliness singular and phantasmal in their

Englishman William Purdom in disguise, his face painted with burnt cork paste, while on a seed-collecting mission in a Tibetan region unfriendly to foreigners, c. 1911.

A watercolour of *P. farreriana*, painted by Reginald Farrer
in the Ta-Tung Alps, Kansu, at a mule-inn on 19 June 1915.

family, very large and ample and round-faced, of a faint blue
lavender so subtle as to be almost a French grey, gradually
suffused with a white radiation from the misty bull's-eye of
intense black-purple at their throat, which continues down
the tube inside and out. And their sad and startling loveliness
is echoed by the keen sad sweetness of their scent.[25]

When he looks up, among boulders 'black as hate' and limestone 'violently bursting aloft in gigantic reefs and spars and slanted towers', there, 'among the dark combes and on the cold sides of those towers', he sees many more specimens, which he now calls 'Mine'.[26]

Farrer explains why the plant hunter cares so deeply to have his or her name joined with that of a garden plant:

Reginald Farrer's grave in the Minshan mountains of Upper Myanmar (Burma).

The collector's dream is to have some illustrious plant to bear his name immortal through the gardens of future generations, long after he himself shall have become part of the dust of their paths . . . To become vividly immortal in the Valhalla of gardeners, one must own a species as vigorous as it is glorious, a thing capable of becoming, and remaining, a household word among English enthusiasts.[27]

P. farreriana is not 'in cultivation' at the moment. Farrer wanted his plant to be grown, to connect with people, but it was 'shy' (the grower's term for recalcitrant species) outside its native territory. It is one of the great Blue Nivalids, lovers of high elevations, limestone precipices and snow.

It is fortunate that E.H.M. Cox travelled with Farrer on his last collecting trip and wrote an account, *Farrer's Last Journey*. Unparalleled travel literature, its pages stuffed with primroses, it is a chance to see Farrer from the point of view of another. Cox offers perspectives on Farrer's essential heroism amid the forceful vegetation on the border between China and Myanmar. It was 'cannibalistic', even cruel, and unsettlingly dense. Overwhelmed, Cox registered a sense of 'lifelessness' in the jungle.[28] Forrest had also found the 'pathlessness' of the forests in Yunnan daunting.[29]

When Cox left to return to Scotland, Farrer had a holiday of sorts, in which he rested in comfort, working on a novel. But he set out again and died at the age of 40 in his camp on one of the cold, wet forest ranges of the Minshan mountains, probably from bronchial pneumonia, although various accounts mention dysentery, diphtheria and alcohol poisoning. For weeks mist and rain limited visibility to just a few metres. His attendant ran for four days over the mountains to get medical help, but Burra Shab Bahadur, as they called him, died, a trouble to no one, his attendant said, subsisting on sips of soda water and whisky.

Many readers and primula enthusiasts have followed Farrer's path. Botanical tours offer trips that retrace his steps in the Dolomites, and at the Harrogate Flower Show in Yorkshire in 2017 there was a re-enactment of his gardening-by-shotgun experiment of shooting Himalayan seeds high on to the vertical face of a limestone cliff.[30] Cox's final assessment emphasizes the power of enthusiasm:

> But make no mistake, Farrer revivified horticulture by his picturesque and dashing enthusiasm at a time when there was a great danger of it again falling into a dignified and somnolent rut. Even today his spirit helps to keep up its vitality.[31]

Farrer did not fit in well with his family or his contemporaries. He adopted Buddhism and quarrelled with rock-garden enthusiasts. He rarely lost his sense of being an outsider, except with plants and with his fellow plant hunter William Purdom, to whom he dedicated *On the Eaves of the World* with the words 'through whom alone it was that these odysseys were made possible and pleasant'. Farrer told Cox, with reference to primulas, that 'my spirit grew quite tame and reconciled to them.'[32] This is perhaps an example of 'biophilia', a word first used by the sociologist Erich Fromm and amplified by the naturalist Edward Osborne Wilson to describe the capacity for love between disparate organisms. Although plant hunting was their livelihood, plant hunters felt an intense connection to their plants that bordered on passion.

Frank Kingdon-Ward

Frank Kingdon-Ward (1885–1958), who worked in the period following the deaths of Forrest and Farrer, has been called 'the last of the great plant hunters'.[33] Early on, however, he had strayed into Farrer and Cox's hunting ground. Despite a background of intense rivalry, they had shared a collegial dinner of 'succulent dishes' made by Dragon, Farrer's cook. Green-eyed and intense, Kingdon-Ward overcame bouts of depression and a fear of heights and cold to live fully the life of the plant hunter, making 22 expeditions to Asia and writing

25 books with evocative titles, such as *Riddle of the Tsangpo Gorges*, *Plant Hunting on the Edge of the World* and *The Romance of Plant Hunting*, and countless articles for the armchair traveller. Like that of Farrer, his writing elevated flowers to icons of improbable beauty on the roof of the world, and plant hunters to heroic figures whose experiences inspire regular retelling.

The son of a self-taught botanist who achieved a professorship at Cambridge but never prosperity, Frank Kingdon-Ward dropped out of Cambridge for lack of funds after two years. He went to Shanghai to work as a schoolmaster, but he was unhappy flogging students. Luckily for him, when Forrest fell out with the seedsman Arthur K. Bulley over late payment, Bulley hired him. Like Forrest, he too travelled with a dog, named Beetle, which he had bought for one rupee. He described it as a 'black long-haired dish-faced bow-legged Bhutanese dog with large appealing eyes and well covered in fleas'.[34] Later Kingdon-Ward was one of the few to make trips with a woman, his second wife, Jean Macklin.

The story of a rose-coloured primrose, never identified by species, shows Kingdon-Ward's persistence and growing appreciation for Tibetan culture.[35] He is in Tibet, having gone 'into camp' at an elevation of just over 3,900 m (13,000 ft), but he descends to the village of A-tun-si to dry and pack seeds. An abbot and several monks come to look at his operation. They have never seen white men before, but are friendly and delight in his microscope. One has brought a primrose with 'bright rose red flowers, deliciously scented'. Kingdon-Ward is smitten, and when he asks for its location, the monk waves to the mountain behind the monastery. Kingdon-Ward is chagrined to realize that he covered that area and must have missed it. Certain that he can find it the next day, he does not press the specimen, but in fact he fails to locate it. He asks the abbot to give the monk, who is a student, a day's holiday to help him find the rose primrose. Twice the abbot refuses. Six weeks later he has still not found the plant, and decides to go back to the monastery to ask again. This time the abbot makes a deal: he asks for money to provide a substitute for the student monk at prayers, and a greeting scarf. Kingdon-Ward and the monk trek off together:

> Approaching the highest peak, the monk outdistanced us and disappeared over the ridge. Tashi and I followed. Arrived at the summit I could see nothing of our guide, and fearful lest he should uproot the Primula, I called to Tashi to find him quickly as I would not countenance the unnecessary destruction of wild flowers even in Tibet.[36]

The monk reappears with the rose-coloured primrose, and Kingdon-Ward realizes that he has had a lesson in seeing:

> After all it grew on the scree which I had dismissed as impossible, and yet explored to make sure! I had been within a dozen yards on my second visit to Ningri Tangor ... Yet deliberately not expecting to see it I had passed it over ... Who dare say now that the Tibetans are not born botanists when they can recognize plants as accurately as this man did?[37]

Kingdon-Ward's descriptions bring the scree alive. This habitat was the last refuge for 'the finest flowers', chief among them primroses. 'Cruel as hell', scree was formed by 'pitiless' weather breaking down limestone peaks into smithereens. He writes: 'a live scree is tense and aggressive; it is all tooth and nail; all hammer and tong', and 'the scree is ever on the move'.[38] On another occasion he climbed and scrambled, bent double, to the clifftop of a fire-charred mountainside and saw the improbable:

> Patches of snow lay about under the trees, and almost the first thing I saw on the warm, black, slimy earth, was a drift of the dwarf purple-flowered Primula eucyclia. This rare and charming rock plant, with deeply cut geranium-like leaves, bears frilly flowers on stems an inch or two high.[39]

Kingdon-Ward's reports of his work as a plant hunter represent a valuable archive. His competitors envied his eagle eye for finding plants and remembering where they were. Few collectors would collect seed from a plant never seen in flower, for it could be 'rubbish'. This meant finding specimens in flower and returning several months later, when the seeds had ripened. He would return to an area that was covered in snow, dig down and find the frozen seed capsules of the plant he wanted.

The discovery that gave Kingdon-Ward the greatest pleasure occurred on his trip to northern Myanmar in 1926. Forcing his way through dense forest, he emerged on an alpine slope in the last half-hour of daylight:

> I can recall several flowers which at first sight have knocked the breath out of me, but only two or three which have taken me by storm as did this one. The sudden vision is like a physical blow in the pit of the stomach; one can only gasp and stare. I stood there transfixed on the snow-cone, in a honeymoon of bliss, feasting my eyes on a masterpiece.[40]

Kingdon-Ward named it *P. thearosa* after the popular Madame Butterfly rose introduced in 1918.[41] It and its four closest relatives have only recently become well known.[42] Virtually inaccessible, they occur on steep banks above 4,000 m (13,100 ft) in the Tibetan borderlands of the eastern Himalayas. Students of the genus *Primula* consider *P. thearosa* and these relatives to be 'the ultimate expression of elegance in that most charismatic of genera', noting that 'the most desirable plants are often the most unobtainable, and much of the glamour of these wonderful subjects results from their sheer inaccessibility'.[43]

Kingdon-Ward was an anxious perfectionist, and more than anyone felt the high stress of the plant-hunting profession. At times his 'eye' was the insecure one of a judgemental artist: 'That Primula you

Overleaf: The tearose primula (*Primula aglemana*) on the Galung La pass, Xizang, in Lhasa, Tibet. See *Primula World* for botanical status of 'thearosa'.

admired so much – is there not an odious flush of magenta in it after all?'[44] Hunger and sleep deprivation led easily to paranoia: 'Are there any plants worth bringing home, or are they all "kag"? Will the seeds germinate? Will the plants be admired, or sneered at, or worst fate of all, ignored?'[45] Alongside the high points, there was almost constant discomfort: clouds of bloodsucking insects, sinister sights at night of phosphorescent fungi 'gorging' themselves on trees, fevers from poisonous rhododendron honey, an unexpected engagement to the daughter of a village headman, made by mistake, and untreated dental problems. His unending financial worries led him to hatch improbable money-making schemes, such as turning papaya seeds into fake caviar. He often had travelling with him young, wealthy patrons who found his taciturnity almost unbearable. Once he didn't speak for three days. But in northern Myanmar he was called Nampan

The tearose primula (*P. agleniana*) photographed in Arunachal Pradesh, India.

Duwa, the Flower Chief, and there were moments when that role suited him, when he felt 'strangely happy and at peace' despite the stress. The hot-water bottle and mug of Horlicks at night helped.[46]

Every spring an article on 'perfect primulas' appears, reminding gardeners that plant hunters brought many primula species from the Himalayas. Forrest introduced the moonlight primrose (*P. alpicola*), the anise primrose (*P. anisodora*) and the orchid primrose (*P. vialii*), among others, and Kingdon-Ward the Tibetan or giant cowslip (*P. florindae*) and Cawdor's primula (*P. cawdoriana*), among others.[47] Farrer's many interesting new species resisted cultivation, being intractable as opposed to simply shy, but many other garden plants bear his name. Two of the earliest primroses to arrive in Europe – *P. denticulata*, in 1861, and *P. japonica*, in 1871 – have thrived in gardens. The former, which is commonly known as the drumstick primrose because of its pompom inflorescence, has adapted so well to Scotland that it is called the Kirrie Dumpling. As for the shy ones, online gardeners' forums facilitate the transfer of minute details of horticultural practice to be shared to keep the species in circulation.

The botanical artist and historian Emma Tennant, in her exhibition 'Plants with Provenance' at the Fine Art Society in London in 2015, paid tribute to the collectors: 'To know something about the plant collectors and explorers who risked their lives to bring us these botanical treasures adds greatly to the romance of gardening.'[48] Scientists pay tribute, too. A recent study at the University of Oxford states that 50 per cent of the world's flora has been discovered by 'the great' plant hunters, who comprise 2 per cent of plant collectors.[49]

Forrest, Farrer and Kingdon-Ward were among the 'great'. Others include a team who also specialized in collecting primroses, George Sherriff and Frank Ludlow. Sherriff introduced 66 species of primula from Tibet and Bhutan, including *P. bhutanica*.[50] Using Google Earth Pro, Pam Eveleigh, creator of the website *Primula World*, gives viewers a bird's-eye view of the route Ludlow and Sherriff took in 1933 collecting primulas in Bhutan.[51] In 1950 Sherriff retired to the magnificent

The Kirrie Dumpling (*P. denticulata*),
photographed by *Primula World*'s Pam Eveleigh.

garden of Ascreavie near Kirriemuir, eastern Scotland, where he was said to grow all the primulas then known. At the exhibition 'The Plant Seekers' held at the Garden Museum in London in 2012, in partnership with the RHS Lindley Library, various artefacts including Forrest's collecting box were on view.[52] Seed catalogues continue to mention the plant hunters in their offerings of Asiatic primulas, hoping to engage gardeners with the romance of remote geography.[53]

Plant hunting is still a profession, and the horticulturalists who grow the seeds found by plant hunters are as indispensable as ever, as are the taxonomists who identify their relationships and habitats. In the words of the RBGE, 'science and horticulture must combine forces to save nature.'[54] At the Flora Malesiana 10 Symposium in Edinburgh in 2016 the theme was Classify, Cultivate, Conserve.[55]

The plant hunters dutifully archived dried specimens for their sponsors, which were often botanic gardens, but their overriding goal was 'introduction': to find new species and collect seeds that would germinate into spellbinding, living plants.

Pl. 88.

1 Primula elatior var polianthus (Burnard's formosa) 2. Primula auricula (the conqueror of Europe). 3. Primula vulgaris (4 double varieties)

3   1   2

Garden treasures that have disappeared: Henry Noel Humphreys's hand-finished chromolithograph of 1) 'Burnard's Formosa, a gold-laced polyanthus that enabled its breeder to buy a cottage; 2) an auricula named the Conqueror of Europe; and 3) several double primroses, after an illustration by Jane Loudon for *Mrs Jane Loudon's Ladies Flower Garden of Ornamental Perennials* (1849).

four
The Well-bred Primrose

You become responsible, forever, for what you have tamed.
You're responsible for your rose.

ANTOINE DE SAINT-EXUPÉRY, *The Little Prince* (1943)[1]

Plant breeders have found the primrose a willing partner in the creation of endless beautiful hybrids, unravelling the history of which is almost impossible. In Sacheverell Sitwell's *Old Fashioned Flowers*, one of the classics of garden literature, he writes that the subject of old primroses and polyanthuses is 'fraught with so many complications that the person who dares to write upon it with only some four or five years' experience behind him runs the gauntlet of endless comment and criticism'.[2] In his book and those of other primrose historians like Barbara Shaw (the Primrose Lady of Yorkshire, 1922–2008), Roy Genders (1913–1985) and Peter Ward, one meets primrose hybrids, mutants, cultivars and seed strains that have vanished, because extinction occurs in the garden as well as in the wild. The story of primrose hybrids and the people who have bred them and cherished them involves chance encounters and the need for perfection.

The Hybrid Swarm

Every primrose seed holds the possibility of new variation, because each is a unique recombination of genetic material from the two parent plants. Further, hybridization often occurs readily — between closely related species and between divergent cultivars, as in the case of the Japanese woodland primrose (*P. sieboldii*) — producing further variation. Gardeners may find that a planting of *P. japonica* will spread an impressionistic carpet of varying shades. In his book *Primula*, John Richards writes:

> In many large gardens where [various species of] Candelabras self-sow, most plants may be hybrid, and in these conditions every individual may differ from the next, resulting in a rainbow of colour. As many of the hybrids are fertile, back-crossing and multiple hybridizations occur; at least one hybrid with four species in its make-up is known.[3]

Botanists call this situation a hybrid swarm. It is a good place to look for new varieties, but the parentage will be a mystery. As we saw in the previous chapter, hybrid swarms complicated the work of plant hunters charged with bringing home true species.

The Anomalous Primroses

The Elizabethans prized what John Parkinson, apothecary to James I in the early seventeenth century, described as the 'Franticke and Foolish' primroses. In the nineteenth century they were much studied as 'teratological phenomena' or 'monstrosities'.[4] Today they are still studied and cultivated, but called variants or 'the anomalous prim-roses'. In *Hybrid: The History and Science of Plant Breeding*, Noel Kingsbury speculates that mutant flowers paved the way for ornamental gardening and ultimately ornamental plant breeding.[5] The artist and plant-breeding critic George Gessert agrees about the inspiration provided by mutant forms. In *Green Light: Toward an Art of Evolution*, he writes:

> One of ornamental horticulture's silliest myths is that garden-ers desire only what is beautiful, tasteful, or harmonious . . .

The reality of ornamental gardens is that they are full of oddities and novelties, puns, kitsch, genetic follies, visual violence, gross stupidity, deception, monsters and whatever else intrigues or captures attention.[6]

Anomalies appear repeatedly in the common primrose, the cowslip and the polyanthus. The Tudors (1485–1603) noticed and named all the odd forms: Jack-in-the-green, jackanapes-on-horseback, hose-in-hose, curled cowslips or galligaskins, clowns, feathers and pantaloons. They saw their own habits reflected in the flowers' oddities, and brought them into their gardens. The flower known as Jack-in-the-green has a lovely green ruff because the sepals are rounded and leafy, and the name is perhaps connected to the foliate Green Man of medieval times.[7] Galligaskins, a variation, has slightly twisted leafy sepals. The calyx of jackanapes-on-horseback has leafy tips but petal-like bases, so that the flower has a bicolour ruff. Jackanapes was the Elizabethan name for someone who made a monkey of himself ('jackanapes' signified a pet monkey). In the hose-in-hose mutation, the sepals of the calyx are transformed into petals so that one flower appears to grow out of another exactly like it. The Elizabethans saw an analogy with the way they wore several pairs of stockings, one appearing above the other with the tops turned down. The pantaloon is a variant of this variant, in which the lower flower has a stripe of green, red or yellow in the middle of each sepal-turned-petal.[8]

Sitwell writes: 'There is no plant that so much suggests the realm of Queen Mab as Hose-in-Hose and Galligaskin; and the pawns with which these moves are made take us back in unbroken descent to the sixteenth century.'[9] At the time he was writing, enthusiasts were still 'prospecting' for the old varieties in Ireland and Scotland:

A pink Hose-in-Hose, found growing in a farm garden in County Kerry, is a lovely flower, and may well be lost in antiquity as to its origins. In an out-of-the-way place, such as a lonely farm in Kerry, plants might easily survive from the eighteenth century or even earlier.[10]

Twentieth century plant breeders have created a hybrid polyanthus-type hose-in-hose that comes true from seed. (Many hybrids do not come true from seed, or are sterile and have to be propagated by division, physically pulling apart plants.) Named the 'You and Me' series (*Primula × tommasinii*), it represents the work of breeders collaborating over several countries and even continents. Its development began after discussions between Dutch plant breeder Kees Sahin and Jared Sinclair, owner of Barnhaven Primroses in Cumbria, northern England. Otka Plavcová of the Silva Tarouca Institute in Pruhonice, near Prague, undertook the breeding work, crossing Barnhaven hose-in-hose varieties and 'Crescendo' polyanthus to create new parent lines. The British plant breeder Simon Crawford then marketed the series. The vibrant cobalt flowers of 'You and Me' Blue appeared on the cover of the Bluestone catalogue in the United States in 2017, indicating the success of the collaboration. Other colours, such as 'You and Me' Cream and 'You and Me' Magenta Lace, are also available.[11]

In 1999 the oakleaf or oak-leafed mutant, with a lobed leaf, was discovered in a commercial nursery.[12] The breeder and geneticist Margaret Webster has worked with it, creating through hybridization the triple mutant feathered/oak leaf/hose-in-hose. Webster has studied the genetic basis of the anomalous primroses for more than 30 years, and holds the National Heritage Collection of Primula (British floral variants) at her home near Bristol in southwestern England.[13]

Pug-in-a-pinner: the doubles

Some say that the most beautiful primroses are the doubles. That was certainly the opinion of the herbalist John Gerard in 1597: 'Our garden double primrose, of all the rest is of the greatest beauty.'[14]

The hose-in-hose anomalous primrose 'You and Me Blue' (*P. × tommasinii*), a recent hybrid representing the collaboration of breeders across several continents.

In double flowers the reproductive organs – stamens, anthers, pistil and ovaries – are transformed into petals. The first mention of a double primrose occurs in the 1580s, when Tabernaemontanus, the father of German botany, described a yellow double primrose called the 'double sulphur', which persisted well into the twentieth century and may still exist.[15] The primrose first mentioned as being tended in a garden was a double. It occurs in the *Herball* (1578) of the English botanist and antiquarian Henry Lyte, who describes it as 'fayre and dubbel'. In the contemporaneous *New Herball*, William Turner wrote: 'There are some grene cowislipped and some dubble, tripel, quadruple, that grow in gardines.'[16] There are semi-doubles, as well. The old name pug-in-a-pinner is apt for the many-petalled types. 'Pinner' was used as early as the sixteenth century to refer to a ruffled woman's cap that encircled the face. Originally bred in China, the pug arrived in Europe at about this time. Some critics deplore the 'petticoatization' effect found in double flowers, but many admire the dense profusion of petals, whereby the primrose earns the 'rose' part of its name.

For more than 200 years varieties of double primrose and poly-anthus proliferated, particularly in the hands of the French, the Irish Quakers and the Scots. Charles E. Nelson, one of the founders of the Irish Garden Plant Society (IGPS), writes: 'It is noteworthy that cultivars of polyanthus and auriculas were perhaps the first ornamental plants deliberately raised, selected and named in Ireland.'[17] In his recent book *A Heritage of Beauty* he describes 5,300 varieties of garden plant raised in Ireland.[18] An effort is underway to source, propagate and distribute each variety to members of IGPS, who will act as 'plant guardians'.[19] Sitwell also stressed the importance of Ireland as natal territory for doubles:

The double primrose 'Blue Ice', introduced by Barnhaven in 2014.

They are at their best in a damp, green climate . . . They come in greatest numbers from six Counties of Ulster, from Limerick, from Dublin, or from the perennially green and damp County Kerry, where they have stayed, unmolested, since the time of Thomas More's Irish melodies, to which, indeed, they approximate in atmosphere and sentiment.[20]

Plant breeders continue to create new doubles, which can occur in the common primrose, the cowslip, the polyanthus, the anomalous primroses and the auricula. Primula 'Dawn Ansell' is a fairly new double Jack-in-the-green primrose, raised by the Welsh breeder Cecil Jones.[21] The Belarina doubles, such as 'Pink Ice' and 'Valentine', bred in Cambridgeshire by David and Priscilla Kerley, who run a family-owned business, are robust, free-flowering plants.[22] Barnhaven Primroses in Plestin-les-Grèves, northwestern France, maintains some of its older varieties, such as 'Miss Indigo' and 'Blue Sapphire', as well as introducing new ones, such as 'Brittany Blue' in 2011, described as having 'the colour of sun-washed doors and shutters of little granite houses in Brittany', and 'Blue Ice' in 2014.[23] Margaret Webster has introduced a number of double-flowered hybrids into the trade. Her hybrid 'Tarragem' (an anagram of Margaret) double, laced polyanthuses, developed in 2008, exert a sumptuous Elizabethan appeal. 'Tarragem Gilded Garnet' has double mahogany-red flowers, each petal laced with pale gold, and 'Tarragem Sparkling Ruby' has bright red, white-laced petals.[24] Micropropagation, a method of tissue culture, has increased the commercial availability of these new hybrids.

Green Primroses

The Elizabethans were interested in green primroses, as have been plant breeders and amateur gardeners since then. Cowslips, common primroses and polyanthuses all produce variants with green flowers. Some are examples of virescence, in which tissues that do not

Primula 'Tarragem Gilded Garnet', a double gold-laced variety,
bred by Margaret Webster and introduced in 2012.

contain chloroplasts (the green-pigmented organelles responsible
for photosynthesis) – such as petals – gain them via mutation. Others
are 'foliaceous', in which the sepals (the green bracts that protect a
flower bud) multiply to flower-like effect.[25] Gerard mentioned 'the
Greene Rose cowslips or double greene feathered cowslip' in his
Herball of 1597.[26] This variant has a large, flower-like feathery calyx
but no actual petals or floral organs. Parkinson named nine kinds
of primrose, singling out the green primrose and the green rose cowslip for special mention. In 1629 he described two single green
primroses and one double green primrose; there has been a search
ever since to find what he saw, and Sitwell writes that 'this is the
great rarity of the Double Primrose world. Its discovery would be
equivalent to the finding of some lost masterpiece by El Greco,
to the restricted world who are interested in that subject.'[27] Some
doubt that a green primrose, whether common primrose or cowslip

or polyanthus, is desirable, except for its rarity and its ancient lineage. However, a green polyanthus-type primrose that appeared on a traffic island in Surrey, British Columbia, a few years ago has star appeal. Noticed by the well-known Canadian gardener Francisca Darts, it is now widely available in the horticultural trade as *Primula* × 'Francisca' (or × 'Francesca' or × 'Green Lace' or *Polyanthus* 'Francisca'). Described variously as jade-green, celadon-green or citrus-green, it has ruffled petals with a long-armed yellow star radiating from the centre.[28]

The Amateur Breeders and Collection Holders

A legion of amateur breeders have achieved renown as hybridizers, among them the Wynne sisters of Tigroney House in Avoca, County Wicklow. Winifred, Emily and Veronica, daughters of a parson and members of the 'first wave' of Irish feminism, are perhaps most famous for reviving Avoca Handweavers, the oldest mill in Ireland (1723), which they inherited in the 1920s, to provide jobs for the impoverished.[29] It was Winifred in particular who raised many new hybrids, among the most famous *Primula* 'Julius Caesar', a 'daughter' of 'Miss Massey', with bronzed foliage and claret-red flowers. It still exists, having been retrieved by the gardening columnist Jane Powers from Winifred's relatives and reintroduced.[30] Winifred raised seedlings, selected new varieties, distributed them and went to shows to promote them. In her diary in 1916 she recounts the difficulties of travelling to an alpine garden show by train, with her show plants and twelve pieces of luggage, two dogs, one canary, eggs and bags of moss. Her niece remembers the Winifred of her childhood as a somewhat stern gardener who quizzed her every morning on the names of the flowers she had left by her bedside each night.[31] Winifred's potting shed and white strawberries symbolized garden romance for her.

Starting with just five plants, the retired dentist Joe Kennedy has taken old Irish varieties and bred new looks for more than 35 years in Ballycastle, County Antrim.[32] The Kennedy Irish Primrose Collection is known for its bronze, chocolate and even dark-purple foliage and

Winifred (born c. 1880) and Emily Wynne, primrose breeders of Avoca, Ireland.

beautifully tinted flowers. Every year Kennedy grew around 2,000 new seedlings, saving only 200 or so. He did not breed for profit, however, and never sold a single primrose. But in 2011 FitzGerald Nurseries of Stoneyford, County Kilkenny, chose to adopt his lines and increase the stock through micropropagation in order to supply the horticultural trade in North America, Europe and Japan. A basket of 'Drumcliff' primroses, the first of the FitzGerald Kennedy line to appear in North America, was presented to the then First Lady Michelle Obama in 2011.[33]

The role of serendipity in the 'birth' of new varieties enhances the feeling of mysterious provenance. Fortunately, eagle-eyed gardeners catch variation in passing as they work. The fragrant *P.* 'June Blake' emerged from the garden of the plantswoman of that name in County Wicklow, and was introduced in 2002. The yellow cowslip-like flowers decorated with orange stripes bloom liberally on 25-cm (10-in.) black stems. *P.* 'Rowallane Rose', with huge hosta-like leaves

Primula 'Julius Caesar', a hybrid developed by Winifred Wynne
in the early 20th century and recently reintroduced.

and tiers of rose-pink flowers, was named after the famous Northern Irish garden Rowallane, where it first appeared as a chance seedling. It craves soggy land.

The notable, redoubtable twentieth-century gardener Margery Fish liked green flowers – she planted a green garden with hellebores and green auriculas – and old-fashioned double primroses. After a career in journalism she became a gardening maven, bringing the cottage garden, with all the old primroses, to the forefront as a classic gardening style. Aware of the dangers of hybridization, she did not allow undue fraternization among her primroses. She writes in *Gardening in the Shade* (1964):

> I would never plant any but the wild primroses in grass, and I am afraid these would not be allowed to grow near any of my named varieties or special ones like the jacks-in-the green and hose-in-hose types which might intermarry and lose their identity.[34]

Other gardeners agree. The well-known garden historian and artist Lys de Bray said so emphatically in *Cottage Garden Year* (1983): 'I always hope that the bees will go back home and brush all the pollen out of their baskets after visiting my Primroses, because I simply do not want a group of False Oxlips, even though they are attractive.'[35] Fish saw to it that her doubles, known to be 'gross feeders', received abundant rotted farm manure. Doubles tend to flower on and on because their reproductive cycle, which would naturally terminate flowering in order to allocate resources to maturing seed, has been altered by the ovaries becoming petals. Doubles cannot produce seeds, but they occasionally produce pollen, which breeders pounce on for breeding purposes. Fish's extensive writings on the old-fashioned primroses kept their history and desirability alive.

The horticulturalist and botanical artist Mary Margaret McMurtrie (1902–2003), described as an 'extraordinarily popular and lovely person', specialized in cottage garden plants, especially double primroses, first in Mannofield, Aberdeen, and later at Balbithan House in Kintore.[36] Like Fish, she nurtured 'the old plants'. She wrote articles, illustrated books on Scotland's wild flowers, roses and heritage plants, and raised new varieties of double primrose well into her eighties. One of her early articles sums up the pleasures of a cottage garden well:

> A garden – and it can be quite a tiny garden – where old plants are treasured can be a delightful place, green and peaceful, full of soft colours and sweet scents: a garden where you can relax. It is so much more restful than one which is a blaze of colour.[37]

Her watercolours evoke the softness of primroses and auriculas, the brushstrokes leaving no sharp edges. She was honoured as the oldest practising artist in Britain by the national charity Counsel and Care for the Elderly as she celebrated her 101st birthday. During the last weeks of her life she was completing artwork for her final book.[38]

The horticultural work of people such as Fish and McMurtrie is now overseen in the UK by Plant Heritage, the world's leading cultivated plant conservation charity.[39] It still falls to volunteers to undertake the care of particular collections, however. Caroline Stone, for example, is the holder of the National Plant Collection of Double Primroses at the Glebe Garden in Cornwall, where she raises doubles in the old ways with plenty of manure from the dairy farm next door.[40] She has repeatedly put out calls for a legendary old gold-laced polyanthus named 'Prince Silverwings', but says the chances of its reappearance are 'vanishingly slim'. The doubles continue to draw attention. In the autumn of 2015 a gardener at the Royal Botanic Garden Edinburgh tweeted about a 100-year-old double, preserved through division, that had come into bloom. Although new varieties continue to appear, the historical associations of the heritage varieties lend a romance that the new ones lack, and new varieties tend to disappear quickly in the hectic pace of commercialism. Until the First

Botanical artist Barbara Shaw's illustration of 'Prince Silverwings', a gold-laced primrose now presumed lost to cultivation, from *The Book of Primroses* (1991).

World War doubles were raised commercially in orchards and under gooseberry bushes with nearby sources of humus and manure. Modern nursery conditions where underplanting is not practical may not be as conducive to their propagation. Doubles that arose as natural sports are observed by some to have more vitality than those fashioned through human hybridization.[41]

The polyanthus reaches a 'Crescendo'

The polyanthus's journey from wild-flower hybrid to 'polychrome princess of the petrol pump' is a story that Noel Kingsbury has told in his essay on the 'Dialectic of the Polyanthus'.[42] The polyanthus, initially a seventeenth-century hybrid of the common primrose, cowslip and oxlip, began a makeover when its early forms hybridized with an immigrant from the Caucasus, John Tradescant the Younger's Turkie-purple primrose. A subspecies of the common primrose (*P. vulgaris rubra*, renamed *P. vulgaris* ssp. *sibthorpii*), it had been brought to England by 1640 and to Paris even earlier. The purple 'blood' from the Caucasian immigrant gave the polyanthus a change in hue, from yellow to brick red, muddy and sepia.[43] The reddish poly-anthus became a popular and well-regarded garden plant that was fairly stable in appearance until Gertrude Jekyll undertook a pro-gramme of hybridization with only yellow and white polyanthuses.

Jekyll laid out her Primrose Garden first when designing garden beds for her property at Munstead Wood in Surrey in the late nine-teenth century. She planted swathes of polyanthus-type primroses against a backdrop of holly, Portuguese laurel, oak and hazel. 'They were best seen in the early evening when they gave the effect of a magical primrose glow, reflected and enhanced by the evergreen screen,' write Martin Wood and Judith Tankard, authors of *Gertrude Jekyll at Munstead Wood* and members of the Munstead Wood Committee for the Royal Commission on Historical Monuments of England.[44]

The enormous number of polyanthus-type primroses in Jekyll's garden provided the perfect opportunity for hybridization. What even-tually became her Munstead strain of 'bunched polyanthus primroses' began with the 'Golden Plover' and a white one that she had found in a cottage garden.[45] These, the great-grandparents of all that came after, needed bulking up, and Jekyll, who strongly preferred 'delicately shaded' primroses, set to work. In her book *Wood and Garden: Notes and Thoughts, Practical and Critical, of a Working Amateur* (1899), she describes her strategies as a hybridizer. She thought she could organize and classify the progeny,

> but gave it up after writing out the characters of 60 classes!
> Their possible variation seems endless. Every year among the seedlings there appear a number of charming flowers with some new development of size, or colour of flower, or beauty of foliage, and yet all within the narrow bounds of white and yellow Primroses.[46]

Gertrude Jekyll in her Spring Garden, Munstead Wood, 1923,
photographed by John Harshberger.

Jekyll worked with them for 50 years, analysing seedlings, choos-
ing the best, culling the rejects and collecting seed, an effective but
slow method called roguing. She was a workaholic, but there was one
aspect of primrose gardening that almost brought her peace – when
she divided her plants:

A boy feeds me with armfuls of newly-dug-up plants, two
men are digging-in the cooling cow-dung at the farther end,
and another carries away the divided plants tray by tray, and
carefully replants them. The still air, with only the very gent-
lest south-westerly breath in it, brings up the mighty boom
of the great ship guns from the old seaport, thirty miles away,
and the pheasants answer to the sound as they do to thunder.
The early summer air is of a perfect temperature, the soft
coo of the wood-dove comes down from the near-wood,
the nightingale sings almost overhead, but – either human
happiness may never be quite complete, or else one is not

philosophic enough to contemn life's lesser evils, for – oh,
the midges![47]

Suttons Seeds acquired her Munstead strain in 1896, and polyanthus
was soon a household name. Jekyll would later write:

> It must have been at about seven years of age that I first
> learnt to know and love a Primrose copse. More than half a
> century has passed, and yet each spring, when I wander in
> the primrose wood, I see the pale yellow blooms and smell
> their sweetest scent – for a moment I am seven years old
> again and wandering in that fragrant wood.[48]

The pace of polyanthus improvement picked up in the twentieth
century as numerous seed companies in the UK worked on compet-
ing strains with names such as 'Giant', 'Brilliance', 'Triumph' and
'Superb'.[49] The blossoms were large and the colours polychrome-
bright. In the U.S. Frank Reinelt, an immigrant from Czechoslovakia
and former head gardener to the Romanian royal family, introduced
the 'Pacific' strain, which became famous throughout the world.
Raised in Capitola, California, it was found to falter in severe win-
ters elsewhere. Sakata Ornamentals in Japan eventually acquired the
seed stock, improved it and released new versions as both bedding
and pot plants. The winter-hardy, brilliant-hued 'Crescendo' strain
developed by the Ernst Benary Seed Company of Germany at the
end of the twentieth century is now one of the favoured 'polychrome
princesses'. There are signs, however, as Kingsbury notes in 'Dialectic
of the Polyanthus', that old-fashioned, subtle hues may soon replace
the ultrabright tones.

Gold- and Silver-laced Polyanthus

In the 1780s, more than 100 years after the appearance of the red
polyanthus, a seedling appeared with a golden centre and a delicate

lace-like edging to each petal. Sometimes the lacing was silver. From their first appearance, gold- and silver-laced polyanthus stimulated hybridizing attitudes. The Florists adopted this type as one of their most treasured flowers. One hundred years later there were 200 named varieties. Historians point out that the lacing was not a yellow, but a true gold, almost as if the edge of the petal has been gilded by hand. The ground colour (the rest of the petal) was a dark red that was soon being coaxed into dark crimson velvet, blackish browns and tortoiseshell colours. Much of the hybridization work was carried out through selection or roguing. The grower's name was listed before the varietal name. The best gold-laced variety for a long while was Pearson's 'Alexander', said to be an excellent 'trusser' or producer of trusses (umbels) with fine large 'pips' (individual flowers). Roy Genders wrote: 'I must say that it is difficult to conceive that anything can be produced more beautiful by the magic wand of nature.'[50] The goal was at least five pips per truss, a light, precise lacing and a deep dark-velvet ground. Less well documented is the silver-laced variety, which never became as popular, although varieties such as the 'Bumble Bee' primrose and P. 'Silver Lace Black' and 'Penumbra' are available today. Margaret Webster recently introduced new ground colours with P. 'Blue Lace Mary' and 'Purple Lace Emmy'.

By the end of the nineteenth century the fevered production of new varieties of gold-laced polyanthus had ceased. Primrose historians blame this on the Industrial Revolution and the decline of Florists, many of whom were weavers working at home, where they could tend seedlings throughout the day. There were societal changes, as well. What the Industrial Revolution and the advent of new leisure activities failed to dismantle, two world wars did. By 1950 the *Year Book* of the Northern Section of the National Primula Society in the UK reported that 'We are going to have a more difficult job of resuscitation here [with the gold-laced varieties] than with the auriculas, as we have so few parents left.'[51] One Captain Hawkes, whose nursery had been bombed during the Second World War and his plants scattered, combed the countryside in its aftermath for remnants of his stock. Some of the few seeds he retrieved were sent to America, to the horticulturalist Florence Bellis, and she in turn shared them, leading to a revival of their fame in the Pacific Northwest.

Florence Bellis and the Americanization of the Primrose

Florence Bellis began breeding primroses during the Great Depression that began in 1929, an unlikely time for promoting flowers. Born Florence Hurtig in New Orleans, she had trained for a career as a concert pianist, but found herself destitute and consumptive as a young woman in Portland, Oregon. In 1935 she married Lou Levy, also from Portland, who had worked as a logger in Washington state. (Much of her early work appears under the name Florence Levy.) She would write that they married because of the Depression or in spite of it. In 1935 they had an offer of free housing in an unheated barn in Gresham, outside Portland. Before moving, carrying their last five dollars, they walked out into a snowstorm to post an order to Suttons Seeds in the UK for five packets of primrose seed, on a whim of Florence's; with the remaining ten cents they bought two candy bars, newly invented in the period following the First World War. Sleeping on hay bales and using orange crates for furniture, they set up housekeeping, accompanied by trays and trays of primrose seedlings; they had no electricity or running water for almost two years. That was the beginning of Barnhaven Primroses. Some years later, after divorce and remarriage, Florence changed her surname to Bellis.[52]

Those first five packets from Suttons yielded the entire genetic stock of the Barnhaven primroses, with the exception of a little new 'blood' introduced in 1947, from the chance offering of one new parent plant. Founded by John Sutton in 1806 as the House of Sutton, on King Street in Reading, Berkshire, Suttons first sold only corn, but it soon diversified into other vegetables and flowers. By 1840 it was Royal Purveyor to Queen Victoria, and in the 1880s was selling large, frilly primroses, such as 'Pearl', 'Moss-Curled Lilac' and 'Ruby King', which looked more like petunias with extravagantly wavy petals. In 1908 Suttons advertised a dark purple version called 'Czar', and later 'Brilliance' and 'Crimson King'. Bellis was interested in colour rather than frills. She once wrote that a friend suggested that it was 'her broken engagement with music' that had led to her obsession with colour. She agreed, writing that 'tone is color heard, and color is tone heard.'[53] In one of her catalogues she described an auricula 'with color tones as richly muted as a cello'.[54]

Bellis said she knew it was her 'destiny' the moment she saw the first flowers of the primroses she had planted the autumn she and her husband had moved into the barn in Gresham. She apparently counted the primroses, because she wrote that there were 1,231 of them. Perhaps, looking at her hillside of primroses beneath the alders and apple trees, she experienced what Europeans had felt so long before, the stabbing sense of renewal, a belief in spring.[55] She had sown the seeds, tended the seedlings and planted them in the earth, and they had flowered. For someone just barely hanging on in the Depression, this would have been a moment of efficacy that symbolized her own 'rebirth'. Through the process of growing plants and working outside she recovered her health. Red-haired and fair-skinned, she admitted to vanity about her complexion, protecting it with special oils during long hours of gardening.

Bellis wrote in a letter to a family member that she had spent her twenties learning to play the music of Brahms. She now turned her hand to pollination. Darwin had used fine camel-hair paintbrushes and gauze bags to separate flowers from insect pollinators in his work with primroses; Bellis looked at the flowers and devised her own technique. She wrote in her book *Gardening and Beyond* (1986):

When I conceived the idea of cross-pollinating my first primroses by hand I had to find a way to do it since it had not been done before. How simple it was to tear down a bloom and find that I held in my hands all the pollen, attached to

The barn that Florence and Lou Levy moved into on Johnson Creek, Gresham, Oregon, which became the first home of Barnhaven Primroses.

the petals, while the female reproductive parts sat in the calyx, completely naked.[56]

She transferred a heavy load of pollen to the desired female parent by hand, and discarded all floral parts so that pollinators would not be attracted any further. Her method of 'emasculation' became 'the wings' of her entire operation. In addition to the paintbrush, she by-passed the tedious bagging required to sequester one flower from another during artificial pollination.

Like Jekyll, Bellis was a workaholic, investing ferocious amounts of energy in hybridizing, and in introducing her Barnhaven primroses to the world, eventually shipping plants throughout the United States and Canada.[57] Her work an act of love more than anything else, she always struggled financially. Her goal in some sense was the Americanization of the primrose. It came to her as 'a fanciful dream', she wrote:

It happened the day I sat on a footbridge over the creek and looked, with stars in my eyes, at my first primroses blooming along its banks under the catkined alders. At that time they were the best available but in my mind I saw them in a Utopian world of color with the series Americanized as the first step toward evangelizing them in this country. So the few bronze shades were thought of as the Grand Canyon series; the few reds as Indian reds; the reddish purples were transformed, then and there, to the Marine Blues of purest hue; the yellows became Harvest Yellows for our ripening wheat fields; white, Winter White, for the fairylands of snow. This was, at that time, the entire color range of polyanthus, the bunch-flowered primroses. Now there are over 140 shades, fixed to come true from seed, the widest color range in their history and, I am sure, that of any other flower.[58]

Bellis had a predilection for 'true' and 'pure' colours. She did not like 'mousey-pink', but was very pleased with her development of the candy pinks: 'I stood before them crying, the beauty too much

Collage of Barnhaven primroses, grown and photographed by horticulturalist Matt Mattus.

to bear.'[59] Even at the end of a long career of hybridizing, she acknowledged that she was still 'obsessed' by colour – 'color has been my ideal and my vision' – and suggested the further development of one of her spice shades, a 'metallic brass', speculating that a name like 'Curry' or 'Turmeric' might do, although turmeric sounded 'sort of nasty', she thought.[60] Today, when the medicinal effects of turmeric make daily headlines, a primrose named 'Turmeric' might sell very well. She believed *Primula* had much more to offer, but she had tired, for 'the hybridizer is not his own master as long as he hybridizes, produces and distributes on a wide scale year after year for what sometimes seems an eternity.'[61]

The 'fixing' of colours was crucial, since most customers want to buy a dependable product, but she did in her catalogues urge customers to buy seed that was only 75 per cent true, for the sake of encountering variation and learning to play with it. After selecting the best cross-pollinated seedlings, she performed line breeding, which forces repeated self-pollination until there is no variation in desired characteristics. We know now that inbreeding in animals can reveal harmful recessive alleles (copies of a gene). When criticized for committing 'the cardinal sin' of line breeding, she delved into genetics and resolutely defended the practice. She felt she had taken 'the quickest route possible to improve the plants, to fix desired characteristics, and to produce hybrids that bloomed true from seed, which, otherwise, is the prerogative of species'.[62] The genetic depth of the genus favoured her work.

Although fragrance ranked above flower size in Bellis's estimation, she did nevertheless wish to adjust flower size to some level of perfection. One of her most famous accomplishments was the Silver Dollar strain of polyanthuses, the name denoting the size of the flowers. She was proud of 'the heavy petal substance of Barnhaven's Silver Dollar polyanthus which insures their beauty in all kinds of spring weather'.[63] She developed them easily in all shades except one: getting Jekyll's 'nickel-sized orange polyanthus' to Silver Dollar size required her most laborious creative intervention.

Bellis's catalogues were masterpieces of proselytization, delivering romance and provenance in enthusiastic prose. Her goal was to spread primroses wherever possible. She was certain of her product. The covers of her catalogues read, 'Famous Primroses from Barnhaven'. She knew they were 'famous' well before they acquired a reputation. She often included an 'In Appreciation' page, where she listed comments from her customers, from Seattle to Maine, almost every state in the union, and up into Canada. Her customers wrote letters of appreciation, such as this one from Big Sandy, Montana:

> When the plants arrived I was in the hospital but my ladies planted them, shading them with an old screen door. You would be surprised what good work a couple of cowpunchers can do. The plants are growing beautifully now with the mark of boot heels still deep in the earth.[64]

When she retired, Bellis sent her seeds to the growers Jared and Sylvia Sinclair in Cumbria, northwestern England. After both maintaining Bellis's stock and creating many new strains, they sent their stock to Angela Bradford in Plouzélambre, Brittany, and she eventually turned her Barnhaven material over to David and Lynne Lawson in nearby Keranguiner, Plestin-les-Grèves. They now maintain the Barnhaven pedigree with the help of their daughter Jodie Mitchell, their son Daniel Lawson and their son-in-law Robert Mitchell.[65] Bellis's legacy also resides in the work of the American Primrose Society, which began in 1941. As the first editor of its quarterly publication, *Primroses*, for which she wrote many articles and which she produced on her kitchen table in the early days, she became known for a lyrical prose style, akin to that of Reginald Farrer.[66]

Hybridizing with *P. juliae*

Barbara Shaw described the discovery of *P. juliae* this way:

> One of the most momentous days in the history of the prim-
> rose must have been the day in April 1900 when Julia Ludo-
> vikovna Mlokossjewicz came across a little purple-flowered
> primula near Lagodechy some eighty miles east-north-east
> of Tiflis in the province of Georgia in the Caucasus.[67]

Some details are precise – it was found near wet stones – and others
less so – the date was 20 April 1900 or 1901.[68] Mlokossjewicz was
the daughter of a Polish aristocrat who was also a botanist and forest
inspector. A specimen had made its way to the Oxford Botanical
Gardens by 1911, sent by Professor Kustensow of the Dorpat Botanic
Garden, who named the plant after the discoverer's first rather than
last name. Little *P. juliae* added a new look and habit to hybrid
primroses. Petite with waxy, heart-shaped leaves and deep-magenta
flowers, it spread via a 'rampant' rhizome and tolerated sun. Soon it
was the most popular garden primrose, and its 'blood' was in every
hybrid, perhaps the most famous being 'Wanda'.

Bellis also described the discovery of *P. juliae* dramatically:

> A waterfall in one of the mightiest mountain ranges in the
> world – the Caucasus, which the ancients said encircled the
> earth as a marriage ring does a finger – successfully hid until
> 1900, a brilliant, star-like, creeping miniature primrose.[69]

Bellis had fun characterizing the 'julianas' or 'julies'. She called them
'mighty midgets' and 'wiggling puppies', and she borrowed words from
a French publication: 'petite, vivace, rampant'. Using *P. juliae* as a pollen
parent because her wooded hillside was too shady to permit the seed of
a mother *P. juliae* to ripen, she created a hybrid line called 'Fireflies'. She
wrote: 'Julianas (hybrids of *P. juliae*) are typically twentieth century,

no sentiment, no fantasy, no cleavage to tradition. And, also typically, their pert gaiety, saucy prettiness and unrestrained generosity make them entirely independent of the past.'[70]

Bellis's close friend Rae Selling Berry furthered the Americanization of the primrose. Her 2.5-ha (6-acre) garden near Portland, Oregon, called for a time the Berry Botanic Garden, eventually contained 61 primrose species, a collection to rival the best of those in Europe.[71] A passionate and inspirational plantswoman, Berry subscribed to the expeditions of such plant hunters as Frank Kingdon-Ward and the duo of Frank Ludlow and George Sherriff, and was repaid in seed from Nepal and Tibet. Her favourite primroses, however, were the natives of the Pacific Northwest. Undaunted by hereditary deafness, she herself explored as far north as the Yukon, and even at the age of 80 she trekked up the Wallowa Mountains in search of Cusick's primrose (*P. cusickiana*), Oregon's only primrose, which she called 'Cookie'. She climbed the Sierra Nevadas in search of the Sierra primrose (*P. suffrutescens*), which she called 'Stuffy'. They were problem children, hard to cultivate. She preferred species to hybrids, but supported Bellis in her work as a friend and primrose lover.[72] Portland State University now maintains the Rae Selling Berry Seed Bank & Plant Conservation Program.[73]

Hybrids that bear the names of individuals and places tell stories and strengthen connections between people and plants. Charles Nelson places a quotation from Hugh Armytage Moore, manager of the Rowallane garden from 1909 to 1917, opposite the frontispiece of his book *A Heritage of Beauty* (2000): 'Yet the gardener who has no sentiment about his plants misses much.'[74] The sense that garden plants form a heritage as rich in history as old buildings and paintings is not new. John Parkinson's seventeenth-century *Paradisi in sole paradisus terrestris* inspired the children's writer Juliana Horatia Ewing to write *Mary's Meadow* (1883–4), a story about children creating a garden, which in turn inspired the formation of the Parkinson Society in 1884. The society's goals were to 'search out and cultivate old garden flowers which have become scarce; to exchange seeds and plants; to plant waste places with hardy flowers; to circulate books on gardening amongst the Members [and] to try to prevent the extermination of rare wild flowers, as well as of garden treasures.'[75]

As woodlands and country settings disappear, we are fortunate that seeds of such treasured wild flowers as the common primrose, cowslip and oxlip are available alongside potted plants of flashy hybrids like *Primula* × *polyanthus* 'Supernova Fire' and 'Blue Zebra'. Every hundred years or so the genus *Primula* 'sports' an innovation like the gold lacing of the polyanthus flower. It undoubtedly has more surprises to offer.

five

The Reckless Primrose

'Concerning the Auricula', he said, masterfully whipping a knife up and down the steel at the sideboard, before carving generous helpings of beef, 'I can become heated. I deplore the illogicality of this attitude, for the beauty and refinement of these flowers should enter the soul of the man who cultivates them. The auricula growers of Britain normally reach a great old age, and as year succeeds year you will see in their faces a deepening serenity and grace. I have known a rose grower, awarded a second place, when expecting a first, sweep his exhibit to the ground and trample upon it in a rage. An auricula grower would merely ask himself where he had gone wrong and resolve to do better in the future.'

HOWARD SPRING, *These Lovers Fled Away* (1955)[1]

The amiable auricula grower speaking here is the fictional Arthur J. Geldersome, Town Clerk of Smurthwaite in the Yorkshire Dales in the early twentieth century. Some 400 years earlier the auricula began its journey from the peaks of the European Alps to the continent's lowlands, where artisans – weavers, lacemakers, cutlers and others – cultivated it assiduously. The auricula is considered the most 'man-made' of flowers. It reached near perfection at the hands of the English working class as early as 1650, and its fame soon spread to the New World.[2] In 1767 Thomas

Jefferson wrote 'auricula' in his *Garden Book*, and his correspondence from that point until 1813 shows several requests for auriculas from his gardening mentor, the Philadelphia nurseryman Bernard McMahon. David Wheeler, plantsman and editor of *Hortus*, has written that

> no other ornamental plant has such an intimate association with mankind. The saga is intriguing, and supreme among the tales of splendour and disappointment are the growers, breeders and exhibitors who have dedicated themselves to that seemingly impossible task: to improve on Nature itself. Many have succeeded.[3]

The auricula had many folk names in early European plant lore. In Switzerland it was *Flublumle*, the little flower that consumes rocks.[4] In German-speaking areas it was *Swindelkraut* or 'giddiness plant': goat and ibex hunters ate parts of the plant to protect against faintness in high places. John Gerard in his *Herball* of 1597 promoted it as a cure for the effects of opium.[5] Another common name was *auricula ursi*, the little ear of the bear, a reference to the muscular, scalloped leaves; in Italy it is still called *orecchia d'orso* and in France *oreilles d'ours*. 'Them reckless plants' is how one of Margery Fish's gardeners referred to her auriculas.[6] The name 'Reckless' developed in Scotland's eastern Borders.[7] The writer D. H. Lawrence, who had an affinity for flowers and particularly primroses, has Lady Chatterley carry a bouquet of velvety auriculas when she goes off to meet her lover. Mrs Flint, the farmer's wife, offers the flowers, saying: 'Recklesses, as Luke called them . . . Have some.'[8] Other country names were ricklers, riclasses, riclous, ariculases and ricklearses.

At one point Geldersome explains to his nephew: 'An auricula will grow, yes. But an auricula that has merely grown is one thing. An auricula that has been cultivated is another.'[9] The root of *cultivate* comes from the Latin verb *colere*, to till. The past participle *cultus* then became *cultivatus* in medieval Latin, and by the early seventeenth century carried the meanings of 'care, labor; cultivation, culture;

worship, reverence'.[10] The auricula called forth all these meanings and became a focus of domestic horticulture in seventeenth- and eighteenth-century England.[11]

The Origin of the Hybrid Auricula: Clusius and his Noble Lady

In 1573 the Holy Roman Emperor Maximilian II invited the Flemish horticulturalist Carolus Clusius (Charles de l'Écluse) to start a botanic garden in Vienna. While botanizing in the high hills, the first to climb the Ötscher, Clusius found *Auricula ursi I* (the yellow-flowered bear's ear) growing on rocks several miles from Vienna, 'where it looks to the North and whence women root cutters fetch bundles of the flowers and sometimes the whole roots'.[12] In the garden of his host family, one Professor Aicholtz and his wife, Anna, he found *Auricula ursi II*, a red-flowered form, which had been given to the professor by 'a certain noble lady'. Encountering greater variation, he eventually described types III to VII. Type III he called 'a brave and beautiful plant', and some he described as flowering under snow. Even though he recognized that they were primulas, he used the names auricula and bear's ears. Carl Linnaeus soon changed the 'Auricula' to 'Primula', but the identity had been fixed. The euphonious 'auricula' remains in use today as the common name. One garden writer has remarked that 'few botanical names sound so beautiful and even-balanced as that of *Primula auricula*.'[13]

Primrose historians wondered about the identities of Clusius's 'noble lady' and the red-flowered *ursi II*, because the crucial step in the creation of the modern hybrid auricula was a hybridization event between a yellow-flowered species and a red-flowered species of primula. But one preferred acidic soil and the other limestone. How had they come together? Some 200 years later another legendary botanical figure – 'the King of *Primula* botanists' Anton Kerner von Marilaun, who held the title of Professor of Natural History and Director of the botanic gardens at the University of Innsbruck in

Auricula ursi IIII,   Auricula ursi v.

Auricula ursi vi.

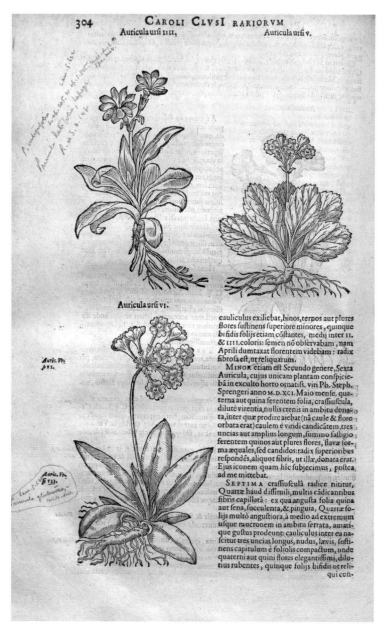

cauliculus exiliebat, binos, terpos aut plures
flores sustinens superiore minores, quinque
bisidis folijs etiam cóstantes, medij inter II.
& IIII.coloris: semen nó observabam, nam
Aprili dumtaxat florentem videbam : radix
fibrosa est, ut reliquarum.

MINOR etiam est Secundo genere, Sexta
Auricula, cujus unicam plantam conspicie-
bá in exculto horto ornatiss. viri Ph. Stæph.
Sprengeri anno M.D.XCI.Maio mense, qua-
terna aut quina ferentem folia, crassiuscula,
dilutè virentia, nullis crenis in ambitu donata, inter quæ prodire aiebat (nã caule & flore
orbata erat) caulem è viridi candicátem, tres
uncias aut amplius longum, summo fastigio
ferentem quinos aut plures flores, flavæ for-
ma æquales, sed candidos: radix superioribus
respondés, aliquot fibris, ut illæ, donata erat.
Ejus iconem quam hic subjecimus, postea
ad me mittebat.

SEPTIMA crassiusculâ radice nititur,
Quartæ haud dissimili, multis cádicantibus
fibris capillatâ : ex qua angusta folia quina
aut sena, succulenta, & pinguia, Quartæ folijs multò angustiora, à medio ad extremum
usque mucronem in ambitu serrata, amari-
que gustus prodeunt: cauliculus inter ea na-
scitur tres uncias longus, nudus, lævis, sustinens capitulum é foliolis compactum, unde
quaterni aut quini flores elegantissimi, dilu-
tius rubentes, quinque folijs bifidis ut reli-
qui con-

Illustration of various 'bear's ears' (*Auricula ursi*), the wild auricula hybrids that Carolus
Clusius gathered near Vienna, from his *Rariorum plantarum historia*, vol. 1 (1601).

the second half of the nineteenth century – would advance both a reasonable identification of the noble lady and a location for where the limestone-loving *P. auricula* and the acid-loving *P. hirsuta* may have met and hybridized.[14] Botanizing above his experimental station in the Gschnitz Mountains, he came across the two primulas growing together in an area where acidic and limestone rock coexisted, near the castle of one of Clusius's many correspondents, Countess Trauttmansdorff, owner of Schloss Trautson and a 'noble lady'. Von Marilaun described the fertile hybrid as *Primula × pubescens*. Although some have criticized his deduction, many feel the mysterious pedigree of the auricula has been solved.[15]

Clusius wrote in *Rariorum plantarum historia* (1601) of his struggles in 'taming' the alpine auriculas for garden culture.[16] He had a large network of correspondents, with whom he freely shared ideas and plants. Although some of the *Auricula ursi* I–VII he had collected languished and died at lower altitudes, those he was able to acclimatize he shared with his horticultural friends all over northern Europe, establishing the auricula as a prized garden plant. *P. clusiana* is named after him.

The Florists

The handcrafting of the auricula began among artisans in the seventeenth century. Many historians believe that Protestant Flemish (Walloon) weavers who came to England in the 1570s fleeing religious persecution by Catholic Spanish rulers brought their handlooms and the first seeds and bulbs of the Florists' flowers in their coat pockets. They settled mostly in northern England, in Lancashire, Cheshire and York. At about the same time French Protestant Huguenots, many also weavers, arrived in Britain, fleeing Catholic persecution in France. Later, another wave of Huguenot silk weavers fleeing France after the Revocation of the Edict of Nantes in 1685 settled in Spitalfields, just outside the City of London.[17] The musical ensemble the Auricula Suite has paid tribute to this story in the twenty-first century. Richard and Louise Duffy-Howard, who created the group,

Chromolithograph (*c.* 1898) of the two species, *P. hirsuta* (now *P. rubra*), top left, and *P. lauricula* (*utea*), top right, that hybridized to create the auricula (*P.* × *pubescens*), from A. Kerner von Marilaun's *Pflanzenleben* (Plant Lives, 1916 edition).

write that their songs and music tell 'of a journey to a new land, a story of love and loss, persecution and a new beginning; inspired by folk tales of the alpine *Primula auricula* and its 16th century journey to England with the Huguenot refugees'.[18]

The term 'Florist' as applied to working-class people who grew speciality flowers as a hobby was first used in 1623, and continues today in auricula-growing circles. The first 'Florists' Feast' was held in 1631 in Norwich, Norfolk. At about this time tulipomania was in full bloom, and there was hyacinth madness as well. Auriculas rapidly gained popularity because they flower so quickly from seed, while tulip fanciers must wait three or more years before their bulbs flower.[19] There were six official Florists' flowers, the first four imports from the Middle East, the tulip, carnation, anemone and ranunculus, joined soon afterwards by the auricula and the hyacinth. The Florists also adopted the polyanthus.

The Ancient Society of York Florists, founded on 20 April 1768, stated in the preamble of its first minute book that 'Happiness' was a primary aim. The founders also manifested the desire to form a community: 'As the taste for Flowers and the disclosing of them to the View of others are most inseparable, we consider these Cultivators as an agreeable Band or Society, who communicate with each other the observations their experience has enabled them to make.'[20] The members comprised apothecaries, cutlers, butchers, comb makers, wharfingers, bricklayers, professional gardeners and scholars.[21] In other words, they were artisans or handworkers, naturals for working as plant hybridizers. Also, because they worked at home they could tend special seedlings, protecting them from weather as needed.

Local newspapers of the day carried accounts and advertisements associated with their activities. One such account read:

On Tuesday last a great Feast of Gardiners call'd Florists was held in the Dog in Richmond Hill, at which were present about 130 in Number; after Dinner several shew'd their Flowers (most of them Auriculas) and five ancient and judicious Gardiners were Judges to determine whose flowers excelled . . . a Gardiner of Barnes in Surrey was so well furnished with good Flowers that the Judge in the affair ordered him two Spoons and a Ladle.[22]

Botanists of the day, however, did not approve of Florists, their feasts or their hybrids. One was Linnaeus, who wrote: 'These men cultivate a science peculiar to themselves, the mysteries of which are only known to the adepts: nor can this knowledge be worth the attention of the botanist.'[23] But it was the work of the Florist Thomas Fairchild, who produced the Fairchild Mule, a hybrid between a carnation and a sweet william, that helped to prove Linnaeus's notions of sexuality in plants. The Gentle Author of Spitalfields has written about Fairchild's gravestone and the auriculas that are still cultivated on windowsills in the area.[24]

Virescence: The Edged Auricula Appears

At the beginning of the eighteenth century a dramatic change occurred in the biology of the auricula. Sir Rowland Biffen, a gifted biographer of the auricula, writes:

> at some time during this period the Auricula started a new and highly distinctive course of development and underwent a series of extraordinary changes which, it is hardly too much to say, converted it into an entirely new plant . . . The result was a flower having no counterpart in the horticultural world.[25]

The change was virescence, a mutation that induces parts of a plant that were not previously green to become so. In the case of the auricula, it was the outermost tips of the petals, which acquired the tougher consistency of leaves and the greenness characteristic of chlorophyll. These auriculas were described as 'edged'. Eventually there were three

Christopher Steele, *Martha Rodes as a Child*, 1750. Steele was just 17 years old at the time, and the auricula had recently been introduced to England.

types: the green-edged, the grey-edged and the white-edged, the colour depending on the amount of farina (see below) overlaying the green portion. Biffen found virescence mysterious, but concluded: 'Anyhow whatever happens and however deeply these matters may be probed into in the future, the finding and the propagation of the first virescence mutation will still remain a thing to wonder.'[26]

The date of this development was imprecise until a portrait by the painter Christopher Steele, on view for the first time in 1987, appeared in London in 'The Glory of the Garden', a joint exhibition by Sotheby's and the Royal Horticultural Society. It showed a young girl, Martha Rodes, in a pale-grey satin gown and matching cap reaching out to a grey-green-edged auricula. The date was 1750. The painting seems deliberately to offer itself as a lesson in observing the auricula. The perfectly round umbel of flowers rises above satiny grey-green leaves. Each flower has a central ring of thick farina, called paste in this context, surrounded by a ring of dark, almost black pigment,

'Auricula', an illustration by John Edwards from *A British Herbal* (1770), showing a perfect 'truss' of blossoms.

which in turn is surrounded by the grey-green edge. Martha's face is serene as she holds up a truss, the name given to the compact head of flowers, which has been cut from the plant to show the underside of the petals. The tip of a red shoe finds echoes in the simple clay pot and a patch of sun setting through a window in the bottom right of the painting. The artist illustrates plant and person as complementary, both refined and exquisite. The striking spherical trusses of the auricula were a favourite subject of eighteenth-century artists.

A Little Light Chemistry: Farina

Farina, a compound that is found almost exclusively in the genus *Primula*, was a crucial characteristic in the fashioning of the show auricula. Biologists believe that farina (from the Latin *farina*, flour), often called meal, protects plants from the stress of high insolation in the alpine environment. Woodland and meadow lowland primroses, such as the common primrose, cowslip and oxlip, lack farina, but many of the Himalayan species show a dusting, as well as cliff-dwelling species such as the bird's-eye primrose and the Scottish primrose. Some species have farina only on young leaves, for which the danger of being burned by the Sun is greatest; their mature leaves show none. The farina is usually white, but sometimes yellow; it can be just a light dusting or very dense, when it is called 'paste' by auricula growers. Different parts of the plant carry varying amounts. The auricula growers of the seventeenth and eighteenth centuries treated it as a form of make-up that could be manipulated for special effect, and they selected seedlings that showed unusual accumulations, creating one strain called the Painted Ladies. These disappeared during the First and Second World Wars, but some growers are trying to re-establish that look. Biffen calls the auricula 'one of the most beautiful foliage plants in existence' because of the decorative effects of farina.[27]

As early as the seventeenth century, 'natural philosophers' such as Nehemiah Grew had begun to think about farina in a scientific way.

Stalked farina glands on the flowers of the fairy primrose (*P. malacoides*),
an annual primrose native to China.

The recent invention of the light microscope had made tiny details
of plant anatomy visible. In *Anatomy of Plants* (1682), Grew suggests
experimental investigation of the 'fine white flour or powder, which
lies over the leaves of some plants, as of Bears' Ear'.[28] The auricula's
farina had literary use, as well. In the opening pages of *The Mill on the
Floss* (1860), George Eliot describes Luke, the head miller, as 'a tall,
broad-shouldered man of forty, black-eyed and black-haired, sub-
dued by a general mealiness, like an auricula'.[29] Eliot may have reached
for this image subconsciously because cottage garden auriculas were
often called Old Dusty Millers. Margery Fish described the Old Yellow
Dusty Miller as 'a lovely thing with its soft yellow flower and white
powdered leaves'.[30] The Old Purple Dusty Miller and Old Black
Dusty Miller were also popular.

One researcher describes *Primula* as 'a genus with fascinating exudate chemistry', referring to the farina-producing glands.[31] Although
some writers still refer to the farina as 'waxy', this term is misleading.

Auricula 'Starling' raised by Chris Gafer in 1980,
shows decorative effects of farina.

Farina is quite different from the epicuticular wax that gives a whitish bloom to various fruits of the rose family, such as plums and apples. Research has shown that in the primula the terminal cell of two-celled glands on the leaf, flower or stem surface extrude snowball mounds of crystalline needles of nearly pure flavone, a secondary compound in a group known as flavonoids. The technical definition of flavone describes it as a 'colorless crystalline aromatic ketone ($C_{15}H_{11}O_2$) found in the leaves, stems and seed capsules of many primroses; *also*: any of the derivatives of this ketone many of which occur as yellow plant pigments in the form of glycosides and are used as dyestuffs'.[32] Fountain-like, the filamentous needles overflow on to the surface of the plant organ in question. This kind of farina is found elsewhere only in ferns, especially the genus *Pityrogramma*.[33]

Auriculas on Stage: The Theatres

Auriculas raised for show need protection from even a single drop of rain, which can dissolve and blemish the pattern of farina, and even early on growers came up with strategies to protect them. In his book *New Improvements of Planting and Gardening* (1717), Richard Bradley wrote:

> Set your Pots upon the Shelves, one above the other in such part of the Garden where Morning Sun may only come on them[,] and as the Flowers are commonly cover'd with a sort of Dust which contributes in great measure to make them Beautiful, some covering must be provided for their Shelter against Rains which are apt to wash it away, and destroy their Colours.[34]

And yet their growers wanted them to have fresh air, and so developed tiered shelving with covers for display. The term 'stage auriculas' came into use, and the protective structures were called 'theatres'. Some were makeshift and homemade, but as they became fashionable, the structures became more elaborate, imposing and built for posterity, especially in the gardens of wealthy collectors, although even monks multiplied auriculas. The 40 Benedictine monks of the Abbey of Tournai in Belgium needed fifteen auricula theatres to display their collection. Information about the monks' 'obsession' comes from the anonymous *Traité de la culture parfaite de l'oreille d'ours ou auricule* (Treatise on the perfect culture of bear's ears or auricula, 1732). The writer is thought to have been Charles Guénin, a tax collector and obsessive Florist, who admitted that an innocent interest in plants could become *folie* (madness).[35] The second edition of his book contains an illustration in which an outlandish figure in a nightcap gestures to an auricula theatre overrun with mice. The caption reads in translation: 'Everyone takes care of his own obsession. The auricula nourishes mine.' The designs were theatrical to say the least, with *trompe l'œil* curtains, proscenium arches and swags.[36]

Auricula historian Patricia Cleveland-Peck's auricula theatre.

When the fad for building auricula theatres in Europe waned, many were removed. Calke (sometimes spelled Caulke) Abbey, a Baroque mansion built in 1701 by Sir John Harpur on the site of an Augustinian priory, now has the oldest original auricula theatre in England. The theatre has been newly refurbished, its shelving painted blue, and the staff of the National Trust, which administers the property, has undertaken to grow on site the more than 140 auriculas needed to fill the theatre. The Auricula Suite premiered there in 2013 to a sell-out audience.

The current resurgence of auricula growers has brought more modest theatres into style. They appear in many shapes and forms, with and without garden gnomes. The multiple Pinterest boards devoted to them show much backyard ingenuity, and indeed a modest theatre made from an old bookcase can fit into a small garden. The Rothschild garden at Eythrope, the dower house of Waddesdon Manor in Bucking-hamshire, maintains a stunning auricula theatre, which, with echoes of Cinderella, displays pumpkins when auriculas are no longer in bloom. The resurgence of interest in the history of the auricula led the New

York Botanical Garden to invite the late Dowager Marchioness of Salisbury, a renowned horticulturalist and owner of Hatfield House in Hertfordshire, to design an auricula theatre for spring display in its herb garden. The theatre began in 2007 and ran for four years.

'Every Florist has his leather-coat': the Many Colours of the Auricula[37]

Auriculas offer the broadest and most surprising colour palette in the floral kingdom. They range from the palest chartreuse, creams, pinks and lavenders to strong, bold hues such as blackish reds, deep purples, greens, murrey, orange, tawny, buff and port. These unusual hues inspire names such as 'Mustard Sauce'. Much of the variety is due to the pink-flowered parent *P. hirsuta* and its pigment, hirsutin, which is found dissolved in a layer of pear-shaped cells on the surface of the petals.[38] Underneath this is a layer that often contains two yellow pigments, both flavones, one lemon-yellow and one buff-yellow, inherited from the other parent, *P. auricula*. The combination creates extraordinary effects. Hirsutin changes colour from crimson to violet to

Elisabeth Dowle's portrait of the auricula 'George Swinford's Leather Coat', from Patricia Cleveland-Peck's *Auriculas through the Ages* (2011).

almost blue depending on the acidity of the cell sap, which in primulas is heritable and independent of soil conditions, and thus amenable to manipulation through hybridizing. Other pigments involved are perlargonin and delphinidin. As Howard Spring's Uncle Geldersome suggests, auriculas inspire eclectic tastes in colour:

> A happy gift, my dear Eustace, that the Auricula bestows upon its lovers is a restrained color sense. The delicacy of the meal, the green that is never flamboyantly green, the purple that is as chaste as the obsequies of kings, these restrain such color outbursts as may be expected of the unredeemed.[39]

The auricula inspired a rich vocabulary of colour words, some now lost or archaic. Gertrude Jekyll, who distinguished between accurate (good) and inaccurate (bad) colour words to describe flowers (she had no use whatsoever for 'golden' to describe any yellow flower), loved the word 'murrey' as applied to auriculas:

> Much to be regretted is the disuse of the old word murrey, now only employed in heraldry. It stands for a dull red-purple, such as appears in the flower of the Virginian Allspice, and in the native Hound's-tongue, and often in seedling Auriculas.[40]

William Salmon, who published *Botanologia: The English Herbal, or History of Plants* in 1710, writes about 'the Murrey Auricula without Eyes', whose colour he describes as deep purple.[41] The murrey shading, often likened to mulberry, can appear black. It has been suggested that auricula growers specifically produced 'black' auriculas during Queen Victoria's long period of mourning after the death of Prince Albert. Salmon lists many other colour categories, among them the flesh-coloured auriculas, the tawny auricula, the hair-coloured auricula, the snow-white auricula, the Virgin's milk auricula and the leather coat auricula, which was chamois-coloured. 'Leather coat' was a name given to an old russet apple of dull, rough skin with reddish-greenish-brownish tints. The *Garden Book* of Sir Thomas Hanmer, completed in 1659 but not published until 1933, lists colour words that have disappeared: aurora for deep orange, bertino for blue-grey, feuille morte and its variant philomot for dead-leaf colour, gilvus for very pale red, gridelin or grizeli (from *gris du lin*) for flax-grey, Isabella for greyish yellow, minimme for the dun colour of a Minim friar's robe, quoist for the colour of a dove's breast, and one called 'needlework pale peach'.[42]

Perfecting the Auricula: 'a difficult aesthetic problem'

The edged auricula, Biffen wrote, gave the Florists an opportunity to engineer perfection: 'In no other flower that I know has the florist made such an attempt to solve what is in reality a difficult aesthetic problem.'[43] The problem: the proportions of a perfect flower. The Florists developed criteria for proportions of the various zones – the eye, the paste, the ground and the edge – known as Standards of Perfection. James Maddock, a Lancastrian nurseryman who moved to London, stated the following in the *Florist's Directory* of 1792:

> The component parts of the pip are the tube (with its stamins [*sic*] and anthers); the eye, the exterior circle containing the ground-colour, with its edge or margin: these should be well proportioned, which will be the case if the diameter of the tube be one part, the eye three, and the whole pip six or nearly so . . . The green edge, or margin, is the principal cause of the variegated appearance in this flower; and it should be in proportion to the ground-colour, i.e. about one half of each.[44]

In 1794 the Florist John Hudson said that 3:5:2:1 was better than Maddock's 6:3:1 ratio, and George Glenny, also a nurseryman, advocated a ratio of 4:2:1 in 1832. Judges were said to walk around with calipers. No one knows how these men arrived at these ratios,

An array of floating blossoms offers a hint of the colour palette of the auricula.

but one current grower with a mathematical bent has studied the Standards of Perfection based on Continuous Proportions ('Rigidly Defined Areas of Uncertainty'), by counting proportions, and by using Euclidean distances.[45] The perfection of the edged auricula seems to be stable right now. Some advances, paradoxically, are re-breeding old varieties that were lost, like the striped auriculas that Derek Parsons of the UK is reintroducing.[46] The important point, Sacheverell Sitwell wrote of the Florists' flowers, was that 'it was essential . . . that they show the workings of men's minds.'[47] The auricula produced unending variation, and the breeder's goal was to harness that to 'divine proportions'.[48]

Although the 'feasts' are different, the shows go on, part of the communal effort to reach perfection. Many eyes turned on an auricula, followed by judging and conversation, help growers and enthusiasts to reach a consensus about aesthetic values. The noted breeder Brenda Hyatt saw the shows as a form of 'testing' of the principles adhered to in a breeding programme.[49] They also strengthen bonds in a diverse community of flower lovers who travel some distances to gather. Modern growers still call themselves Florists, and speak of finding 'spiritual' meaning in annual show days. One such Florist wrote that 'the more I write the less I understand the welter of pleasurable emotions that are generated in the company of florists and flowers so far from my home', when 'the auricula publicly commands our fealty and devotion as befits one of such floral eminence and pedigree.'[50]

The auricula lends itself to the propagation of named varieties. In an article in *The Florist and Pomologist* in 1880, D. T. Fish of Hardwicke praised the border auricula, a group adapted for the garden bed rather than the show table, for their sturdiness and productivity.

Bill Lockyer with w&s Lockyer's Auricula Specialists' gold-medal winning plants at the 2015 Chelsea Flower Show.

In rich soil the offsets (little plantlets at the base of the main stem) will root and produce new plants. By this means, Fish writes, 'the units of Auriculas become tens; the tens, hundreds; the hundreds, thousands.'[51] An offset is genetically identical to its parent. Fish waxed eloquent over one characteristic of the auricula that we have not yet mentioned:

> The perfume is also of the sweetest, richer and fuller than that of any other members of the primrose family, and reminding one of a sort of trinity of odours, composed of valley lilies, primroses, and violets. Hardly any pleasure within the entire range of horticulture can prove more rich and satisfying than that of brooding over an Auricula bed or border at early morn or dewy eve, inhaling their fragrance, and marking their infinite variety of flower and foliage.[52]

He also notes that the border auriculas are 'vigourous as cabbages, and neither snow, wind, nor rain, nor any weather, can mar their rich beauty, nor rob them of their sweet fragrance'.[53]

Finding Names for So Many Auriculas

The names bestowed upon varieties of auricula through the centuries provide cultural signposts and commemorate public as well as private memories. When the appearance of the edged varieties hastened the pace of hybridization, naming became an important part of the business end of the process. The grower James Douglas as a young boy in Kelso, Scotland, saw six auriculas at a show in the 1840s; 56 years later he had 15,000 varieties in his firm, House of Douglas. His article for the *Memoirs of the Royal Caledonian Horticultural Society* is very much a list of names, indicating the importance of lineage and pedigree.[54] Those that have 'passed away' he does not name. Breeders often wrote of 'the blood' of an auricula, as if it had achieved personhood through the process of hybridization.

'Stjärnhimmel' (Starry): an auricula made from a cross, involving 'Starling' by Swedish auricula breeder Ray Molin-Wilkinson.

The earliest named varieties, 'Rule Arbiter', a green edge, and 'Hortaine,' a white edge, appeared in 1757. The derivation of 'Hortaine' is most likely Norman. One William Berte paid a fine in the bailificy [bailiwick] of Hortaine, Normandy, in 1208.[55] Other eighteenth-century names were 'Potts's Eclipse,' which led to a series of botanical Eclipses, notable among them 'Cockup's Eclipse'. The breeder's name might precede the varietal name, so there were 'Taylor's Plough-boy', 'Taylor's Glory', 'Taylor's Incomparable', 'Taylor's Victory' and 'Taylor's Alexander'. Thus 'Stretch's Alexander' was grown by a different breeder, who also raised 'Stretch's Victory'. By 1821 some notable grey edges had appeared, such as 'Lancashire Hero', 'George Lightbody' and 'Richard Headly'.[56]

The ever-growing number of auriculas meant the quest for names covered a broad swathe of human activities and desires, from battles to war heroes to place names to ideals of beauty. Using the name of 'some great Family or conspicuous Person' struck John Laurence in 1726 as a 'Way of boasting and triumph'.[57] But more reprehensible was the habit of giving new names to old varieties. Samuel Gilbert, married to Minerva, daughter of the prominent Florist John Rea, wrote a book called the *Florist's Vade-Mecum* (1682) expressly to 'the disadvantage of the Mercenary Flower Catchers about London or some that are of the same stamp scattered up and down the Countrey, Fathering new names on Old Flowers to enhance their price'.[58]

With each succeeding generation new sources of names appear. Allan Guest writes of a breeder whose day job was in the electrical generating industry and who named his auriculas after power stations.[59] The varietal names of auriculas are archived in horticultural literature, lending context, at once historical and elusive, to the other-worldly aura of these plants.

Potting Media

In quite a different way, much can be learned about the culture of the times in recipes for auricula potting media. Florists were publishing treatises with cultural advice right and left in the eighteenth and nineteenth centuries. Thomas Hogg, Florist of Paddington, whose nursery was on the site of the present-day Paddington railway station, was a schoolteacher happily turned Florist for his health in the early nineteenth century. He writes: 'I have known persons, at the turn of life, at the age of forty-five, or fifty, commence flower growing, as the current of their blood was beginning to flow more evenly.'[60] He became quite the expert on auricula compost, although for him it was an inexact science:

Where a large stud of Auriculas (to use a Yorkshire term) is kept, it seldom happens that the same sort of compost precisely is made use of two years together; this is very often my case. I frequently, as opportunities occur, deposit in the same heap, the dung of sheep, horses, cows, poultry, and pigeons, night-soil, and blood from the slaughter-house, and turn and mix the whole up together.[61]

It is a tribute to the hardiness of the auricula that it could survive this rich diet. Most modern recommendations are simple: loam, composted manure, perhaps sand. Hogg criticized James Maddock's recipe for being 'too complex and difficult to be prepared by anyone who is not conversant with fractional parts'. Maddock, who had devised the ratios for floral perfection, was at home with fractions. His recipe called for '½ Rotten cow-dung, two years old; ⅙ Sound earth of an open texture; ⅛ Earth of rotten leaves; ¹⁄₁₂ Coarse sea or river sand; ¹⁄₂₄ Peaty or moory earth; ¹⁄₂₄ Of the whole, ashes of burnt vegetables'.[62] Hogg's criticism does seem justified.

Another of Hogg's contemporaries and a nearby nurseryman was his friend and rival Isaac Emmerton the Younger (his father of the same name also grew auriculas), who added some ingredients, noted with astonishment by Brenda Hyatt:

I find the soil mixture recommended by Isaac Emmerton almost beyond belief, but he obviously had great faith in it. The mix consisted of sugar, baker's scum, nightsoil, sand, yellow loam (preferably from molehills) and goose dung steeped in bullock's blood.[63]

Emmerton forced a client to obtain two geese and a gander and to start stockpiling their dung. The smell of the pile when mixed with the bullock's blood caused an outcry in the close quarters of the London neighbourhood, especially among the women. Hogg wrote about this client in his *Supplement to the Practical Treatise on the Culture of Florists' Flowers; Containing Additional Directions and Improved Modes of Cultivating the Auricula, Polyanthus, Tulip, Ranunculus, Heartsease, Carnation, Dahlia* (1833).

Sir Thomas Love Peacock, the genial 'Laughing Philosopher', business-man and prolific writer, in his novella *Headlong Hall* (1815) imagined 'a philosophical auricula falling into a train of theoretical meditation' on its diet, in a conversation of men debating the merits of vegetarianism. The speaker asserts that although the auricula might work itself into 'a profound abomination' of bullock's blood, sugar-baker's scum and other 'unnatural' ingredients, it would soon realize that it was 'retrograde' to forsake the Emmerton diet for something 'natural' when it was compared to more beautiful auriculas nourished by animal products.[64]

Auricula Biographers

The auricula's status in the human sphere shows in the number of its distinguished biographers. Sacheverell Sitwell became a horticultural critic with the writing of *Old Fashioned Flowers* in 1939, illustrated in fantastical style by John Farleigh. 'This first moment of seeing a Stage Auricula is an experience never to be forgotten,' wrote Sitwell after viewing one at a Royal Horticultural Show.[65] His writing on the aesthetics of the auricula articulates what many feel but few can express.

Later in the twentieth century the auricula was fortunate to fall into the collaborative hands of the flower historian Reverend C. Oscar Moreton and the illustrator Rory McEwen. Their book *The Auricula: Its History and Character* (1964) is, like *The Temple of Flora*, a grand, large-format work, produced in a limited edition of 500 copies.[66] Little is recorded about the Reverend except that he was the father of the well-known diplomat Sir John Moreton and must have had a passion for flowers. Moreton and McEwen first collaborated on *Old Carnations and Pinks* (1955), which McEwen illustrated when he was just 23, still at Cambridge. The book jacket states that 'This book has been produced in the conviction that the auricula is one of the most beautiful and fascinating of all the cultivated flowers.'[67]

Sir Rowland Biffen's *Auricula: The Story of a Florist's Flower* appeared in 1951. Biffen, who was director of the Plant Breeding Institute in

Elisabeth Dowle's portrait of the auricula 'Catherine' from Patricia Cleveland-Peck's *Auriculas through the Ages* (2011).

Cambridge from its founding in 1912 until his retirement in 1936, gained fame breeding new varieties of wheat using the newly discovered Mendelian genetics. In his own garden, working with his wife, he bred strawberries, peas, delphiniums, gladioli and auriculas, his 'most constant love'. His book on auriculas, published posthumously, was the jewel in the crown of a distinguished life. He completed the rough draft days before his death in 1949. A model of gracious, economical, informative prose, *The Auricula* is a classic, a treasure to read and reread. Biffen, writing during and after the Second World War, worried about the future of the auricula in a troubled world, but he hoped that 'surely,

A greeting card by 'Romany Soup' showing the complementary nature
of peacocks and auriculas.

however badly things may go, there will always be many who can find
their happiness in contemplating the mysterious haunting beauty of
this, the most perfect of all the flowers which human efforts have
brought into existence.'[68]

Inspired by Sitwell's comment that 'Mere photographs of the
Auricula convey nothing whatever of its qualities,' the garden writer
Patricia Cleveland-Peck and the botanical artist Elisabeth Dowle
produced a new classic, *Auriculas through the Ages: Bear's Ears, Ricklers and
Painted Ladies* in 2011.[69] Cleveland-Peck climbed to the top of the Kitz-
büheler Horn in the Austrian Alps to find wild auricula species, learned
medieval French and Latin, and visited many archives to complete the
most comprehensive history of the auricula to date.

Elizabeth Kent devotes a chapter in her book *Flora Domestica; or, The Portable Flower-Ggarden* (1831) to the auricula.[70] It is written from the point of view of a woman who, having received many gifts of potted plants that then died, wants her readers to do better maintaining 'a potted garden in pots'. She writes: 'There is no flower more tenderly cherished by its cultivator', whom she terms an 'Auriculist', and quotes verses from the poem 'Spring' by the seventeenth-century writer Heinrich von Kleist in which he describes a peacock as jealously stalking auriculas that are 'rayed in sparkling dust, and velvet pride, Like brilliant stars in splendid row'.[71] Kent tells us that the auricula repays cultivation, noting that 'It has been affirmed that Henry Stow of Lexden, near Colchester, a noted cultivator of these flowers, had one plant with no less than one hundred and thirty-three blossoms upon one stem.'[72] She emphasizes that, although the extravagant beauty of the auricula has earned its residence in stately homes and theatres, its true place is where it started:

> The Auricula is to be found in the highest perfection in the gardens of the working class, who bestow much time and attention upon this and a few other flowers, as the tulip and the pink. A fine stage of these plants is scarcely ever to be seen in the gardens of the nobility and gentry, who depend upon the exertions of hired servants, and cannot therefore compete in these nicer operations of gardening with those who tend their flowers themselves, and watch over their progress with paternal solicitude.[73]

These are the many growers who inspired Spring to create Uncle Geldersome.

six

Cult Primroses from the East

At the end of the Edo Period, people became interested
in not only beautiful flowers but also unusual plants with
unusual appearances or shapes of leaves and flowers. These
were called 'cult plants'.

AYAKO NAGASE, 2011

W hen Europeans first arrived in China and Japan, they
were astounded by the flora and state-of-the-art
horticulture. During the Edo period (1603–1868),
Japan was said to lead the world in floriculture.[1] China was its equal.
The Chinese primrose (*P. sinensis*) and the Japanese star or snowflake
primrose (*P. sieboldii*) quickly achieved cult status on being introduced
to the West. By the end of the nineteenth century Europe was infatu-
ated with exoticism. For 70 years the Chinese primrose was second
only to the pelargonium as a windowsill and conservatory plant. However, the two World Wars changed their fates, and that of horticulture
in general throughout Europe.[2] Untended plants and lack of seed
collecting led to the demise of thousands of heritage plants. Buildings
could be 'rebuilt', but not the genomes of unique cultivated plants.

P. sinensis

P. sinensis has been called 'one of the greatest mysteries of British
horticulture'.[3] The Chinese primrose first appeared in England as a

152

drawing, sent home by John Reeves in 1819, and it caused excitement among horticulturalists.[4] Reeves had gone to Canton in 1812 as an assistant tea inspector. A frequent correspondent of Sir Joseph Banks of Kew, he hired Chinese artists to paint flowers, and sent the paintings to the Horticultural Society, of which he was an active member. He interested himself in the flora around Canton and Macao (travel in China was restricted severely to only a few miles outside the two ports), and became so influential in the introduction of the country's flora to the West that he was called 'one of the Nestors of Horticulture'.[5] Once he was adept in preparing plants and seeds for travel and instructing shipboard personnel on their part in keeping the plants alive, he sent living material. His introduction failed, but one plant arrived in 1821 on board an East India tea ship under the command of one Captain Rawes.[6] Rawes gave it to a relative in Bromley, south of London, where it flourished. In 1922 John Potts, a gardener for the (now Royal) Horticultural Society (RHS) working in China, sent a large quantity of seed, and soon Chinese primroses were spreading by the thousands across Europe, where they were pampered in glasshouses from the Netherlands to France.[7] The flower's capacity for producing unusual variation made it a 'cult' favourite among amateur growers, who held shows, particularly in the north of England, devoted solely to its display.

Chinese primroses were amenable to the Victorian enthusiasm for nurturing flowers 'under glass'. They are classified as tender perennials, and will flower throughout the year if kept in a greenhouse. Like other primroses, the Chinese primrose is prone 'to sport', that is, to produce atypical forms or novelties. Starting with the ivy-leaved and the palm-leaved forms, genetic mutation produced variations that took the primrose leaf into uncharted territory. In 1860 a fern-leaved sport appeared that took horticulture's fancy. In the 1880s new leaf forms appeared that were given names such as moss-curled, parsley-leaved, crispifolia and kale-leaved. Flower petals could be lobed, as in the wild-type *stellata* varieties, or heavily frilled (*fimbriata*). Further, there were flaked flowers, pure white with small streaks of colour.

Primula sinensis, from John Lindley's *Collectanea botanica* (1821).

Flower doubling and gigantism added to the party. Soon the seed company Suttons and Sons was knee-deep in stunning varieties of the Chinese primrose, including 'Crimson King', 'Coral Pink', 'Blue Star' and 'Double Duchess'. It became very busy crossing novel varieties to see how human intervention could influence variation. In his history of the Chinese primrose and Sutton's work with it, Arthur Warwick Sutton (1854–1925), grandson of the owner and founder, describes one example of the variation that occurred: 'In 1886 we obtained a double lilac mottled flower, deeply fringed, curled foliage with bronze edges. This feature only lasted two years and then disappeared.'[8]

Taming 'sports' was, and still is, a difficult business. Plant breeders must conduct countless crossing trials over many years to stabilize new traits in sturdy plants, and even then can be unsuccessful. F1 seed (resulting from the first generation after a hybridization event) is genetically unstable and prone to sport. Gardeners must order new F1 seed each year if breeders cannot stabilize the desirable traits.

Between 1900 and 1930 the Chinese primrose became one of the most intensively studied model organisms for the new science of genetics. It is easy to see why geneticists adopted it to test the inheritance of Mendelian characters: more was known about it than about any other plant. The biologist William Bateson, who coined the term 'genetics', spent many years studying the species, and served with Sutton on a joint committee of the RHS and the Royal Society's Evolution Committee. The latter was formed in 1893 to conduct 'statistical enquiry into the variability of organisms'.[9] Bateson and Sutton brought their work on the Chinese primrose to the public with the help of the Linnean Society in 1904. A public presentation of 240 specimens created a vivid display of the variation found in just this one species.[10]

Mystery surrounds the wild form of the Chinese primrose, if one even still exists. The plant material sent to Europe in the first half of the nineteenth century comprised a variety cultivated for centuries.[11] A wild form was reported to have been introduced to Britain in 1895, having been found by the plant hunters Jean Marie Delavay, Reginald Farrer and others on the limestone cliffs of the Yangtze gorge at Yichang.[12] However, Bateson reported in 1914 that the cultivated form and this wild form were intersterile, a condition that precludes their being the same species. Further, the wild form (called *P. rupestris*

Primula sinensis Sabine ex. Lindl. var. hortensis, from Jean Linden's *L'Illustration horticole* (1888).

A plate from William Bateson's *Mendel's Principles of Heredity* (1909), illustrating heredity in *Primula sinensis.*

when considered a separate species) is fairly stable in morphology, rather than variable. A number of hypotheses attempt to explain all this. Perhaps the cultivated and wild forms diverged through centuries of separation to become distinct species.[13] Perhaps the introduction that led to the European populations of the Chinese primrose carried a mutation that hindered their reproduction with the non-mutant wild form. Or perhaps the specimens that arrived in Europe had particularly high rates of mutation.[14]

The Chinese primrose has all but disappeared from the horticultural scene in North America and Europe since the end of the Second World War. A 'tender' perennial, it was expensive to keep in conservatories, and, like its close relative *P. obconica*, it could be allergenic, its hairs causing nasty rashes in some gardeners. It is possible that plant breeders, in becoming so enamoured of mutant forms, fostered varieties so ruffled, doubled and crisped that the true charm, even identity, of the Chinese primrose was missing. The public might have lost interest in a primrose that looked like an overbred petunia or poodle. But dedicated primrose lovers still put the call out for seeds, perhaps to start a new breeding programme to restore its character.[15] And geneticists are still probing its secrets. In 2016 researchers in China sequenced the entire genome of the chloroplast (the structure that contains chlorophyll and therefore enables photosynthesis) of the Chinese primrose.[16]

P. sieboldii

Introduced to England in the 1860s, the Japanese Star Primula [*P. sieboldii*] soon became popular and it thronged the mighty conservatories over the next fifty years. It truly sparkled in the lamplight and peeped prettily through the ferns at many a lady with the after ball vapours . . . Its career was ruined by the Kaiser. The milk white hands with the blue veins that once caressed piano keys through aching ballads now rolled patriotic bandages and served cups of tea to bright blue wounded soldiers in the stripped conservatories.[17]

In fact, the Kaiser did not entirely ruin the centuries-long cultivation of *P. sieboldii*. Although perhaps not peeping through ferns at elaborate balls any longer, hundreds of new varieties have replaced those that were lost. About the same time as the auricula reached near perfection in Europe at the hands of Florist weavers in Britain, a similar 'florist' movement arose in Japan, and the reverential cultivation of *P. sieboldii* began and flourished throughout the Edo period. In the process a simple wild flower became 'civilized', an object of beauty for show. *P. sieboldii* caught the attention of Edo horticulturalists because the flowers resembled those of cherry trees, hence the common name *sakurasou* (variously *sakurasoh* and *sakurasoo*; *sakura* means cherry blossom and *sou* is the word for herb). Although it is sometimes called, in translation from the Japanese, the 'traditional primrose', 'eightfold primrose' or 'Japanese star primrose', most gardeners in North America and Europe now call it simply 'sieboldii'.

Philipp Franz von Siebold was born in Bavaria and educated at the University of Würzburg. In 1823 he arrived in Dejima, an artificial island in the bay of Nagasaki, constructed during the Edo period as Japan's point-of-entry trading post with the outside world. Employed as a physician and scientist in the service of the Netherlands (Dutch) East India Company, Siebold introduced Western medicine to Japan, setting up a medical school on Nagasaki. He also introduced the country's flora and fauna to Europe, including the now infamously invasive Japanese knotweed (*Fallopia japonica*) and the magical *P. sieboldii*. Banished from Japan after being accused of spying, Siebold left in 1829 with 12,000 specimens, which are now housed in the National Herbarium of the Netherlands in Leiden. Because of his influence as a doctor, *rangaku* (the study of Western medicine via translation from Dutch texts) became popular in Edo-period Japan. Siebold left a daughter there, and she became the country's first practising female doctor, and eventually a court physician to the empress.

During the Edo period Japan's isolation encouraged floriculture, especially in central Tokyo. All classes of person, including samurai,

Primula sieboldii by Kawahara Keiga (1786–1860), who depicted flora and fauna on the artificial island of Dejima in a style blending Japanese and Western influences.

Shunman Kubo (1757–1820), *Sakurasou*, woodcut showing *P. sieboldii* seedlings growing in a box, with a mature plant in pot to the upper right.

priests, poets and commoners, became involved in the craze for potted plants and unusual cultivars. Although it is a wild flower of wet streams in gently mountainous woodlands, *P. sieboldii* adapted easily to pot culture, and soon unusual cultivars were being displayed in traditional handmade pottery in bamboo structures, much like the auricula theatres, called *sakurasou kadan*. Each *kadan* has five shelves, each holding eight pots. One of the oldest cultivars still available today is 'Nankin-kozakura', which means 'the cherry blossom primrose of Nankin'; it was listed by Ihei Ito, a nurseryman of Tokyo in about 1733. Just as in Britain, nurserymen charged large sums for cult flowers and speciality pots. One such nurseryman, Hantei-Kinta, published the catalogue 'Soumokukihinkagami' in 1827, listing 1,000 cult species.[18]

Although both have a cult status, 'sieboldii' is the antithesis of the auricula. Its foliage is delicate rather than muscular, the leaves yellowish-green rather than grey-green, the flowers delicate, snowflake-like and varying in shades of white to pale lilac to violet to magenta, never brown or murrey-toned like the auricula. Sacheverell Sitwell observed that the auricula has the classical stillness of porcelain.[19] 'Sieboldii', on the other hand, is made for breezes; it's frilly and it dances. One popular cultivar today is 'Pink Snowflake'. Few would name an auricula 'pink snowflake', just as few would name a *sakurasou* a 'leather-coat', one of the popular auricula names in eighteenth-century Britain. But just as the Western Florists collected and propagated the endless variations of the auricula, so the Japanese florists collected and encouraged the variations of the *sakurasou* through selection of novel

Barnhaven's *Primula sieboldii* 'Trade Winds'.

forms and hybridization. Sitwell, who felt the auricula was almost entirely man-made, wondered what the Japanese florists, whose skill was legendary, would have created with it.

There are currently well over 400 named varieties or cultivars of *P. sieboldii*; hundreds more have been lost irretrievably during times of war and civil strife, but some take on a second life. Many that are currently offered are new seed strains derived from varieties developed in the 1970s by Barnhaven (UK), such as 'Apple Blossom', which was introduced in 2016 by Barnhaven of France.[20] Their names reflect character, appearance and heritage: 'Akatonbo', for instance, means red dragonfly. Other names of seed strains evoke the ethereal nature of *P. sieboldii*: 'Romance', 'Dancing Ladies', 'Trade Winds', 'Pale Moon' and 'Nirvana'. This last is described as a 'light marshmallow pink with smooth, rounded petals'.[21] Infinite shades of pink abound: 'Blush Pink', 'Sorcha's Pink', 'Spring Blush' and 'Martin Nest Pink'. 'Snowbird' artistically combines feathered petals and whiteness. Its cultivars are most often sold as 'White' or 'Snowflake', while 'Snowdrop', with its drooping petals, strangely mimics its well-known namesake (*Galanthus* spp.).[22] Planted en masse, *P. sieboldii* carries subtle woodland effects into garden settings.

Reverence for the *sakurasou*

Reverence for the *sakurasou* comes in as many shades as does *P. sieboldii* itself. There are many stories of ordinary gardeners finding themselves smitten by the infinite variations of colour and form, lured into amazingly fine levels of discernment. As in the case of the auricula, the human connection with the *sakurasou* often starts as a *coup de foudre*, when the sight of a particular blossom strikes at the intellectual, emotional and spiritual centre of a person. One such story has been told by Tomoshige Hirota in 'The Sakurasou, the Mountain and Me'.[23] He often climbed Mt Kongo-zan (elevation 1,125 m/3,700 ft) in Osaka Prefecture, Japan, with his mother, and every spring he bought twenty *sakurasou* plants from the Takagamo Shrine there. Soon he had

Primula sieboldii 'Noboruko'.

1,000 plants representing 400 kinds of *sakurasou*, and he continued to increase his collection as secretary of the Naniwa Siebold's Primrose Association. Cultivating the flowers symbolizes for him the enduring bonds that connect 'sieboldii', the mountain, his mother (who is now dead) and himself.

P. sieboldii has a distinctive place in Japanese culture. At special festivals devoted to the *sakurasou*, volunteers place vases of 'sieboldii' in railway stations. There are also primula preserves, for example one in Urawa City (Saitama, to the north of Tokyo), and in a land of many beautifully decorated manhole covers, there is a particularly striking one adorned with images of 'sieboldii'.

P. sieboldii as a Model System

P. sieboldii is native to eastern Siberia, Mongolia, northern China, Manchuria, Korea and Japan. Although preferring moisture, it tolerates extreme cold, heat and drought, simply shedding its foliage to avoid hot, dry summers. It has a clonal habit, meaning that it spreads by underground rhizomes, resulting in large patches that are genetically identical (known as genets or clonal colonies). When segments of the rhizomes break or rot, in a process called 'splitting', a 'daughter' results, called a ramet. While genets can live for a long time, the daughter ramets live for about a year before producing gemmae (sing. gemma), resting underground buds that result in new plants. Specific cultivars can be conserved by cutting pieces of the rhizomes, a form of vegetative propagation. New variation appears with the planting of a single seed. Sometimes the chemical compound colchicine can be applied to produce triploid and tetraploid plants, which have the advantage of robustness.

Now endangered in the Japanese archipelago, 'sieboldii' is the subject of intense scrutiny by ecologists trying to understand the factors affecting its future in the wild. Loss and fragmentation of habitat as a result of human-engineered development have obliterated some populations and interfered with a healthy genetic balance among those that remain. Although bumblebees, butterflies and hoverflies visit *P. sieboldii*, the most effective pollinators, given the flower's pin-and-thrum architecture, are the queens of the long-tongued bumblebee, such as *Bombus diversus tersatus*. After hibernating over winter, these queens begin their activity outside the nest just as the flowering season of 'sieboldii' begins. The structure of the flower and the geometry of the bee's body are an effective match for achieving 'legitimate' cross-pollination. The queens, conveniently for ecologists, leave claw marks on the petals, indicating their presence in the environment and their work as pollinators. However, the loss of pollinators is a major factor in low seed set and thus the loss of new individuals and overall genetic diversity. In one nature reserve near the urban area of Greater Tokyo, ecologists monitored a patch of 'sieboldii' flowers for sixteen continuous hours and failed to log a visit by any insect.[24]

P. sieboldii has been used as a model system for studying the flower shapes bumblebees prefer. Its flowers are flat and radially symmetrical, and have a distinctively deep notch on the petal head. Researchers developed artificial flowers based on them, and found that bumblebees can be trained in the laboratory to visit flowers of a certain shape and size. Although this does not yet translate into behaviour in the wild, bumblebees showed a clear preference for deep petal notches and extremely narrow petals.[25]

Biologists have also studied how 300 years of intense cultivation have affected the genomes of 'sieboldii' cultivars. Focusing on the effect of domestication on petal shape and size variations compared with these characteristics in wild populations, they found that cultivars showed more variation than wild plants in traits associated with symmetrical characteristics, and that there was an overall increase in size and diversity of form. Head notches were shallower and the petals larger and more fan-shaped than in the flowers of wild 'sieboldii'.[26] Domestication is an evolutionary process that can conserve genetic potential and benefit the wider community.

Biologists and horticulturalists realize the importance of conserving the genetic resources of both the cultivars and the wild forms of 'sieboldii'. Wild forms depend on insect pollinators, and cultivars depend on human intervention. A particular cultivar can be maintained only through the continual division of pieces of the rhizome of a 'mother' plant. The Agricultural and Forestry Research Center of the University of Tsukuba in Ibaraki Prefecture has been working to conserve 'sieboldii' cultivars since 1980. In cooperation with the not-for-profit organization Tsukuba Urban Gardening, it started the Primrose Foster Parent programme. After training, a volunteer citizen acts as 'foster parent' to 'foster children' – in this case twenty 'sieboldii' cultivars. The 'parents' update university staff periodically, and once a year the city's botanic garden mounts a show of the whole collection. Analogous to 'citizen science' programmes throughout the world, in which birdwatchers, for example, add their data to Christmas counts, this 'citizen horticulture' programme may be one of the few where humans actively 'foster' plants.

Siebold's legacy in Japan received renewed recognition because of his connection with the primrose *P. kisoana*, known in Japan as *kakko-so*. Siebold named it after Mt Kiso, where he first found it. Now it survives in the wild only in shaded alpine areas of Narukami Mountain, near the city of Kiryu on Honshu. The Kakko-so Preservation Society of Kiryu has become active in protecting this population, educating the public and protesting against the construction of woodland roads. Biologists are assisting pollination to increase seed set, and reintroducing seedlings in this remaining population.[27] The journalist Akiko Minosaki of the *Kiryu Times* wrote a series of articles in the late 1990s describing her visits to Leiden's National Herbarium (Rijksherbarium), carrying seeds and sixteen specimens from Kiryu to plant in the Von Siebold Memorial Garden there. She writes: 'Planting the flowers will form a new bridge of friendship between Japan and the Netherlands, [and] Kiryu and Leiden.'[28] These efforts were part of the build-up to the 400th anniversary of Siebold's arrival at Dejima. *P. kisoana*, which is available in the horticultural trade in North America and Europe, symbolizes one of the first encounters in the continuing process of globalization. Its rose-mauve flowers and dense covering of downy white hairs on shapely light-green leaves add a soft presence in the garden.

As China and Japan gradually opened their doors to the outside world, primroses were among the first immigrants to the West. As they travelled from their place of origin, they found niches at points of contact among horticulture, science and commerce. New chapters are still being added to the stories of their journeys.

seven
Writing the Primrose

'Now, mind you don't talk with and notice your cousin too much,' were my whispered instructions as we entered the room. 'It will certainly annoy Mr Heathcliff, and he'll be mad at you both.'

'I'm not going to,' she answered.

The minute after, she had sidled to him, and was sticking primroses in his plate of porridge.

EMILY BRONTË, *Wuthering Heights* (1847)[1]

Wuthering Heights is a dark and stormy novel, almost entirely unrelieved by anything light or bright, until the scene near the end when Catherine sprinkles common primroses into the porridge of wild young Hareton. Indeed, new life is about to begin, ending the cycle of death and tragedy. Catherine and Hareton will marry on a New Year's Day. One critic has written that the common primroses here represent 'sunshine', and another that the primrose-strewn porridge foretells the transformation of the Heights into 'a haven of tranquility' and the renewal of domesticity.[2] Such is the symbolic power of the primrose. Writers have used primroses in text as transformative metaphors, as mirrors to self and as near-equal organisms whose literal presence is transformative. Most often they reached for the common primrose (*P. vulgaris*), because of its abundance and constant character. The written primrose has enlivened many pages.

168

'The child's flower in the childhood of life' is how the Victorian poet and writer William Allingham (husband of the painter Helen Allingham, whom we met in the Introduction) described the common primrose in a sonnet.[3] Anne Pratt, an influential flower writer and painter of the same period, wrote of another association: that people 'have welcomed the early flower, welcomed it all the more because they could find it by vale or hill, by wood or river'.[4] The common primrose and the cowslip signified the land, childhood, spring and home for people of all classes. It was primrose time even in the city, when bunches of violets, common primroses and cowslips were sent from Cornwall to London for sale. But picking a cowslip or common primrose for a grandmother or finding it near one's doorstep formed the deepest memories. Mary Baker, the author of *Primrose Time: A Cornish Childhood Remembered* (1993), describes moving from London to Lelant, near St Ives:

> And on the bank of one narrow footpath by the vicarage garden, a small gully overshadowed by presently leafless, dripping trees, we found our first primroses, pale and dainty. The pathway where they grew was called Skidney and the name sounds right for what it was – narrow, steep and slippery. Those primroses were Cornwall's first offering to me and the sight and scent and feel of primroses will even now, so long after, recall the innocence of those days.[5]

For almost all Victorian writers, the common primrose could do no wrong. In *Field Flowers: A Handy-book for the Rambling Botanist, Suggesting What to Look For and Where to Go in the Out-door Study of British Plants* (1870), Shirley Hibberd wrote that 'we look upon primroses as upon people who never have chilblains or bad tempers', although he was at times more poetic, calling them 'angels that went astray after the daughters of men ages ago'.[6] Near the beginning of *Rebecca* (1938), Daphne Du Maurier describes the spring wild flowers surrounding Manderley: the stately daffodils, the vibrant crocuses, the bluebells,

Luigi Schiavonetti, *The Primrose Seller*, 1793, stipple engraving print after Francis Wheatley.

while 'the primrose was more vulgar, a homely pleasant creature who appeared in every cranny like a weed.'[7] By 'vulgar' she probably means 'common', the sense carried in the plant's specific epithet 'vulgaris'. However, an abundance of benign species brings comfort. It was not rarity but rather abundance that made people feel so attached to the common primrose. Like green grass, blue sky and white clouds, the pale primrose presented itself copiously at a vulnerable time. The goliard poets of the twelfth and thirteenth centuries had expressed fears about seasonal change in the line 'When Spring starts to fail us, Is winter far behind?'[8] The reappearance of the common primrose meant that failure had been averted once again. Du Maurier notes, insightfully, of the common primrose that 'although a creature of the wilds it had a leaning toward civilization'.[9] It could 'smile' in a jam jar of water in a cottage window for a week or so.

Rural Curates Pen Descriptions of Primroses

The eighteenth-century parson-naturalist Gilbert White faithfully recorded in his journal the appearance of flora and fauna at his vicarage. On 26 March 1787 he wrote: 'Transplanted some of the best, blowing seedling polyanths from the orchard to the bank in the garden.' On 16 May 1790 there was much fruitfulness: 'One polyanth-stalk produced 47 pips or blossoms. Mrs Edmund White brought to bed of a boy, who has increased the number of my nephews & nieces to 56.' On the other hand, on 7 April 1793, 'The chaffinches destroy the blossoms of the polyanths in a sad manner.'[10] Aside from his lovely language, White's precise observations bearing dates add to our understanding of phenology, the timing of seasonal phenomena in the natural world. Such data help us to interpret changes in the face of global warming. White lived out his life as the curate of his grandfather's vicarage in Hampshire, where he had been born.

A century later Reverend Francis Kilvert wrote about common primroses in his diaries describing life as a rural curate in the Welsh Marches. Easter was primrose time, and Easter Day 1870 (17 April) was especially beautiful:

> There was a heavy white dew with a touch of hoar frost on the meadows, and as I leaned over the wicket gate by the mill pond looking to see if there were any primroses in the banks but not liking to venture into the dripping grass suddenly I heard the cuckoo for the first time this year . . . The village

lay quiet and peaceful in the morning sunshine, but by the time I came back from primrosing there was some little stir and people were beginning to open their doors and look out into the fresh fragrant splendid morning.[11]

Kilvert had definite ideas about how graves should be decorated. He did not like cut flowers stuck into holes in the ground around a grave without design, and was proud of guiding his parishioners to decorate the tops of graves with what he called 'primrose crosses'.

Prose Writers Remember Millions of Primroses

H. E. Bates is known for fiction such as *The Darling Buds of May* (1958) and the collection *My Uncle Silas* (1939), and for non-fiction essays describing the Northamptonshire countryside. It was at the home of his real-life Uncle Silas, a man of 'aggravated wickedness and cunning', that he encountered his first woodland: 'It was a paradise of a million primroses. They crowded everywhere, often attracting many small birds around them, all through the wood and outside of it, very big and rich in that black earth. We took baskets to gather them.'[12] In the last chapter of *Through the Woods* (1936), 'Primroses and Catkins', he describes an early spring in thinned woods:

> Primroses appear miraculously on the cleared ground, in short-stemmed tufts that thicken rapidly. Here, we gather primroses all winter, even for Christmas Day. We have gathered them in January, by moonlight, when they seemed like flecks of earth-bound moonlight themselves. They seem extra precious, these winter primroses. Rain-blanched and small and frost-browned, they are often very poor; but they are symbolic. They are living bits of sunlight. They are indomitable. Nothing can suppress them. For such flimsy-petalled soft flowers they have an astonishing tenacity and toughness. They come up through the snow. They almost thrive on it:

so that as the snow melts it seems to melt not into water but into flowers, into fresh tiny flower-flakes of palest yellow.[13]

An avid gardener, Bates wrote many books about flowers, among them *Flowers and Faces* (1935), *A Love of Flowers* (1971) and *A Fountain of Flowers* (1974). He captures the joy of encountering the abundance of cowslips and the pleasure of picking them in his short story 'The Cowslip Field' (1959). A young boy goes cowslip-picking with Pacey, a dwarfish country woman. She is thick-legged, has a large, furry mole under her right eye and uses country dialect, which the boy corrects querulously. In turn, she corrects the boy when he can't tell the difference between a buttercup field and a cowslip field. Bates captures the spirit-altering sight of the latter:

> He knew he had never seen, in all his life, so many cowslips. They covered with their trembling orange heads all the earth between himself and the horizon. When a sudden breeze caught them they ducked and darted very gently away from it and then blew gently back again.[14]

When the boy observes the cowslip chains the pair have made on Pacey's hair, he has a revelation about the nature of beauty.

Poets

A brief survey of famous primrose lines from the fourteenth to the seventeenth century gives a sense of contrasting interpretations, often reflecting the writer's personality.[15] In the late fourteenth-century *Miller's Tale* Geoffrey Chaucer describes a carpenter's wife: 'She was a primrose, and a tender chicken/ For any lord to lay upon his bed,/ Or yet for any good yeoman to wed.' Chaucer was known for his ribald earthiness, whereas Edmund Spenser, author of the epic poetical allegory *The Faerie Queene* (1590), respected the primness of the common primrose in describing a young lady: 'As fairer nymph yet never saw mine eie/ She is the pride and primrose of the rest.' In the next century the visionary Henry Vaughan also inferred a saintly interpretation in his poem 'Thou that Know'st for Whom I Mourn': 'it was my sin that forc'd thy hand to cull this primrose out.'

For the seventeenth-century poet John Donne, it was not the mesmerizing yellow but the five petals that focused his thoughts in 'The Primrose, Being at Montgomery Castle upon the Hill, on Which It Is Situate'. The title attracts our attention to this particular primrose. The first stanza reads:

> Upon this Primrose hill,
> Where, if heaven would distil
> A shower of rain, each several drop might go
> To his own primrose, and grow manna so;
> And where their form, and their infinity
> Make a terrestrial galaxy,
> As the small stars do in the sky;
> I walk to find a true love; and I see
> That 'tis not a mere woman, that is she,
> But must or more or less than woman be.[16]

The poem has been interpreted as one that expresses Donne's cynical views of female constancy in matters of love. In mythical lore a five-petalled flower represents woman, and each petal stands for the major stages in her life: birth, initiation, consummation, repose and death. Five was also the number of infidelity in the 'language of flowers'. Donne spends the next two stanzas wondering how likely it is that he will find a six- or four-petalled primrose; either would represent a faithful woman. Critics have made much of the 'numerological dalliance' in the poem.[17] In the first stanza Donne visualizes raindrops turning into primroses, joining those on the ground, all of them signifying manna from heaven.

The scholar Molly Mahood, former professor of English literature at the University of Kent, became an expert on the poetry of primroses; her magnum opus is *The Poet as Botanist* (2008). A noted Shakespearean authority, she glossed every line in which he mentioned the common primrose, cowslip or oxlip.[18] Shakespeare knew his flowers with the eye of a botanist, differentiating clearly between the cowslip and the common primrose. The red spot at the base of each cowslip petal had not escaped his attention. In *A Midsummer Night's Dream*, a fairy tells puckish Robin Goodfellow of her busy peregrinations in search of cowslips (*P. veris*):

> I do wander everywhere,
> Swifter than the moon's sphere;
> And I serve the Fairy Queen,
> To dew her orbs upon the green.
> The cowslips tall her pensioners be:
> In their gold coats spots you see;
> Those be rubies, fairy favours,
> In those freckles live their savours:
> I must go seek some dewdrops here
> And hang a pearl in every cowslip's ear.[19]

In his *Flora Londinensis* (1777–98), William Curtis praises Shakespeare for this description, which shows 'how pleasing the most trifling appearances in natural history may be rendered by an imagination like his', while calling the mistakes of poets, who, 'in general, have not sufficiently attended to the works of Nature', 'reprehensible'.[20]

Many, however, have wondered why Shakespeare ever wrote the phrase 'the primrose path of dalliance'. Mahood calls his use of the primrose in this context 'startling'.[21] Others agree. The First World War poet Edmund Blunden wrote 'An Annotation' protesting at Shakespeare's phrasing, which he quotes below the title. The poem's opening lines address the primrose: 'Emblem of early seeking, early finding,/ Frailness whose patience stills the moody cries/ Of old Time struggling through chaotic skies.' It concludes: 'Your paths are peace, they comfort and not burn,/ There young Love strolls, old Adage stares in ponds./ With what strange wrong was Shakespeare mocked when he/ So tossed you to the hooves of infamy?'[22]

When the primrose and cowslip became free of religious connotation, they took on poetical symbolic ones, easily becoming innocent, virginal maidens. However, Mahood points out that primroses have long since attracted 'polarized meanings': 'Yet despite such associations, in other contexts a hint of the voluptuous hangs about primroses. Shakespeare's Venus seduced Adonis on a primrose bank.'[23] Shakespeare repeated his 'startling' primrose phrasing in several of his plays. In *Macbeth* he writes of 'The primrose way to the everlasting bonfire' (II, iii), evidently finding the phrasing useful. In 'Regeneration' (1650), a metaphysical poem by Henry Vaughan, a young narrator clouded with 'sin' goes for a walk: 'It was high spring, and all the way/ Primrosed and hung with shade.' He has a change of heart when sitting on a primrose-covered bank.[24]

Mahood also became an authority on the primroses of Wordsworth and Darwin, writing, 'it so happens that the greatest poet and the greatest scientist of the nineteenth century both paid much heed to primroses.'[25] And she pays close attention, as well, to developing the notion of the poet-botanist, particularly those who looked at primroses. Flowers had 'ensnared' poets from the earliest times, but the exciting developments in botany in the mid-eighteenth century gave poets much more material to work with. William Wordsworth may have framed the question with the few now-famous lines in his long narrative poem 'Peter Bell: A Tale in Verse' (1819). It tells the story of an insensitive, rough hawker of pottery who lives the outdoor life but gains no spiritual insight from his closeness to Nature:

> In vain, through every changeful year,
> Did Nature lead him as before;
> A primrose by a river's brim
> A yellow primrose was to him
> And it was nothing more.[26]

Walter Hood Fitch, *A Primrose by a River's Brim.*

The story of 'poor' Peter Bell, who could not see significance in the common primrose, became a commonplace reference in the nineteenth century. A few decades later the art critic John Ruskin would distinguish three kinds of poet based on their ways of seeing the primrose:

> So then, we have the three ranks: the man who perceives rightly, because he does not feel, and to whom the primrose is very accurately the primrose, because he does not love it. Then, secondly, the man who perceives wrongly, because he feels, and to whom the primrose is anything else than a primrose: a star, or a sun, or a fairy's shield, or a forsaken maiden. And then lastly, there is the man who perceives rightly in

spite of his feelings, and to whom the primrose is for ever nothing else than itself – a little flower, apprehended in the very plain and leafy fact of it, whatever and how many soever the associations and passions may be that crowd around it.[27]

Ruskin declares that the first is not a poet at all, the second a middling poet and the third the true poet. He was fascinated by botany, and wrote and illustrated a book on alpine and Arctic plants. His poet categories may seem simplistic today – one cannot easily classify poets, any more than one can plants – but he does raise the question of 'meaning' in a poet's use of a flower. Ruskin's own appreciation of plants as simply plants took an odd turn when his 'revulsion against insect pollination . . . drove him to declare war on science in his final series of lectures at Oxford'.[28]

Wordsworth became obsessed with the significance of a 'tuft' of primroses. In 1802 his sister Dorothy wrote in her journal about a walk from Grasmere to Rydal with their close friend Samuel Taylor Coleridge: 'We all stood to look at Glow-worm Rock – a primrose that grew there and just looked out on the road from its own sheltered bower.'[29] In 1808 Wordsworth wrote a poem about the sighting, 'The Primrose of the Rock'. He set it aside and came back to it in 1829. The copy made by Dorothy bears the subtitle 'Written in March 1829 on seeing a Primrose-tuft of flowers flourishing in the chink of a rock in which that Primrose-tuft had been seen by us to flourish for twenty-nine seasons.'[30] It was published in 1831 and includes historical context:

> What hideous warfare hath been waged,
> What kingdoms overthrown,
> Since first I spied that Primrose-tuft
> And marked it for my own;
> A lasting link in Nature's chain
> From highest heaven let down![31]

Not satisfied, he continued working on it for the rest of his life, hoping to incorporate it into his magnum opus, *The Recluse*, which was never finished. This longer version of the 'The Primrose of the Rock' from 1831 was finally published in 1949 as the 500-line poem 'The Tuft of Primroses'. In it, the tuft had become 'a Queen' and, as Mahood writes, 'In such inflated language Wordsworth seems to be asking more of *Primula vulgaris* than it could give.'[32] Here, verbiage buries the tuft entirely. In his manuscript Wordsworth crossed out the image 'large as the moon', evidence that he knew he was over-reaching himself. Mahood suggests that the loftiness of his language in 'The Tuft of Primroses' is out of scale with his experience and with the biological identity of the common primrose. In his simple, short poem 'A Farewell', he may have said all that needed to be said about the primrosed Glow-worm Rock: 'Here with its primrose the steep rock's breast/ Glittered at evening like a starry sky.'[33] Wordsworth's brother John had written to him about seeing primroses at night on the Isle of Wight.[34]

The writer and flower lover D. H. Lawrence critiqued Words-worth's attitudes about the significance of the tufted primrose in an essay in *Reflections on the Death of a Porcupine and Other Essays* (1925):

> This is bunk. A primrose has its own peculiar primrosy iden-tity, and all the oversouling in the world won't melt it out into a Williamish oneness . . . The primrose will neither be assimilated nor annihilated . . . It has its own individuality, . . . but its very floweriness is a kind of communion with all things: the love unison.[35]

Wordsworth mentioned primroses in many poems, but his inability to articulate the meaning of the tuft on Glow-worm Rock suggests that the primrose had become only a symbol, dead and weighty. His friend Coleridge sensed and articulated the dangers of overreliance on Nature's manifestations as emblems and revelations:

John Ruskin's drawing of a primrose leaf; watercolour and body colour over graphite on wove paper, before 1872.

Never to see or describe any interesting appearance in nature, without connecting it by dim analogies with the moral world, proves faintness of impression. Nature has her proper interest; and he will know what it is, who believes and feels, that everything has a life of its own, and that we are all one life.[36]

In 1818, in one of his famous letters, John Keats used the primrose as an analogy to make a similar point:

We hate poetry that has a palpable design upon us . . . Poetry should be great & unobtrusive, a thing which enters into one's soul, and does not startle it or amaze it with itself but with its subject. – How beautiful are the retired flowers! How would they lose their beauty were they to throng into the highway crying out, 'admire me I am a violet! Dote upon me I am a primrose!'[37]

During stays on the Isle of Wight, where he loved to write, Keats was so impressed by the presence of primroses underfoot that he suggested it be called 'Primrose Island' – 'that is, if the nation of Cowslips agree thereto, of which there are diverse Clans just beginning to lift up their heads and if and how the Rain holds where that

Birds eye abate'.[38] 'Birds eye' is shorthand for the bird's-eye primrose (*P. farinosa*).

The Rathe and Pale Primrose

Coleridge had his own primrose poem, 'To a Primrose. The First Seen in the Season', wherein he queries the pallor:

> But, tender blossom, why so pale?
> Dost hear stern Winter in the gale?
> And didst thou tempt the ungentle sky
> To catch one vernal glance and die?[39]

Many of the early poets make a connection between the primrose's pale yellow and sickness. Francis Bacon, the father of experimental investigation and author of the eccentric *Sylva sylvarum; or, A Natural History in Ten Centuries* (1626/7), reprinted ten times in the seventeenth century alone, asked why the primrose flowered so early. Bacon believed that an understanding of human nature could be found in appetites.[40] Extending this to the plant kingdom, he asked why the primrose has an 'appetite' for the cold. He decided that 'prime-roses', among other early flowerers, 'are all cold plants, which therefore (as it would seem) have a quicker perception of the heat of the sun increasing, than the hot herbs have'.[41] The why of the primrose's early appearance is deeply embedded in its genetic history, as is its pallor, which poets have noted for hundreds of years. The Reverend Charles Alexander Johns, a Cornishman and keen-eyed naturalist of the Lizard Peninsula in Cornwall, wrote in his *Flowers of the Field* (1853) that 'The colour of the flowers is such as to have a name of its own; artists maintain that primrose-colour is a delicate green.'[42] Sometimes the flower is extremely pale, revealing dark-green veins.

The two most famous flower passages in all of English poetry, according to Mahood, mention both qualities of the primrose.[43] In *Lycidas* (1637), John Milton mentions 'the rathe primrose that forsaken

Dorothy Wordsworth, journal writer and sister of William Wordsworth, *c.* 1820.

dies', and in *The Winter's Tale* Shakespeare describes 'pale primroses that die unmarried'. The now archaic word *rathe*, the root of *rather*, meaning sooner, meant 'early'. The primrose relies on long-tongued pollinators, such as bees, bumblebees, butterflies and bee flies, for fertilization. Truly, if the flowers are out before the pollinators – as is often the case with the first primroses – they will die unfertilized or 'unmarried'. Perhaps true poets do have an ecological sense.

Poets who draw on the associations of the primrose with its habitat and landscape find the deepest meaning in its presence. John Clare often wrote of primroses near Helpston in rural North-amptonshire, earning the acclaim of critics even now as 'the poet of the environmental crisis – 200 years ago'.[44] His first collection was published in 1820, just a year after Wordsworth's 'Peter Bell'. Clare made frequent references to primroses in his poems. He described their early appearance with the eye of an ecologist, even at the age of sixteen, when his sonnet 'To a Primrose' was published in the *London Magazine* of January 1820. The opening lines describe the earthy setting:

> Welcome, pale primrose, starting up between
> Dead matted leaves of oak and ash, that strew
> The every lawn, the wood, and spinney through,
> 'Mid creeping moss and ivy's darker green![45]

A schoolboy picks the flowers 'enchantedly', and a shepherd stops singing at the sight of the primroses. Few, if any, sixteen-year-olds would write or want to read such a poem now, but Clare wrote from observation, and the poem allows the modern reader to wonder about a time when schoolboys picked flowers and shepherds sang.

Later, when Clare had grown into a young man of dalliance, he wrote 'Primroses', a poem with deeper tones. The first line reads: 'I love the rath primroses pale brimstone primroses', and the poem ends:

> Spring time is come love primroses bloom fair
> The sun o' the morning shines in thy bright hair
> The ancient wood shadows are bonny dark green
> That throw out like giants the stovens between
> While brimstone primroses like patches o' flame
> Blaze through the dead leaves making Ivy look tame
> I love the rath primrose in hedgerows & closes
> Together lets wander to gather primroses —[46]

His repeated descriptions of primroses as fiery and flame-like show how vividly he saw the natural world. At about the same time, in Scotland, Robert Burns was writing 'The Primrose', a poem that described the 'languid, pensive, pale' visage of the flower, made so because 'The sweets of loves are wash'd with tears'.[47] This well-known poem may have informed the primrose's meaning in the Victorian language of flowers.

Another poet who celebrated primrose and landscape was Edward Thomas, one of many who were killed in the First World War. In one of his early poems, 'March', which begins 'Now I know that Spring will come again', he describes the hard birth of spring and primroses torn and buried by hail. He asks: 'What did the thrushes know? Rain, sleet, hail,/ Had kept them quiet as the primroses.'[48] While it may go without saying that primroses are quiet, Thomas pays attention to their silence. He had a naturalist's eye, and chose walking over bicycling to give him time to observe:

> But walking I see every small thing one by one; not only the handsome gateway chestnut just fully dressed, and the pale green larch plantation where another chiff-chaff was singing, and the tall elm tipped by a linnet pausing and musing a few notes, but every primrose and celandine and dandelion on the banks.[49]

In 1913, however, he did take to his bicycle, chasing spring from London to Somerset and compiling observations that became *In Pursuit of Spring*, recently republished with his own photographs.[50] The final chapter is called 'The Grave of Winter'. In the Quantocks, on the north side of Cothelstone Hill, he finds himself under 'a low-arched rainbow' and notices a fallen bouquet:

> By the side of the road were the first blue-bells and cowslips. They were not growing there, but some child had gathered them below at Stowey or Durleigh, and then, getting tired of them, had dropped them. They were beginning to wilt, but they lay upon the grave of Winter. I was quite sure of that. Winter may rise up through mould alive with violets and primroses and daffodils, but when cowslips and bluebells

Stamp designed by Peter Newcombe, issued by the Post Office on 21 March 1979.

have grown over his grave he cannot rise again: he is dead and rotten, and from his ashes the blossoms are springing. Therefore I was very glad to see them.[51]

Cowslips do flower later than common primroses and are brighter yellow, emphatic evidence of the death of winter. England's Poet Laureate Ted Hughes called Thomas 'the Father of us all'.[52]

Thomas died in 1917 during the Battle of Arras. Mahood concludes her survey of primrose poetry with the statement that 'the first major war of the twentieth century had given the coup de grace to poems about primroses.'[53] The context of the primrose had changed as soldiers came across them in the ravaged landscape of Europe. In a letter to his fiancée, Vera Brittain, from somewhere in France on 20–21 April 1915, the poet Roland Leighton wrote:

Your last two letters came, one last night and one the night before, and I read them by candlelight sitting on the little wooden bench outside my dug-out. I am sitting with them now writing this, while the sun shines on the paper and a bee is humming round and round the bed of primroses in front

185

of me. War and primroses! At the moment it does not seem as if there could be such a thing as war.[54]

The primroses are real, and so is the horror of war. Leighton describes how a bullet whistled past his head as he was shaving, how he stumbled on the decayed body of a British soldier sunk in a marshy area near a sunlit wood, and how the company had lost its first man the day before, shot through the head. He himself would soon die, shot by a sniper in Louvencourt, France, while Brittain would become the celebrated author of *Testament of Youth* (1933). When writing the letter, perhaps Leighton remembered primrosing as a child with his sister Clare, who lived a long life and became a famous engraver.

The world wars and increasing urbanization ended the trajectory of primrose poetry that began in the Renaissance, reached a high point in the work of Shakespeare, Donne, John Clare and others, lapsed somewhat into sentimental moralizing in the Victorian era, and appeared here and there in the twentieth century. However, real primroses were the go-between when the American poet May Sarton wanted to meet Virginia Woolf. In 1937 Sarton sent her first volume of poetry and a bunch of primroses to Woolf, and was invited for tea.[55] A few years later, as Europe struggled against Hitler, she wrote to Woolf asking whether she would donate a manuscript for an auction in the United States raising money to help refugees from Germany. In conclusion, Sarton wrote: 'I wish you were near and that I could send you the primroses that I saw in a shop and gave to my mother instead.'[56] In Woolf's play *Freshwater* (1935) – about her relatives and Alfred, Lord Tennyson, set on the Isle of Wight – there are numerous light-hearted references to 'the primrose path'.[57]

Ted Hughes, who is seen as a successor to Thomas, wrote in *Gaudete* (1977) that 'A primrose petal's edge/ Cuts the vision like laser.'[58] This observation was new and apt, indicating that more remains to be said.

eight
Picturing the Primrose

❧

I paint flowers as a way of getting as close as possible to
what I perceive as the truth, my truth of the time in which
I live. This mostly means looking, looking and thinking.

RORY MCEWEN, *The Colours of Reality* (2013)[1]

The work of depicting primroses has focused people's attention in productive ways for centuries. A cowslip bloomed in the *Paradiesgärtlein* (Little Garden of Paradise, 1410), a painting on oak panel by the Upper Rhenish Master. Pink, yellow and red primroses flowered in the Unicorn Tapestries (1495–1505).[2] In *The Science of Describing*, his book on the archiving of natural history in words and images in the Renaissance, the scholar Brian Ogilvie writes that 'naturalists formed a community of curious observers', devoted to making tangible their 'impulse to describe and love the particular'.[3] Medieval herbalists had relied on collections of dried plants known as the *siccus hortus*, 'dry garden', for reference. Carolus Clusius, the 'tamer' of auriculas (see Chapter Five), dug up plants on his travels, replanted them in his garden in Leiden, the Netherlands, and created comprehensive life histories based on his observation of living plants.[4] Clusius wrote to one of his correspondents that

It is not possible to do great things with a little sprig of dried plant material, you need an effort like mine . . . I have suffered a lot in growing my plants, nourishing them and seeing them from beginning to end – it is then we find all their qualities, so that the painter with his brush and I with my pen can extract from them all the information possible.[5]

Finding 'qualities' – Clusius's words capture the nature of the quest of the visual artist, an effort that is new each time a new observer contemplates his or her chosen flower.

Prayer books: the books of hours

The presence of the common primrose and the cowslip in *Les Grandes Heures d'Anne de Bretagne*, commissioned in about 1503 by Anne of Brittany, queen of France, indicates their importance as palliative plants. One of the richest and most powerful women of her time, married to two kings in succession, Anne led a complicated political and personal life. Scholars have studied her library, and the connection between female book ownership and political power at the time.[6] By all standards, *Les Grandes Heures* is the most sumptuous of the tens of thousands of books of hours (illuminated prayer books) that were commissioned by wealthy nobility in the Middle Ages. It is a large book, measuring 30.5 by 20 cm (12 by nearly 8 in.), of 476 pages, lavishly illuminated, as compared to the smaller *Petites Heures d'Anne de Bretagne* and the *Très Petites Heures d'Anne de Bretagne*, which were designed for use while travelling.[7] The primrose illuminations by the miniaturist Jean Bourdichon – although unnaturally elongated to fit the constraints of their position as panels in the margins – have a realistic, resonant beauty.

The herbals

Thousands of copies of hundreds of illustrated herbal texts appeared in the sixteenth century.[8] The need to identify useful medicinal plants, and the lack of vocabulary for describing botanical details, created a requirement for images and image makers. The first illustrations were

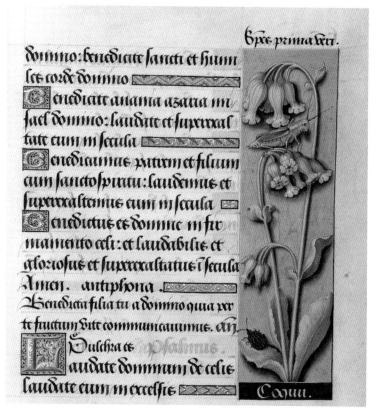

Cowslip (*P. veris*) from *Les Grandes Heures d'Anne de Bretagne.*

crude woodcut copies of pictures from Dioscorides's *De materia medica* (*c.* AD 60), the authoritative herbal manual for 1,500 years.[9] It was illuminated in the sixth century and copied many times by hand, often with additional notes. Pedanius Dioscorides was born in Anazarabus, in the Cilician region of Turkey, and travelled throughout the Roman Empire as a surgeon in Nero's army. On the way he collected plants, made concoctions and tested his herbal remedies on soldiers. His pithy descriptions left room for subsequent editorial embellishment. In 1544 Pietro Andrea Gregorio Mattioli (Mattiolus) produced a six-volume version of Dioscorides's herbal that became a bestseller. Some 32,000 copies in 60 editions were sold during his lifetime.[10] Considered an excellent but quarrelsome botanist, Mattiolus – who is

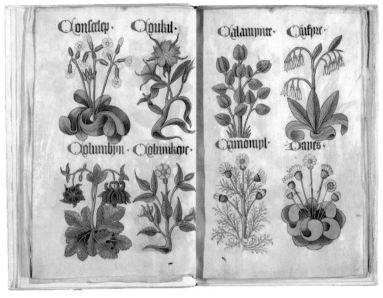

Woodcut from the *Helmingham Herbal* and *Bestiary* (*c.* 1500) showing the cowslip (top left, labelled 'Conscelep') and the oxlip (top right, labelled 'Colvirkeye').

also remembered for testing poisonous plants on prisoners – used his influence to sideline his rivals and enhance his own reputation.

Errors and misinformation multiplied as versions appeared in different languages, and continual redrawing led to images that were 'debased, even invented, and in many cases unrecognizable'.[11] A mystery plant called 'Herba Britannica', which had cured Roman soldiers on the Rhine of a disease similar to scurvy, caused much discussion. The commentators, who included the English botanist William Turner and a Dutch physician, advanced differing opinions on its identity, one candidate being the auricula (*P. auricula*). In 1825 a historian of medicinal plant substances lamented 'the mortifying uncertainty that involves the history of ancient plants'.[12]

The drawings of the cowslip (labelled 'Conscelep') and the oxlip (labelled 'Colvirkeye') that appeared in the *Helmingham Herbal and Bestiary*, on the other hand, are recognizable if stylized.[13] Completed in about 1500 at Helmingham Hall in Surrey, home of the Tollemache family, it is an important record of Tudor knowledge of natural history. A work of gouache and watercolour on parchment by an 'unidentified hand' using pen and ink, it perhaps served as a pattern book for decorating the hall (then called Creke Hall), or as a children's primer. Now in the Yale Center for British Art in New Haven, Connecticut, it was said to have been the banker Paul Mellon's favourite book among his collection of British art. A variant twin of this book is in the Bodleian Library, Oxford.[14]

One of the earliest naturalistic woodcut portrayals of the cowslip appeared in the herbal of Otto Brunfels, *Herbarium vivae eicones* (Living Pictures of Plants), in about 1530. The woodcut artist Hans Weiditz (also known as Johannes Guidictius or Gauditius) created an exquisite free-form cowslip that almost seems to move.[15] At about the same time, Albrecht Dürer, star of the Northern European Renaissance, was making coloured drawings of turf both small and large, 'das kleine Rasenstück' and 'das grosse Rasenstück', respectively.[16] In these studies (practice pieces for larger works) he rendered the

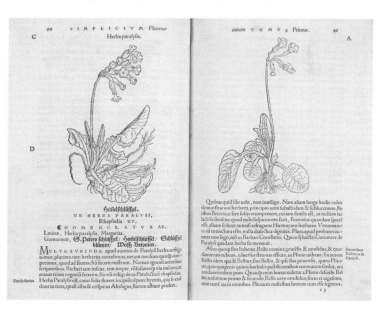

From Otto Brunfels' *Herbarium vivae eicones* (1530): Hans Weiditz's woodcut images of the cowslip (left), named here as *Herba paralysis*; and perhaps an oxlip (right), which was also used to treat spasms, cramps and paralysis.

Albrecht Dürer, *Tuft of Cowslips*, 1526, gouache on vellum.

various species present in the sod with almost photographic clarity.[17] His 'Tuft of Cowslips' appeared in 1526, a work of gouache on vellum measuring just 19.3 by 16.8 cm (7½ by 6½ in.). As a nature study, it is timeless, showing the cowslip as it looks now.

Gherardo Cibo's Oxlip

The recent rediscovery of two manuscripts of Gherardo Cibo's version of Mattiolus's herbal, *Commentarii a Dioscoride* (1568), in the British Library released an extraordinary oxlip (*P. elatior*) from obscurity.[18]

Illustration by Gherardo Cibo of the oxlip (*P. elatior*) for Andrea Mattioli's edition
of Dioscorides' *De materia medica* (1568).

Cibo, the well-connected product of a Genoese papal family, travelled widely in the service of the army, the Church and diplomacy before retreating to pursue a life of botanical study in Arcevía, a hill town in the Marche region, on the Adriatic coast of Italy. His 2,000 dried specimens comprise the oldest surviving herbarium, dating from 1532. Living near his elderly mother and sister, a Benedictine nun, he became the ideal of the Renaissance 'dilettante', or 'curioso'. He was intensely interested in medicinal plants, and botanized widely, preparing pigments and herbal remedies from local plants and engaging in community service, starting a grain reserve for the destitute during a plague. He portrayed plants that were common in central Italy, but showed them as part of 'a much more vast universe whose serene and harmonious rhythms' he felt deeply.[19] His plant portraits include landscape features, weather phenomena and 'vivacious little human figures' going about their business. The scholar Lucia Tomasi writes: 'In this "theatre of nature" a certain figure recurs again and again – that of the herbalist equipped with his little sack and hoe'.[20] In effect, he created a visual autobiography. Cibo's artistry and ecological focus have attracted twenty-first-century attention, bringing him out of the obscurity he had needed to complete his work.[21]

Elizabeth Blackwell's *Curious Herbal*

The eighteenth-century Scottish artist Elizabeth Blackwell was one of the most remarkable people to portray the cowslip and primrose in an herbal. The daughter of a prosperous stocking merchant in Aberdeen, she married a man whose reckless, devious schemes created continual financial disasters. His posing as a doctor, despite having no formal training, caused them to flee to London, where he launched himself as a printer without apprenticeship, leading to heavy fines and a spell in debtors' prison. In order to support herself and her son, the enterprising Blackwell decided to create a herbal that would encompass the plants then arriving from North and South America. She gathered support for the project, installed

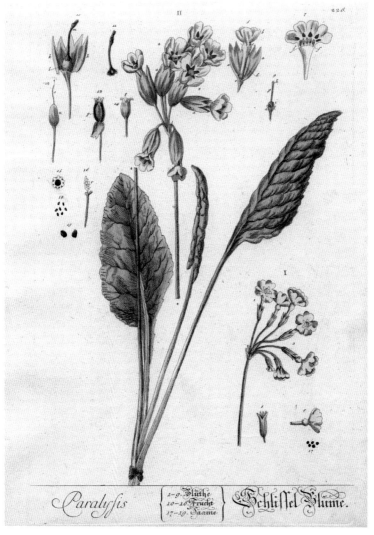

Elizabeth Blackwell's illustration of the cowslip (*P. veris*) for *A Curious Herbal* (1737–9).

herself in rooms near the Chelsea Physic Garden, drew her specimens from life and took them to her husband in prison, where he identified them and wrote text. She issued four plates each week from 1737 to 1739, completing in the process 500 drawings, which she engraved herself on copper plates and coloured by hand, work usually carried out by a team of men.

Blackwell's successful marketing of *A Curious Herbal* to booksellers led to generous royalties, which earned her husband's release from prison. After more reckless ventures he fled to Sweden and became court physician to the king. But he was hanged for meddling in politics just as Blackwell was leaving England to join him, having sent him money throughout the six years of his absence. She lived for ten more years, and died alone in 1758. *A Curious Herbal*, which was reprinted many times in several European countries, is considered a masterpiece.[22] Her cowslip of 1767 is graceful and winsome, and clearly shows dissected thrum flowers as pointed out by Philip Gilmartin in his study of heterostyly in *Primula*.[23]

The *Florilegium* and the *Hortus*

Herbals sold well for several hundred years. When verbal descriptions became sophisticated enough to describe a specific plant accurately, florilegia began to replace herbals as popular plant books.[24] Images became naturalistic rather than analytic as the wealthy sought to archive the evanescent floral beauty of their gardens.[25] Plants had been shown flattened, with various parts in unnatural positions; it was now time to document beauty. The word *florilegium* arose in the medieval period to refer to an anthology (a Latinized version of the Greek *anthologia*, a collection of flowers), using the Latin roots *legere*, 'to gather', and *flos*, 'flower'. An interchangeable term for an illustrated flower book was *hortus*, Latin for 'garden'. An elaborate system of patronage arose that created a new job title: flower painter. Many painters began their careers after freeing themselves from punishing apprenticeships in gardening, calico design and apothecary work as young teenagers.

Many long hours over the drawing board were required to achieve the level of productivity that would supply an income.

The auricula quickly took on a starring role in florilegia. Auriculas dance across the pages of Alexander Marshal's *Florilegium*, the only florilegium to survive from seventeenth-century England. Little is known about Marshal. He spoke French perfectly, having lived for some years in France, but seemed to have had no permanent residence in England, although he had several gardens at other people's houses. For a time he worked on a florilegium for the famous John Tradescants elder and younger. The Tradescants' museum in Lambeth, south London, contained a flower book of 'Mr Tradescant's choicest Flowers and Plants, exquisitely limned in vellum, by Mr Alex: Marshall [*sic*]'.[26] For more than 30 years Marshal worked on his own florilegium, which included a fair number of insects, since he was known as a 'stupendous' entomologist as well as a horticulturalist. Miniaturized for the folio pages (460 × 333 mm/18⅛ × 13⅛ in.), many of his depictions show striped auriculas in a variety of colours. They are of historical as well as artistic interest, since by the mid-eighteenth century the 'Painted Ladies' and edged varieties had overtaken the striped auriculas in popularity. One of his correspondents wrote that Marshal 'had a Picturary of his owne Herbary for wh[ich] hee had beene offered upon a Table 300 pieces of gold, but would not'.[27] Upon his sudden death, the florilegium passed to his wife, whose relatives eventually gave it to the Royal Library of King George IV. Considered a fine 'limner', the self-taught Marshal was so well known for the vibrant pigments he made from flowers that the Royal Society asked him to share information on their composition.

Primrose historians look to these florilegia to discern trends in the development of the auricula in particular. The Badminton Florilegium (1710) of Mary Somerset, Duchess of Beaufort, for example, reveals the development of virescence.[28] At the age of 69, after two marriages and eight children, Mary began a new career upon inheriting Badminton House in Gloucestershire in 1700. The widowed duchess turned to botany and horticulture. She planted seeds from

Striped auriculas illustrated in watercolour by Alexander Marshal for his personal florilegium, which he worked on for over 30 years.

Barbara Regina Dietzsch (1706–1783), *Garden Auricula with Caterpillar and Pale Clouded Yellow Butterfly*, body colour on black ground on vellum.

around the British Empire in her newly invented 'tropical stove' or greenhouse, and her twelve-volume herbarium is a record of the plants she grew.[29]

The stakes were high for plant portraitists as they worked to satisfy their wealthy patrons. In eighteenth-century Nuremberg Barbara Regina Dietzsch, member of an artist dynasty, learned to engrave and paint, with her sister and five brothers, in the workshop of their father, the draughtsman and etcher Johann Israel Dietzsch. The seven children all became artists. Barbara's work, noted for its clarity and finish, was in demand by engravers, and was also used as payment among fellow artists, a sign of great respect.[30] As was her custom, she painted her 'Primula auricula (hybrid) with caterpillar and pale clouded yellow butterfly' against a black background, which accentuates its satiny, pale-blue petals. A delicately haired caterpillar embraces the stem while the butterfly perches on dainty black feet, casting a slight shadow on the willow-grey leaves. It is a perfect still-life, a pictured silence.

The seductive auricula achieved more fame at the hands of the incomparable Georg Dionysius Ehret. At about the same time as Dietzsch, Ehret made a hand-coloured engraving of an auricula named 'Fille Amoureuse' (Girl in Love; 1743). While Dietzsch's auricula poses with its caterpillar like an ethereal wild flower against the black background, Ehret's amorous auricula has taken on the make-up of the 'self' auricula, where the 'paste' of the base of the petals con-trasts with the light-blue outer portion of the petals, a sky-and-cloud look suggesting a chaste but fervent love. Ehret made another por-trait of a 'Fille Amoureuse' in 1757, this time with an orange butterfly. In contrast, his portrait of the claret-coloured auricula 'Duke of Cumberland' has a distinctly masculine feel. 'Fille Amoureuse' has disappeared from the horticultural trade, but Ehret's image, courtesy of Fine Art America, has become a classic image of love, available as a print, duvet cover, cushion, tote bag and shower curtain – a tribute by popular culture to one of the most eminent plant portraitists and his model.

George Dionysius Ehret, 'Fille Amoureuse', 1743, body colour on vellum.

Several of the best-known, most iconic images of auriculas come from *The Temple of Flora* (1807), the third volume in the *New Illustration of the Sexual System of Carolus von Linnaeus*, a work conceived by Robert John Thornton. Thornton gave up Church studies for medical botany and, having inherited a family fortune after the death of his parents and older brother, planned a lavish work of obsessive veneration for Linnaeus, who was second only to God in his eyes, for (as Linnaeus himself said), while 'Deus creavit, Linnaeus disposuit' (God created, Linnaeus organized). Unfortunately, the Napoleonic Wars interfered with the fortunes of Thornton's subscribers. Napoleon's Berlin Decree of 1806, which blocked trade between Europe and Britain, undermined the economy. Thornton tried many schemes to keep

Pierre-Joseph Redouté, *A Bouquet of Auriculas*, 1837, watercolour on vellum.

his monumental work afloat, including a 'Royal Botanical Lottery for fostering the fine arts and sciences', but had to abort the volume with only 28 plates completed. He died destitute. Even abbreviated, *The Temple of Flora* is a remarkable work. Its images of the auriculas are prevalent in popular culture today.

The illustrators who honoured the auriculas in the eighteenth century left a record of varieties that will never be seen again. Although he is best known for his roses and lilies, Pierre-Joseph Redouté painted the auricula many times. In his watercolour *A Bouquet of Auriculas* (1837), auriculas glow with radiant colour, even now lighting up the dark wall in the National Gallery of Art in Washington, DC, where the painting resides. Pancrace Bessa, Redouté's student and eventual competitor, instead captured the statuesque nature of the auricula by painting the potted plant, where the substantial corporeality of the leaves captures the plant's *objet d'art* quality, poised for admiration. Bessa is known for perfecting the technique of stipple engraving.

Walter Hood Fitch, illustration of *Primula magellanica*, the only South American primrose.

In the nineteenth century, when more of the general population became attuned to the intrinsic beauty of their native flora, artists tried to capture primroses as wild flowers rather than civilized beauties. Between 1777 and 1798, *Flora Londinensis*, the brainchild of the apothecary-turned-botanist William Curtis, was published in six volumes. Its purpose was the identification of local wild plants.[31] In it, William Kilburn's portrait of the common primrose (*P. vulgaris*), like Dürer's of the cowslip, captures the 'genius' of the living plant. Kilburn started out as an apprentice to a calico printer in Dublin, and eventually, after an interlude working for Curtis, became a highly successful calico designer and printer in London.

Walter Hood Fitch and the South American Primrose

Like Kilburn, Walter Hood Fitch started out as an apprentice in the textile industry, designing patterns for fabric in Glasgow. Prodigiously prolific, he became the most famous botanical artist of the nineteenth century. At about the age of fifteen Fitch was bought out of his apprenticeship by William Jackson Hooker, then a professor of botany in Glasgow. Fitch completed more than 10,000 drawings during the course of his career, and he became the sole artist for Kew Royal Botanic Gardens when Hooker was appointed its director in 1841. Hooker's son Joseph Dalton Hooker was among the plant hunters sending pressed specimens from exotic places to Kew's herbarium. On his first collecting trip he found *P. magellanica* in the Straits of Magellan. Fitch had a genius for conjuring a lifelike appearance from dead, flattened material and the collector's written description. He developed a method of creating better 'models' out of desiccated herbarium specimens, reconstituting the plant material in water and studying several specimens before drawing a 'typical' example of the species in question. Fitch had this response to critics:

> Botanical artists require to possess a certain amount of philosophical equanimity to enable them to endure criticism for as

no two flowers are exactly alike, it is hardly to be expected
that a drawing should keep pace with their variation in size
and colour.[32]

Later Fitch would illustrate J. D. Hooker's primulas collected in the
Himalayas. For relaxation, however, he liked to make sketches of local
plants, such as the common primrose. In 1877, after many years of
service, he left Kew abruptly over a disagreement about pay with J. D.
Hooker, who had succeeded his father as the garden's director. Despite
incredible productivity throughout his life, Fitch did not earn financial
independence until Benjamin Disraeli gave him an annuity of £100
in recognition of his services in the field of botanical illustration.

Anne Pratt and 'the gentle stranger'

Among the 70,000 artists of the Edwardian and Victorian periods,
a number of industrious women practising botanical art gave their
close attention to primroses.[33] One of these was Anne Pratt, who drew
the plants brought home from the fields by one of her sisters for their
herbarium (Anne herself had physical problems that limited her
mobility). This practice, combined with studying botany with a family
friend, led to a vigorous career exploring wild flowers in writing and
illustration. In 1840, fearing the displeasure of her mother (although
by this time an adult herself), she surreptitiously published her first
book, *Flowers and their Associations*. Her later works, such as *The Flowering
Plants and Ferns of Great Britain* (1855–66), were monumental efforts of
several thousand pages requiring sustained effort over decades, and
inspired many people to botanize.[34] Her books are available online,
with her colour illustrations and text relaying the history and lore
of the common primrose, cowslip and auricula. In one account Pratt
relates the story of a primrose in full bloom arriving in Australia in
1856: 'the sensation excited by it as a reminiscence of fatherland was
so great, that it was necessary to protect it by a guard.'[35] A newspaper
account of the day refers to the primrose as 'the gentle stranger'.[36]

J. R. Dicksee after Edward Hopley. *A Primrose from England*, 1856, engraving.

Some 3,000 people came to see the primrose escorted off the boat by armed guards. While its passage to Australia was in part intended as a test of the newly invented Wardian case, the primrose had also been sent to allay the homesickness of British immigrants in their new country. The flower depicted is white, which implies that it was a hybrid polyanthus, rather than the common primrose.

Although the English painter Edward Hopley had never been to Australia, he created an emotional rendering of the primrose's welcome that was shown at the Royal Academy in London in 1855. The painting was so popular that a lithographed version by John Robert Dicksee achieved fame as well. Hopley clearly imagined a nativity scene, with the primrose as the object of worship. Recently displayed at the Bendigo Art Gallery in Australia, Hopley's painting reminds viewers of the many forces involved in immigration and colonization. The primrose emigrated successfully, a well-documented case of dispersal.[37] By contrast, the Australian-born Elizabeth von Arnim, who emigrated to England as a young girl, wrote several novels in which characters abroad have longings for primroses. In *Mr Skeffington*,

Anne Pratt.

set in New York, the beautiful Fanny Trellis (played by Bette Davis in the film version in 1944), feels 'Vague longings for pure, cold, solitary things like primroses, and moss, and little leafless copses'.[38] Von Arnim often mentioned primroses in her well-known *Elizabeth and her German Garden* (1898).

'Bird's Nest' William Henry Hunt

Primroses and the mossy bank became a popular subject for art in Victorian England. Along with birds' nests, they appeared frequently in a subgenre of nature painting said to have been 'invented' in the 1830s by 'Bird's Nest' William Henry Hunt. Hunt developed a sophisticated use of gouache for rendering vivid, realistic portrayals of miniature natural landscapes. Also called 'Hedgerow Hunt', he had whole chunks of primrosed banks transported into his poorly lit 2 by 2-m (7 by 7-ft) studio so that he could examine every minute detail.[39] Imitators abounded, and critics eventually grew tired of the genre. One wrote: 'Some of our minor artists exhibit every year a countless number of birds' nests, lying among Primroses that are painted pea-green, but as they grow in the hedges, they are everywhere of the same Pale Primrose colour.'[40] It was not easy to get the colour right, as one writer of that period noted:

> To paint a faithful portrait of the 'rathe primrose', the world's artists require the finest talent in blending their Indian yellow, aureolin, emerald green, and Prussian blue because a tint of indescribable beauty resides in its pale golden hue never found in other yellow flowers.[41]

Primrose-yellow was used as a distinctive colour name by 1844, its hue variously defined as a light to moderate yellow or greenish yellow.

The Engraved Primrose

Wood engravers have long had an affinity for primroses. Like black-and-white photography, engraving in black and white has a way of revealing what cannot be seen in the presence of colour. Although photography replaced wood engraving as a means of reproducing artworks and illustrations, wood engraving has remained as an art form for fine book illustration. Agnes Miller Parker, who was born in Ayrshire, and her husband, the artist William McCance, also Scottish, became members of the London group of artists called the Vorticists.[42] In illustrating H. E. Bates's *Through the Woods* (1936) and *Down the River* (1937), celebrating the countryside of North-amptonshire, Parker adopted the vignette style of presenting natural history first used in the eighteenth century by Thomas Bewick. Her engraving complements Bates's deep admiration for the common primrose. Parker's 'Birds and Primroses' captures the topography of the crinkled leaves of the primrose more beautifully than almost any other artwork.

Parker's equally famous contemporary Clare Leighton also lent her imaginative vision to primroses. In *Four Hedges: A Gardener's Chronicle* (1935), her book about gardening month by month in the Chiltern Hills of Buckinghamshire, the first chapter, 'April', begins with an engraving of the cowslip and ends with one of an auricula.[43] She writes that cowslips just managed to gain a footing on the cold clay soil of the Chilterns by April. That auriculas could do so by the end of the month advertises their hardiness. 'Picking Primroses', both essay and engraving, appeared in her book of essays *Country Matters* (1937).[44] She remembers the picking of common primroses with fear. In the countryside surrounding a family home near Yarmouth, common primroses were few, occurring only in a few private woodlands.

Clare Leighton, 'Picking Primroses', an illustration for *Country Matters* (1937).

For her Easter-time birthday, 'Old Nurse' insisted that she and her brothers go poaching for primroses:

> In the rituals of our childhood's year, my iced birthday cake needed to be surrounded by stolen primroses. No mere flora, they had been gathered with the ecstasy of great fear . . . It was queer how this strict Baptist, normally so straitlaced and upright, would fling aside her moral scruples and organize this reckless trespassing.[45]

The owner comes upon her picking in his woods and smiles, but the next day he puts up barbed wire. For Leighton, primrosing would forever mean 'that extravaganza of emotion, fear'. Other twentieth-century wood engravers who have portrayed the primrose include the iconoclastic Gertrude Hermes ('A Spring Bouquet'), Yvonne Skargon, Monica Poole and Howard Phipps.[46] Poole's 'Herbage' is held by the Victoria and Albert Museum in London. Skargon made many illustrations for David Wheeler's *Hortus*, and her primrose engravings are now in the hands of private collectors.

The Perennial Primrose

Entire books about primroses have benefited from the observational and artistic genius of botanical artists. Brigid Edwards completed 116 coloured paintings, comprising most of the species in cultivation, for John Richards's *Primula* (1993), and the critic Ian Burton praised her 'creative act of attention'.[47] Describing herself as inspired by Ehret, Edwards has written that 'to draw is to explain', and that the goal is 'revelation'.[48]

Barbara Shaw, the author and illustrator of *The Book of Primroses* (1991), came to art through horticulture. She gardened at Tan Cottage in Cononley, North Yorkshire, and became known as the Primrose Lady for her knowledge, the result of twenty years of research and taking notes. Her large collection of primroses officially became the

Rory McEwen's
grey-green auricula,
the cover of the
Revd C. Oscar
Moreton's book
*The Auricula: Its History
and Character* (1964).

Collection of *Primula*, Section Vernales and its cultivars in the North,
part of the National Collection for the Conservation of Plants and
Gardens, which was formed in 1978. Self-taught, she began by setting
herself the task of painting all the flowers in her garden. Before long
she had become a primrose historian, painter and botanist.

Close observation taught Shaw botany. She learned that older
primrose leaves are generally smoother than the first puckered leaves
of spring – but that occasionally the opposite is true. Leaf colour
varies depending on whether the leaf is above or below a neighbouring leaf. Leaf margins vary, too: 'This is particularly noticeable

Computer-imaged auricula from David Esslemont's *Florilegium Solmentes.*

when drawing in the leaves of *P. juliae* – some have teeth like dragons while others appear to have no more than gums, and one leaf alone may vary from smooth to toothed.'[49] Flowers also have a tendency to be more anomalous later in the season: 'with primroses, late flowers may not be by any means typical. In the autumn quite a variety of doubles become semi-single, and plain and singles become semi-double, fringed or frilled in a most frivolous fashion.'[50] Shaw's goal was to capture the 'personality and behaviour' of each plant, from each hair to the faintest flush of a floral tint.

The illustrations made by Rory McEwen for C. Oscar Moreton's *Auricula: Its History and Character* (1964; see Chapter Five) capture the uncanny beauty of the flower. A retrospective of his botanical studies at Kew Gardens in 2012 brought him forward as an icon for the next century of botanical artists. Redouté and Ehret inspired his work, he recalled, and, whether 'illustrator' or 'artist' – a distinction that is sometimes made by critics – his influence has been profound. Viewers have said that the devotional, even 'religious' aspect of his plant portraits has moved them to tears. At his peak McEwen painted for eight hours a day, but a brain tumour cut short his career when he was just 50 years old.[51]

Auriculas still figure prominently in the work of contemporary artists. José Escofet, following the tradition of Dietzsch and Ehret, shines an exacting light on show auriculas using oil paint on wooden panels. Mary Fedden was celebrated for her modernistic still-lifes featuring objects in the foreground and distant landscapes in the background. Her *Auriculas and Lunch* (2007) shows two potted auriculas on a floor, with a view beyond to two darkened figures seated at an outdoor table in front of an olive-green hill, bare but for two slight ribbons of conifer-green. The purple-and-white eyes of the auriculas present an effective contrast. *Flora 2003* by Lizzie Riches, an artist inspired by Elizabethan themes and imagery, is a portrait of a woman wearing a garland of auriculas.[52] Other contemporary artists include John Morley, a ruralist who includes portraits of named auricula varieties ('Remus', 'Sirius', 'Pink Lady') in his repertoire.

The botanical artist Hazel West-Sherring calls the auricula one of the classic subjects.[53] Her portrait of 'the incredibly luminous' auricula 'Sissinghurst Blue' from her series 'The Auricula Collection', inspired by her own collection of show auriculas, appears in the illustrated *Sissinghurst Flora* published by the National Trust in 2018.[54] The contemporary artist David Esslemont includes several auriculas in his *Florilegium Solmentes*. Elisabeth Dowle, who made 60 plates for Patricia Cleveland-Peck's *Auriculas through the Ages*, paints in watercolour on paper and vellum. For the auricula studies, she worked from her own collection as well as using specimens from speciality nurseries and private breeders. The *Highgrove Florilegium* (2008–9), the first British royal florilegium, contains one of her apple portraits.[55]

Other illustrators whose representations of common primroses, cowslips and their relatives leave a valuable historical record for the future include the Reverend William Keble Martin and Roger Banks. Martin read botany at Oxford and then served in France as a chaplain during the First World War, before becoming Archpriest of Haccombe in Devon. Encouraged to refrain from visiting his parishioners too often, he turned to illustrating the wild flowers of the countryside around him. He published *The Concise British Flora in Colour* in 1965 at the age of 88, with more than 1,400 illustrations.[56]

Roger Banks was among the most unusual of those who painted the primrose and its relatives. He led a full life, filled with eccentricity.[57] Interestingly, a stay in Antarctica after university was instrumental in his learning to paint wild flowers in watercolour. A newspaper garden correspondent, he opened his own garden to the public, calling it the 'Shabby Garden' and promoting the beauty and culinary value of weeds with informative labels. He illustrated *Living in a Wild Garden* (1980) and *Old Cottage Garden Flowers* (1983), both valuable resources. His last post was as harbourmaster of Crail, a fishing village in Fife, eastern Scotland. He was a throwback to the Elizabethan herbalists, and revivified early plant lore, finding a reference to the 'primerole' (primrose) and 'prime veyre' (cowslip) in the Anglo-Norman *Treatise* (*Le Tretiz*) of Walter of Bibbesworth, written in the mid-thirteenth century: 'Primerole et prime veyre/ Sur tere aperunt Entems deveyre.'[58] The treatise is written in Old French as a long poem, and was addressed to a French mother living in England who needed to improve her English. Covering a wide range of practical household matters, it was intended to be read aloud to her children as a tool for teaching the language. In addition to citing the medicinal value of primrose and cowslip, there is a passage that mentions 'gathering primroses/ To make garlands for schoolmen who, with boasting that's not worth a fennel-stalk,/ With blade or virl know how to attract a silly woman'.[59] It was a popular text for several centuries.

Like poets, visual artists use the common primrose's symbolic power to seek meaning. In 1896 the Danish artist Harald Slott-Møller

Harald Slott-Møller, *Spring*, 1896, oil on wood.

painted the haunting 'Spring', in which common primroses and crows symbolically oppose each other. His compatriot the philosopher Ole Fogh Kirkeby calls it his favourite painting, and critiques its melancholy and the complexity of spring as it straddles life and death.[60] The painting is now in the Hirschsprung Collection on Stockholmsgade, Copenhagen.

Floral art is a way of growing plants into perpetuity, creating virtual perennials that never die, and members of the primrose family continue to challenge the human desire to document what they see.[61] Specimens differ depending on their particular habitat, and new hybrids quickly replace older ones. Botanical artists therefore serve history as well as beauty. In 2016 the Irish Garden Plant Society and the Irish Society of Botanical Artists collaborated on the project *Heritage Irish Plants: Plandaí Oidhreachta*, in which botanical artists were commissioned to portray heritage plants, both old and new, bred in Ireland. The resulting book honours both breeders and artists, fostering the long-standing connection between horticulture and art.[62] Picturing a primrose by hand continues to be one of the best ways to represent an encounter between a unique person and a unique plant. This work is open to all. Botanic gardens offer courses in botanical art, many books provide instruction, and YouTube videos offer primrose-specific tutorials.

nine
The Beneficial, Versatile, Influential, Positive Primrose

> But in the real world of Earth, trees are wildlife just as deer or primroses are wildlife. Each species has its own agenda and its own interactions with human activities.
>
> OLIVER RACKHAM, *Woodlands* (2012)[1]

From the early days of human civilization, the roots, leaves and flowers of the common primrose, the cowslip and, to an extent, the oxlip, when mistaken for the other two, became elements in fashioning a positive, supportive belief system. Their abundance – there were millions and millions across Europe and Eurasia – forced attention. They 'spread out over the land [making it] almost lemon-coloured for they are the colour of lemons', wrote Jacob Meydenbach of the common primrose of Europe in *Hortus sanitatis* (1491), the first natural history encyclopaedia.[2] Konrad von Megenberg had described the common primrose as Mary's flower, 'the delicate flower of the field who stands on the road of Grace', in *Das Buch der Natur* (Book of Nature, 1349–50).[3] And they were medicinal and edible. It is generally agreed that the plant Pliny the Elder named 'dodecatheos' ('of the twelve gods') in the first century AD is the common primrose. He called it the 'one remedy' because 'taken in water it is a cure, they say, for maladies of every kind.'[4] Many of the interactions and associations that began so long ago continue today.

Common Names Reveal a History of Associations

Names tell stories. Widespread throughout Europe, the common primrose, the cowslip and the oxlip shared many names that archive folklore and medicinal properties: artetyke, arthritica, buckles, crewel, drelip, fairy cups, herb Peter, herba paralysis,[5] key flower, keys to Heaven (*Himmelschlüssel* in German), Lady's frills, Mayflower,[6] milk-maid, Our Lady's keys, palsywort, paralysis, paigle, paigil, passwort, peggle, pimerose, plumrocks, plum-rocks, primet, primrose, prumorole, St Peter's herb, St Peterwort, petty mullein, polander, pug-in-a-primmel, simmeren, spink, spring flower, summerlocks, Virgin Mary's cowslips.[7] Names applied to double primroses and cowslips included beef and green, butter rose, hen-and-chickens, hose-in-hose, Jack, Jack-in-box, Jack-in-the-green, jackets-and-petticoats and King Charles-in-the-oak.

The name 'cowslip' (*P. veris*) has an especially long etymological history. The poet John Ciardi describes the word 'cowslip' as a 'fossil poem', and credits the Anglican Archbishop of Dublin and amateur etymologist Richard Chenevix Trench as the creator of this term for folk names using picture words: for example, 'daisy' for 'day's eye'.[8] Ciardi writes: 'The [cowslip] is most commonly found in meadows used by cows, and tends to grow close to one of the pancakes that slip out of the cow. Evidence and surveillance: where the cow slips, there slip I.'[9] The cowslip's other names, such as 'fairy cups' and 'keys to Heaven', convey other associations. The Swedish have an entirely different fossil poem name for the cowslip, *guldviva* (catsboots).[10] In Russian the cowslip is *baranćik*, 'little lamb', and in Irish it is *Bainne bó bleachtáin* (cow milk).[11]

Before the name 'cowslip' settled into its familiar spelling, there were many variations: cowslap, cowslippe, cowislip, cus-slippe ('oxan-slippan' was used for oxlip), coosloppe, coostropple, cow's leek, cow's-mouth, cow's-troop and cowslek, to name just a few. The Old English cow's leak means cow's plant, but one early source states that cows do not eat cowslips, despite the plant's abundance in meadows.[12] Etymologists believe coostropple reflects a comparison to 'the plaits of a cow's throttle' and cus-slippe a comparison to a cow's lip, while coosloppe reflects the resemblance of 'the wrinkled leaves and calyx . . . [to] the corrugated surface of a calf's stomach' ('keslop' was a country term for calf's stomach, which was added as rennet in cheese-making).[13]

In 2015 the naturalist and writer Robert Macfarlane noted with dismay that 'cowslip' had been dropped from the Oxford Junior Dictionary, along with 'acorn'.[14]

Scientific Names Carry their Own Associations and Problems

In botany and zoology, each species has an italicized binomial name. The person who first describes the type specimen of a species has the honour of having his or her (usually his) name directly after the binomial, unitalicized. Linnaeus's system ensured that people's names were joined forever in a partnership with plant and animal species. The cowslip is *Primula veris* L., which recognizes the fact that Linnaeus named it first. The common primrose's binomial is *Primula vulgaris* Hudson after the eighteenth-century apothecary William Hudson, who was knowledgeable about plants, molluscs and insects as well. The oxlip's binomial is *Primula elatior* Hill. A colourful, contentious poly-math, 'Sir' John Hill and spent sixteen years writing an enormous botanical treatise, *The Vegetable System*, published in 26 volumes between 1761 and 1765, with 1,600 plates that he etched himself. He gained the 'Sir' when the king of Sweden knighted him for introducing the Linnaean system of classification to England.[15]

In 1737 the German botanist Johann Jacob Dillenius wrote: 'We all know that botanical nomenclature is an Augean stable,' in other words, a mess of Herculean proportions.[16] The problem of redundant naming, known as synonymy, arose as botanists in different countries speaking different languages encountered specimens and assumed the role of primary discoverers. One species of primrose had more than twenty different Latin binomial names applied to it. Some species 'disappear' because their names are really just synonyms for previously named species. Gardeners may fall in love with an account of a particular primrose in a magazine, for example the beautiful burgundy *P. abschasica*, and go on the hunt, only to be told it is no longer considered a species and has vanished from the trade.[17]

Nomenclatural confusion was good for primroses, however, because in 1886 it prompted the first of a series of Primula Conferences. The account in *The Garden* reads:

> No better plants could be chosen for creating a charming exhibition than the Primroses, and if confusion in nomenclature be one of the reasons for holding the conference in question, then assuredly it would be difficult to find a genus of plants so confused both in gardens and herbaria as the Primroses in respect to their names and identity. Botanists, indeed, consider the genus to be one of the most intricate with which they have to deal, on account of the singular tendency of Primulas to become intercrossed.[18]

The writer goes on to say that, while the daffodils are in a state of 'chaotic confusion', the entire lot of primulas – the polyanthus, the auricula, the species and the natural hybrids, 'distributed throughout the northern hemisphere from Japan to California' – present unique conundrums.[19] Additional conferences were held in 1906, 1913 and 1928, and their scope went beyond the mere solving of nomenclatural problems. A writer in *The Gardeners' Chronicle* reporting on the first conference notes of one speaker:

> Professor Foster confessed to a love for the whole family from the common Primrose to the most civilized Auricula, and expressed a hope that cultivators of one or a few species would not treat others contemptuously which appeared to be less attractive to their individual taste.[20]

The appreciation of primroses engendered disinterested, broad-minded attitudes.

The Primrose of Fairy Tale and Fairyland

The primrose, whether common primrose, cowslip or oxlip, takes on the role of a key to treasure in many myths. In Norse mythology, it could open the door to the hall of the goddess Freya, the Key Virgin. There are many versions of a Christian myth adopted from Germanic mythology in which the Apostle St Peter, drowsy or agitated, drops the golden keys to Heaven's gates. On Earth they become *Schlüsselblume*, key flowers, or *Himmelschlüssel*, keys to Heaven. Although it was said they could open the way to treasure caverns in the high mountains, most often the reward was spiritual rather than material. In a different storyline the Alpine Germanic goddess Bertha (Perchta), sometimes synonymous with Hulda or Mother Nature, used cowslips to lure children to her hall. Good children found treasure covered in cowslips; bad children faced evisceration. In Germany, as *Heirathschlüssel*, they were the keys to marriage, and as *unserer Frauenschlüssel*, they were the keys of the Virgin Mary.[21] In the early twentieth century Manfred Kyber wrote the fairy tale 'The Key of Heaven', which tells the story of a wealthy but insensitive king who, after successfully undergoing three trials of enlightenment, each one causing a cowslip to bloom at his feet, finally gains entry to Heaven.[22]

Primroses connect people to fairyland. Ariel, the 'airy spirit' in *The Tempest*, reveals that 'In a cowslip's bell I lie.'[23] The writer and folklorist Terri Windling offers lore from Devon about the common primrose:

Primroses guard against dark witchcraft if you gather their blossoms properly: always thirteen or more in a bunch, and never a single flower. On May Day, small primrose bouquets were hung over farmhouse windows and doors to keep black magic and misfortune out, while allowing white magic to

Primroses have colonized a sculpture at the Lost Gardens of Heligan, Cornwall.

enter freely. Primroses were braided into horses' manes and plaited into balls hung from the necks of cows and sheep as protection from piskie [pixie] mischief on May Day and Beltane. Hedgewitches made primrose ointment and infusions for 'women's troubles' (menstrual cramps) and 'melancholy' (depression), while oil of primrose, rubbed on the eyelids, strengthened the ability to see faeries.[24]

Primroses in the garden attract fairies, but if they die, beware fairy anger. According to some authorities, fairies do not like yellow flowers in hedgerows, but that does not deter common primroses from populating such places. They retain a central role in the current resurgence of interest in herbalism and hedgewitchery.

The Healing Primrose

Hildegard von Bingen was a visionary medieval healer known for her admiration of the green world, embodied in her notion of *viriditas*. She thought highly of the beneficial properties of primroses, and wrote in her medical treatise *Physica* (1155) that

> Primrose (hymelsloszel) is hot . . . this plant takes its strength especially from the power of the sun, when it checks melancholy. When melancholy rises in a person, it makes him sad and agitated in his moods. Airy spirits notice this, and rush to him, and by their persuasion turn him toward insanity. This person should place primrose on his flesh, near his heart, until it warms him up. The airy spirits dread the primrose's sun-given power and will cease their torment. A person

Primrose carved by Chris Wood for the cloisters of Iona.

223

whose head is so oppressed by bad humors that he has lost his sense should shave his hair and place primrose on top of his head. He should bind it on and should do the same thing to his chest. If he leaves these bindings on for three days, he will return to his senses.[25]

Scholars believe she meant the cowslip here, although she was writing hundreds of years before cowslips and common primroses were clearly distinguished. Meydenbach's *Hortus sanitatis* promoted the cowslip for soothing headaches and catarrh, rejuvenating elderly folk, warding off winter chills and quieting trembling limbs.[26] Primrose oil added to wine or dribbled in the ears brought the palsied to their senses, and the orange spots on the throat of the cowslip flower were thought, through the doctrine of signatures, to indicate that it was useful for clearing spotty skin.[27]

The Renaissance herbalists William Turner, John Gerard and Nicholas Culpeper carried these recommendations forward. All parts of the cowslip and common primrose – flower, leaf and root – were tested for curative effects. As an overall sedative for insomnia, hyperactivity and 'phrensie', the cowslip and the common primrose had few herbal equals.[28] Gerard specifically advised a concoction of both the common primrose and the cowslip boiled in wine for ailments of the lungs. For migraine, he recommended inhaling juice from the roots, and for 'phrensie' he advised a 'dyet' of common primrose leaves steeped in rose and betony waters with salt, pepper, sugar and butter, taken morning and night.[29] Turner made the following comment on the cosmetic use of the plants:

> Some weomen we find, sprinkle ye floures of cowslip wt whyte wine and after still [distil] it and wash their faces wt that water to drive wrinkles away and to make them fayre in the eyes of the worlde rather than in the eyes of God, Whom they are not afrayd to offend.[30]

A century later Culpeper was less judgemental:

> they [primroses] remedy all infirmities of the head coming of
> heat and wind, as vertigo, false apparitions, phrensies, falling
> sickness, palsies, convulsions, cramps, pains in the nerves,
> and the roots ease pains in the back and bladder. The leaves
> are good in wounds and the flowers take away trembling.
> Because they strengthen the brains and nerves and remedy
> palsies, the Greeks gave them the name Paralysio. The
> flowers preserved or conserved and a quantity the size of a
> nutmeg taken every morning is a sufficient dose for inward
> diseases, but for wounds, spots, wrinkles and sunburnings an
> ointment is made of the leaves and hog's lard.[31]

The link between these herbalists and the present is the nineteenth-century physician William Thomas Fernie, whose classic work *Herbal Simples Approved for Modern Uses of Cure* (1895) is still in print.[32] An enthusiast in several areas, he practised water cure therapy, popular in industrialized areas during the Victorian era, at Tudor House in Great Malvern, Worcestershire, for a time.[33] Modern herbalists, such as Juliette de Baïracli Levy and Matthew Wood, support the use of the cowslip and common primrose as a nervine (a plant remedy with anaesthetic and calming properties), as well as recommending it to soothe conditions such as sciatica and sunburn.[34]

The medical herbalist and plant spirit healer Carole Guyett, who works from her herb centre, Derrynagittah, in County Clare, Ireland, uses the common primrose as spiritual and bodily medicine, in the tradition of Hildegard and Gerard. The common primrose first inspired Guyett's ongoing work in plant diet ceremonies. She writes that the common primrose 'has a very clear, pure healing energy that washes away extraneous mental activity and brings feelings of deep peace. It clears away obsessive thinking.'[35] In her practice, the common primrose is again the key flower, but one that unlocks treasure within the self. She is well versed in primrose biology, and wonders

'Freya's Key: Unlocking Ancient grief, Winter's Sorrow', showing
common primrose surrounded by cowslips, an illustration
by Fiona Owen for *Weeds in the Heart* (2016).

whether heterostyly may be 'a reflection of Primrose's role in the
evolution of consciousness'.[36] A friend who sent her common primroses from the Isle of Islay in Scotland advised her to plant them in
various sacred places in Ireland because 'they act like acupuncture
needles for the land and Her energies'.[37]

Guyett reminds us that the common primrose is the herb of Bealtaine (also Beltain or Beltane), the Gaelic May Day festival. Druids relied on the common primrose to ward off evil. In 1792 Barrow Hill in London was renamed Primrose Hill when druids gathered there for a revival, their first sacred meeting in modern times, and they still meet there in recognition of its sacred status.

Chemical analysis of the genus *Primula* began in the 1830s, when Dr Robert Thomson reported the identification of primulin, an anthocyanin pigment that can be extracted from the roots of the cowslip.[38] In 1930 it became the first crystalline plant pigment to be isolated, by the brilliant young chemical geneticist Rose Scott-Moncrieff. The genus has a number of unique flavones, the crystalline compounds that form the basis of yellow and white pigments. Modern analysis has identified triterpenoid saponins and phenolic glycosides in the roots – useful for treating inflammation, laryngitis and bronchitis – and lipophilic flavonoids in the flowers and leaves, good for epilepsy and convulsions.[39] The beneficial effects of primrose concoctions first documented in the Middle Ages still invite research.[40]

Traditional Tibetan healers use primroses to combat fever and diarrhoea, while ethnoveterinarians in Saudi Arabia use the Abyssinian primrose (*P. verticillata*) to treat fever in camels, and as a general tonic.[41] First found by the Swedish plant explorer Peter Forsskål in 1762 in what was then known as Arabia, the Abyssinian primrose made its way to glasshouses at Kew, where in the 1890s it met the buttercup primrose (*P. floribunda*), originally from the Himalayas. They spontaneously created a fertile hybrid, which is now available in the trade as the Kew primrose (*Primula* × *kewensis*).[42]

The Edible Primrose

Cowslips and common primroses had a prominent place in the Renaissance kitchen garden as salad greens.[43] Leonardo da Vinci liked the flavour of raw common primrose leaves, but found them somewhat indigestible. Boiled, he wrote, they were good for stones in the bladder.[44] Common primrose leaves feature in primrose pottage, a popular vegetable stew recipe mentioned in *A Noble Boke off Cookry ffor a Prynce Houssolde or Eny Other Estately Houssolde*, which combines them with almonds, saffron, rice and honey. In *The Compleat Angler* (1653), Izaak Walton describes a dish of minnows and primroses:

> in the spring they make of them excellent minnow-tansies; for being well washed in salt, and their heads and tails cut off, and their guts taken out, and not washed after, they prove excellent for that use; that is, being fried with yolks of eggs, the flowers of cowslips, and of primroses, and a little tansy; thus used they make a dainty dish of meat.[45]

The long list of the primrose's use through the ages in recipes covers butter, cakes, cheese, cordials, cream, curd, oil, pickles, puddings, syrup, tarts, vinegar and wine. Crystallized common primrose flowers are a favourite decoration for many confections. In the Easter Masterclass of the *Great British Bake Off* in 2013, Mary Berry demonstrated how to crystallize them to decorate a simnel cake, a cake that dates back to medieval times and is known for its religious symbolism.[46] Now it is most often baked for Mothering Sunday or Easter. Modern foragers of the common primrose, who must be ecologically minded to stay in business, recommend pulling the corolla out of the calyx without disturbing the reproductive parts, so that seed can set if pollination has already occurred. Lucinda Warner, who runs the Whispering Earth website, decorated her Easter Merriment Cake in 2017 with pink and yellow common primrose flowers.[47] It is also possible to attempt a primrose meringue nest cake made with primrose honey and decorated with baked primrose flowers.[48]

Cowslip Wine and Tissty-tossties

Cowslip wine has a long history of proponents. Alexander Pope wrote in the eighteenth century that 'If you need rest, Lettuce and cowslip wine probatum est.'[49] The slightly narcotic properties of the flower petals give rise to a wholesome, medicinal cordial even considered suitable for children. In *Recipes from an Old Farmhouse* (1966) Alison Uttley, creator of the children's books featuring Little Grey Rabbit (first published in 1929), describes the day-long gathering of enormous numbers of cowslips by the whole family, and the separation of the peeps, the yellow petals, from the rest of the flower:

> At night, we sat in the kitchen pulling the peeps from the flowers. The stalks and calyces like pale green lace were thrown on a sheet spread on the floor. The 'peeping' continued all evening, until bedtime, when it was finished. Then the real making of the wine began.[50]

An Easter Merriment Cake, decorated with pink and yellow primroses, made by herbalist Lucinda Warner.

A recipe from George Hartman's *Family Physitian* of 1696 needs no changes:

> Having boil'd your Water and Sugar together, pour it boiling hot upon your Cowslips beaten, stir them well together, and let them stand in a Vessel close cover'd till it be almost cold; then put into it the Yest beaten with the Juice of Lemons; let it stand for two days, then press it out with as much speed as you can, and put it up into a Cask, and leave a little hole open, for the working; when it hath quite done working stop it up close for a Month or Six Weeks, then Bottle it. Cowslip Wine is very Cordial, and a glass of it being drank at night Bedward, causes sleep and rest.[51]

In *Cider with Rosie* (1959), Laurie Lee's account of growing up in Slad, Gloucestershire, after the First World War, one of the two competitive wine-making grannies, Granny Wallon, makes a memorable cowslip wine. Lee first describes the 'honey rich pungent smell' of the flowers filling her kitchen – and parsnips, since she had to bulk up her brew with some additives. A year later it was ready:

> Through the kitchen window she'd fill up our cups and watch us, head cocked, while we drank. The wine in the cups was still and golden, transparent as a pale spring morning. It smelt of ripe grass in some far-away field and its taste was as delicate as air. It seemed so innocent, we would swig away happily and even the youngest guzzled it down. Then a curious rocking would seize the head; tides rose from our feet like a fever, the kitchen walls began to shudder and shift, and we all fell in love with each other.[52]

Making cowslip wine as a family activity is unusual now. People have moved away from the countryside and its customs, and fears grow of endangering a wild flower that has suffered habitat loss. Moreover,

Molly Brett, *Primrose Procession*, 1950s.

the picking of sufficient quantities to make wine was laborious and best done by a small army of children.

The making of cowslip wine inspired a host of children's illustrations, especially among illustrators for the Medici Society, which was begun in 1908 to offer inexpensive and high-quality colour reproductions to members. In 1930 it began to offer greetings cards. One member of the society, Molly Brett, spent 60 years writing books, for which she made more than 500 paintings. Her *Primrose Procession* from the 1950s shows hedgehogs, mice and a rabbit carrying baskets of primroses along a primrose path, presumably for the making of cowslip wine. Angus Clifford Racey Helps began his career writing illustrated stories for his daughter, who was evacuated from London to the countryside during the Second World War. In his painting *The Toast*, a merry group of animals and insects sits around a toadstool drinking cowslip wine. In her book of nursery rhymes first published in 1922, Beatrix Potter portrayed the rabbit Cecily Parsley, surrounded by wine-making apparatus, pouring an apronful of cowslips into a large bowl.

Tissty-tossties were balls of cowslip flowers made by children. In *Children and Gardens* (1908) Gertrude Jekyll described their construction:

Racey Helps (1913–1970), *The Toast.*

two children would hold a string tight between them, while a third hung cowslip flowers along it. When it was gathered tightly, the result was a floral Koosh ball that would be tossed to prognosticate various things, such as the village of origin of a future suitor.[53]

The Pickable Primrose

Primroses have been called the child's flower because of the association with picking them. Mothering Sunday, a centuries-old tradition in the UK, was traditionally the day on which working-class children, who often entered service at the age of ten, were given the day off to visit their mothers and many brought them flowers.[54] The original 'mother', however, was the Church. Anne Thackeray Ritchie (daughter of the novelist William Makepeace Thackeray), who was herself noted as writer, memoirist and keeper of her father's literary papers and reputation, captured in a letter the romance of picking primroses. Here she is with her grandchildren 50 years after her own first experience:

A letter from Pinkie came with yours with a bit about long long ago when he had been as a boy to that very wood where we went yesterday to gather the Primroses – It seemed so extraordinarily beautiful & the childrens figures passing between the slender trees & the golden shining flowers quite reckless with light and profusion.[55]

The Wiggins, Teape & Co. paper mill in Ivybridge, Devon, began the pre-First World War practice of sending bunches of common primroses, picked by schoolchildren, to its customers. The children – who collected at weekends, often storing the flowers in family baths – were paid fivepence a bunch, and clients received two bunches, each with five leaves. There were different decorative insert cards each year. In the 1960s environmental concerns led to a rotation of picking sites, and continuing pressure against the 'pillage' of primroses ended the programme in 1989.[56] However, a later study by botanists debunked the idea that picking primroses causes a decline in population numbers.[57]

Some native plant societies and wild-flower organizations now encourage the picking of flowers in suitable areas, because the experience of touching and smelling encourages bonding that would not take place without the physical contact. Uprooting entire plants will affect a population, but a little picking will not hurt, it is thought.[58] In 2010 the village of Lambley in Nottinghamshire revived the tradition of Cowslip Sunday, held on the first Sunday in May. At the height of its popularity, in the mid-1850s, coachloads of people had come from Nottingham to the village – which struggled economically at the time, subsisting on a stocking-frame cottage industry – to buy cowslips gathered by children for wine-making.

The political primrose

The curious, and touching, friendship between Queen Victoria and Benjamin Disraeli led to an explosive appearance of the common primrose on Britain's political stage in the late nineteenth century. It started simply in 1881, when the queen sent a modest wreath of common primroses for Disraeli's coffin, with the message 'His favourite flower'.[59] When 19 April was officially declared Primrose Day, in commemoration of his death, the nation began a near orgy of yearly primrose gathering for celebratory wear, wreaths and graveside tributes.[60] Victoria and Disraeli had long shared an affection for the common primrose. For years she had sent him baskets of primroses from Windsor Castle and her palatial residence Osborne House on the Isle of Wight, and he replied with thank-you notes. Primroses carpeted the Isle of Wight, and Disraeli's estate, Hughenden Manor in Buckinghamshire, had nearly 610 ha (1,500 acres) of woodland filled with primroses. In one letter, he wrote that he liked 'primroses so much better for their being wild: they seem an offering from the fauns and dryads of the woods.'[61]

There was money to be made from primrose bouquets. Businessmen, ladies, cabmen, errand boys, nursemaids – everyone wanted to wear primroses, and the popularity of picking and wearing these flowers for Primrose Day led to worries about their scarcity. One journalist wrote: 'Primrose Day is leading to the extirpation of the primrose: and unless the eccentric craze changes, the last primrose is likely to take its place with the "last rabbit" in the British Museum.'[62] There were other problems ahead as the primrose entered the political arena. In 1883 a group of conservatives, capitalizing on the popularity of Primrose Day, founded the Primrose League to foster enthusiasm for the Conservative (Tory) Party. There were honorific titles, and the image of the common primrose figured prominently on decorations, badges and jewellery. Primrose League 'Dames' bicycled around the countryside proselytizing Tory views to farmstead women.

However, the primrosed statesman Disraeli and the Primrose League also inspired resentment, and this woodland flower symbolized political controversy for the first time as Disraeli's Jewish ancestry raised the spectre of anti-Semitism. Editorials abounded on the subject of the common primrose and Disraeli. One A. E. Dangerfield of Cheltenham was an eloquent fan of both:

How exquisite the salver-shaped Corolla, the notched heart-shaped petals; how lovely the foliage, intersected everywhere

Ralph Todd (1856–1932), *Primrose Day*, 1885, oil on canvas.

Disraeli's 'Primrose Tomb' at Hughenden, Buckinghamshire, UK.

by 'tiny hollows and green ravines' that appear far more beautiful when the leaf is held up between the eye and the radiant sunshine . . . No wonder the great D'Israeli made this modest bloom his favourite flower, for if ever Mysticism is taught by perennial roots, it is by the primula, and the Mysticism is precisely like that of the Jewish people.[63]

After 121 years of activity, the Primrose League was disbanded in 2004.

The Popular Primrose

Many threads are woven together in the associations between primroses and people. Shakespeare's phrase has kept the primrose alive in popular culture, and people who cannot picture an actual primrose wonder about the symbolism of the path. Politicians continue to use the phrase.[64] In 1875, 22 years before *Dracula*, Bram Stoker wrote his first book, *The Primrose Path*. It describes the tribulations of Jerry O'Sullivan of Dublin, a decent family man who moves to London to work as head carpenter in a theatre. His career deteriorates, however, and in a horrific denouement he kills his loyal wife with a hammer and then cuts his own throat with a chisel.[65] In the film *Primrose Path* (1940) Ginger Rogers plays a young woman from the wrong side of town, Primrose Hill, in love with a clean-cut young man. The subject matter, which included alcoholism and prostitution, provoked censorship, perhaps preventing Rogers from winning an Academy Award for her role in the film.[66]

Writers still use the phrase to title their work – for example John Mortimer's short story 'Rumpole and the Primrose Path' (2002) – and for some the path is without tribulation. The country music singer Jerry Wallace's 'Primrose Lane' was a hit in 1959. In films such as the BBC's *Cranford* (2007) and *The Quiet Man* (1952), symbolic primrose bouquets pass between characters. Suzanne Collins, the author of *The Hunger Games* (2008), draws on the 'prim' part of the name and the medicinal value of the common primrose to name the protagonist Katniss Everdeen's sister, a gentle soul with a talent for healing. After Prim's death, Peeta plants primroses in front of Katniss's house. When long-beleaguered Edith in *Downton Abbey* (2010–15) has a daughter, she names her Primrose, suggesting a new beginning.

The American journalist and politician Albert Olaus Barton's *Story of Primrose, 1831–1895* (1895) describes the 'element of romance' in the naming of a small town in Wisconsin. The 'chivalrous' pioneers allowed the 'ladies' to choose a name. One lady, the first woman to arrive, chose 'Primrose' after a song her father liked to sing, beginning 'On Primrose Hill there lived a lass.' An opponent felt this was 'too sweet', and suggested Hillsburgh, but a vote of the larger group determined that Primrose was not 'too sweet'.[67] In the census of 2000, some 682 people were recorded as living in Primrose, Wisconsin.

'Primrose' has also become a popular name for meritorious organizations, schools and foundations, but 'cowslip' is less so. In the U.S., Primrose Healthcare concentrates on Hepatitis C, and in the UK, the Primrose Foundation delivers breast cancer services. Invoking the phrase 'positively primrose', the foundation pays tribute to the common primroses growing along the lanes and hedgerows of Cornwall and Devon as symbols of hope. On its website it quotes the distinguished horticulturalist Geoffrey Smith: 'If I had to grow one flower, it would be the primrose. It is so complete, the lovely green and pale yellow complement each other. So optimistic.'[68]

Many writers echo this sentiment. In 'The First Primrose', one of the 100 or so sketches published in *Our Village* in the 1820s and 1830s, Mary Russell Mitford describes a walk through her village, Shinfield in Berkshire. She sees a clump of early primroses on an island where they cannot be reached or picked, 'looking as if they could feel their happiness'.[69] While all flowers offer rewards, primroses seem particularly successful as models of happiness that inspire renewal and the spirit of solicitude.

The variations that keep appearing in primroses – both cultivated hybrids and species – make news at the prestigious RHS Chelsea Flower Show year after year, exciting successive new generations of growers. Brenda Hyatt's display of auriculas there in 1982 created a new wave of appreciation, and a variety of the black primrose *P. melanantha* 'Moonshine' appeared on the Kevock Garden Plants stand in the Great Pavilion in 2011.[70] A white version of the orchid primrose, *P. vialii* 'Alison Holland', surprised visitors to the show in 2016.[71] An antique black auricula was one of the favourites in the Biodiversity Heritage Library's Halloween Tumblr posting 'Page Frights! – Black Flowers' in 2016.[72] This capacity for innovation inspires similar behaviour in people, and primroses engage humans seeking to embellish their own agenda. The American gardener Nancy Ross Hugo explains how the growth potential of the cowslip influenced her behaviour:

Photographer Tony Evans (d. 1982) glued the common primrose (*P. vulgaris*) to his finger for this iconic photograph of 1978.

I have just given away my one thousand three hundred and eleventh cowslip and am still feeling sad that there are others in the yard that need dividing, but I haven't the energy to divide them. This feels like having money sitting around under a mattress when it could be in a bank collecting interest, but there is a limit to the amount of investment banking a gardener can do.[73]

PRIMULA AURICULA NIGRA
FLORE PLENO.

L. Stroobant ad. nat. viv. del. & sc.   Ch. lith. & gravure Horto Van Houtteano.

A Halloween favourite: *Primula auricula nigra*.

In 1888 the anonymous author, 'L.S.B. (F.R.S.)', of 'On Growing Primroses' in the *Selborne Magazine* wrote: 'If one had to select the flower, which would be the most pleasing to the greatest number, it would be the primrose.'[74] The writer refers here to the common primrose (*P. vulgaris*), and is an impassioned defender of it in every way. L.S.B. believes that readers of the magazine must cultivate and spread primroses in order to prevent its 'rapid extinction' from exploitation ('tens of millions') for London flower-selling markets. He or she rails against flat garden landscapes, arguing that primroses do not 'approve of that monotonous flat piece of earth . . . wrongly called a garden'. But with a mossy bank and a little neglect the gardener can propagate 'hundreds and thousands' of primrose plants, and should take them to town in pots for friends, who ought to know to replant them in their gardens.[75] This vision has come true in the current habit of selling potted primroses worldwide in spring. It is estimated that the business associated with raising and selling primroses, organizing shows and continued exploration amounts to $50 million annually.[76]

The *Selborne Magazine* writer was also right about the popularity of the common primrose. In 2015 the conservation organization Plantlife.org conducted a Favourite Wildflower Vote in the UK.[77] The common primrose came in first in Scotland, Northern Ireland and Wales, and was a close second to the bluebell (*Hyacinthoides non-scripta*) in England. One voter explained that common primroses are 'just perfect, and could not be improved in any way'.[78]

Many people have taken the primrose path. Botanical explorers and wild-flower enthusiasts trek into remote areas, creating valuable photographic databases and collecting seed where possible. Artists and scientists study primroses to discern patterns of beauty and evolution. The horticultural work of plant breeders, seed merchants, nurseries, specialist societies and botanic gardens keeps members of the genus *Primula* in cultivation, from garden to garden and from generation to generation.[79] And then there are the growers, who secure the benefits of cultivation. In 1970 Josephine Nuese, who gardened in Cornwall, Connecticut, and wrote a weekly garden column for the *Lakeview Journal*,[80] described her near-end-of-life gardening agenda:

> When I am an old, old woman with long grey moustaches, a baggy tweed suit, stout boots and a cane (what do you mean, when?), I shall have a whole garden of primroses. All kinds. Each growing in its preferred spot . . . A garden of primroses is especially recommended for the elderly because it needs little care. The small plants are so light and so easy to handle, so easy to divide every few years, need so little attention, that most primrose-gardening can be done sitting down; all you need is a trowel and a low stool . . . Another delight in growing primroses from seed is that they often produce sports (i.e., mutations, variations in form, habit or color) which may often turn out to be a primrose the likes of which no one has ever seen before. This is one of the most exciting things which can happen to a gardener and sets you up among the experts – in your own estimation anyway.[81]

For most the path is a labour of love as the work of co-evolution and co-domestication continues to shape relationships between kingdoms.[82] The primrose path takes turns through places both accessible and inaccessible, from seeps and weeping walls to supermarkets and high-level genetics labs, from the Straits of Magellan to the extreme elevations of Ladakh in the northwestern Himalayas.[83] It is unlikely that all its secrets will ever be revealed.

Paul Curtis (b. 1941). *Two Beaches and a Primula.*

Timeline

c. 25 million years ago	*Primula* solidifies its genetics in the eastern Sino-Himalayas
AD 77–9	Pliny the Elder describes *dodecatheos* (thought to be the common primrose, *Primula vulgaris*) as the 'one remedy' for all bodily ills
1155	Hildegard von Bingen recommends medicinal properties of the cowslip and the common primrose in *Physica*
1250s	Walter of Bibbesworth includes the cowslip and the common primrose in a list of medicinal plants in *Le Tretiz*, a poem describing Anglo-Norman life
1495–1505	Primroses abound in the Unicorn Tapestries
1526	Albrecht Dürer makes 'Tuft of Cowslips'
c. 1602	Shakespeare pens the phrase 'primrose path' in *Hamlet*
1603	First Florists' Feast celebrating the auricula held in Norwich, UK
1750s	Virescence, a mutation in the auricula, appears, leading to the edged varieties
1753	Linnaeus circumscribes the genus *Primula* and groups the cowslip, common primrose and oxlip as a single species

1780s	Lacing appears in the polyanthus, leading to gold- and silver-edged varieties
1821	A specimen of the Chinese primula (*P. sinensis*) arrives in England aboard an East India tea ship under the command of Captain Rawes
1831	William Wordsworth publishes 'The Primrose of the Rock'
1856	The first primrose plant arrives in Australia in a Wardian case
1860	Henry Doubleday writes a letter (30 May) about the Bardfield oxlip to Charles Darwin
1861	Darwin reads a paper on pin-and-thrum primrose flowers to the Linnean Society, London
1877	Darwin publishes *The Different Forms of Flowers on Plants of the Same Species*, reporting his studies on heterostyly and speciation in *Primula*
1881	Queen Victoria sends common primroses to Hughenden, Disraeli's home, on his death on 19 April, which is henceforth celebrated as Primrose Day
1886	First Primula Conference held in South Kensington, London
1896	Suttons Seeds, UK, starts selling seed of Gertrude Jekyll's Munstead 'bunch' primroses (a type of polyanthus)
1935	Florence Levy (Bellis) buys five packets of primrose seeds from Suttons Seeds, which form the entire basis of her Barnhaven breeding stock
1941	The American Primrose Society is formed in Portland, Oregon, with Bellis as first editor of its quarterly publication
1966	Bellis retires, sending her Barnhaven seed stock to Jared and Sylvia Sinclair in Brigsteer, Cumbria, UK

1986	Publication of G. K. Fenderson's *Synoptic Guide to the Genus Primula*
1990	Barnhaven Primroses moves to Plouzélambre, Brittany, in the care of Angela and Keith Bradford
1993	John Richards's *Primula* appears, with a second edition in 2003
2000	Barnhaven Primroses moves to Plestin-les-Grèves, Brittany, in the care of David and Lynne Lawson
2000	Pam Eveleigh launches the Primula World website with a species gallery, field notes and accounts of *Primula* exploration past and present
2007	Schoolchildren begin planting oxlip seedlings grown at Writtle College to restore the Great Bardfield oxlip population, which had dwindled to twelve plants
2011	Publication of Patricia Cleveland-Peck's *Auriculas through the Ages: Bear's Ears, Ricklers and Painted Ladies*, illustrated by Elisabeth Dowle
2015	Dr Philip Gilmartin documents observations of portrayals of heterostyly made from 1583 onwards, centuries before Darwin's research began in the mid-nineteenth century
2015	Dr Elena Conti and her colleagues at the University of Zurich report the draft genome of the cowslip (*P. veris*) as part of their research on heterostyly
2016	Gilmartin and colleagues at the University of East Anglia isolate the *S* locus supergene specific to the thrum flower in the common primrose (*P. vulgaris*)

References

Introduction: The Primrose Path

1 William Shakespeare, *Hamlet*, 1.3, 47–51.
2 The scape is a dedicated flowering stalk for hanging flowers, which are attached to it by their own individual small stalks called pedicels.
3 See M. G. Karlsson, 'Primrose Culture and Production', www.horttech. ashspublications.org, accessed 1 June 2017.
4 See Noel Kingsbury, 'Polyanthus: The Polychrome Princess of the Petrol Pump', *The Telegraph*, 2 February 2014, www.telegraph.co.uk.
5 See R. Miller Christy, 'The Garden Polyanthus: Its Origin and History', *Journal of the Royal Horticultural Society*, XLIX (1924), pp. 10–24; and Ruth Duthie, 'The Origin and Development of the Polyanthus', *The Plantsman*, VI (1984), pp. 28–32.
6 Peter Ward, *Primroses and Polyanthus: A Guide to the Species and Hybrids* (London, 1997).
7 William Miller Christy, 'The Origins of the Hybrid *Primula elatior* × *vulgaris* Demonstrated Experimentally in the Field, with Notes on Other British Primula Hybrids', *New Phytologist*, XXI (1922), pp. 293–300.
8 Karlsson, 'Primrose Culture and Production'.
9 See www.sakataornamentals.com.
10 Jennifer Botkin Phillips, 'The Power of a Primrose Plant', *Pasack Valley Community Life*, 15 March 2013, www.jenleetalk.blogspot.com.
11 Emily Tennyson, *The Farringford Journal of Emily Tennyson, 1853–1864* (Isle of Wight, 1986), pp. 53, 56, 89, 104, 124.
12 Dan Pearson, 'Life in the Woods', *Gardens Illustrated*, 233 (April 2016), pp. 72–7.
13 John S. Harrison, 'The History of the Primrose and the Polyanthus', 1976, www.harislau.co.uk.
14 In the foreword to Barbara Shaw, *The Book of Primroses* (Newton Abbot, Devon, 1991).
15 The enthusiast Pam Eveleigh has said that the 'extraordinary details' found in the genus *Primula* inspire her work as a primula scholar and hunter (see 'Primula World', *Primroses: Quarterly Journal of the American Primrose Society*, Summer 2015, pp. 5–8); see also Jennifer Connell, 'An

Intrepid Plantswoman and Primula Hunter', www.threedogsinagarden.
blogspot.com, 6 May 2015.

1 The Naturalist's Primrose

1 Frank Kingdon-Ward, *In the Land of the Blue Poppies: The Collected Plant-hunting Writings of Frank Kingdon-Ward*, ed. Tom Christopher (New York, 2003), p. 138.
2 See John Richards, *Primula*, 2nd edn (Portland, OR, 2003), for a discussion of the evolutionary history of the genus *Primula*.
3 Ibid., p. 29.
4 Susan Kelley, 'Plant Hunting on the Rooftop of the World', 2001, www.arnoldia.arboretum.harvard.edu; see also David Boufford, 'Hengduan Mountains, China: Not All Diversity is Tropical' (lecture), www.youtube.com, accessed 15 June 2017.
5 Zheng Weilie et al., 'The Germplasm Resources and the Habitat Type of Primroses on Sherjila Mountain in Tibet', *Acta Horticulturae Sinica* (1992), www.en.cnki.com.cn.
6 Quoted in Charles Lyte, *Frank Kingdon-Ward: The Last of the Great Plant Hunters* (London, 1989), p. 72.
7 Léon Croizat, *Manual of Phytogeography: An Account of Plant Dispersal throughout the World* (1952). Available at www.books.google.com.
8 'The Mysterious Primula of Omta Tso', https://primulaworld.blogspot.com, accessed 25 October 2017; see also Martin Walsh, 'In Search of Sherriff's Blue Poppy', Alpine Garden Society Dublin Group newsletter, 65 (Winter 2016), pp. 12–16, www.alpinegardensociety.ie.
9 Theodore F. Niehaus, *A Field Guide to Southwestern and Texas Wildflowers* (Boston, MA, 1984), p. 300.
10 'Cave Primrose (*Primula specuicola*)', www.desertusa.com, accessed 16 February 2016.
11 Richards, *Primula*, p. 280.
12 '*Primula specuicola* Rydb. Cave Primrose', Navajo Nation Department of Fish and Wildlife, www.nndfw.org, accessed 1 March 2016.
13 Pam Eveleigh, '*Primula specuicola* in Utah', https://primulaworld.blogspot.com, accessed 8 May 2017.
14 Richards, *Primula*, 2nd edn, p. 103.
15 'Mealy Primrose – *Primula incana*', Montana Field Guide, www.fieldguide.mt.gov, accessed 15 February 2017.
16 'The Flora of Nunavik: Seashore Flora', *Turnivut (The Cultural Magazine of the Nunavik Inuit)* (Winter/Spring 1994), p. 48.
17 Jacob B. Davidson and Paul G. Wolf, 'Natural History of Maguire Primrose, *Primula cusickiana* var. *maguirei* (Primulaceae)', *Western North American Naturalist*, LXXI (2011), pp. 327–37.
18 United States Department of Agriculture, Natural Resources Conservation Service, 'Maguire Primrose Plant Guide', www.nrcs.usda.gov, accessed 15 September 2017.

19 J. B. Davidson et al., 'Breeding System of the Threatened Endemic, *Primula cusickiana* var. *maguirei* (Primulaceae)', *Plant Species Biology*, XXIX (2014), e55–e63.

20 Graham Avery, 'Clarence Bicknell and Reginald Farrer, 19 July 1910', www.clarencebicknell.com, accessed 1 June 2016.

21 Noel Kingsbury, *Garden Flora: The Natural and Cultural History of the Plants in your Garden* (Portland, OR, 2016), p. 262.

22 Richards, *Primula*, p. 93.

23 Ibid.

24 G. Casazza et al., 'Polyploid Evolution and Pleistocene Glacial Cycles: A Case Study from the Alpine Primrose *Primula marginata* (Primulaceae)', *BMC Evolutionary Biology*, XII/56 (2012).

25 G. Casazza et al., 'Phylogeography of *Primula allionii* (Primulaceae), a Narrow Endemic of the Maritime Alps', *Botanical Journal of the Linnean Society*, CLXXIII (2013), p. 637.

26 G. Casazza et al., 'Distribution Range and Ecological Niche of *Primula marginata* Curtis (Primulaceae)', *Plant Biosystems*, CXLVII (2013), pp. 593–600.

27 Davie Sharp, '*Primula scotica*: A Weel-faured Scots Floorie', *Rock Garden*, CXXVIII (January 2012), pp. 30–36, www.files.srgc.net.

28 '*Primula scotica* Scottish Primrose', www.chilternseeds.co.uk, accessed 1 March 2016.

29 See 'Scottish Primrose *Primula scotica*', www.scottishwildlifetrust.org.uk, accessed 13 June 2018; 'Primroses on Papay!', www.rspb.org.uk, accessed 21 February 2016.

30 Roger Banks, *Old Cottage Garden Flowers* (Kingswood, Gloucestershire, 1983), p. 25.

31 Richard Mabey, *The Cabaret of Plants: Forty Thousand Years of Plant Life and the Human Imagination* (London, 2016), pp. 31, 33.

32 Ibid., p. 28.

33 'Carniolan Primrose (Primula carniolica)', www.vlada.si, accessed 19 February 2018.

34 '*Primula scandinavica*', www.iucnredlist.org, accessed 15 January 2016.

35 Richards, *Primula*, p. 250.

36 See Pam Eveleigh, 'The Real Primula involucrata (P. boveana)', Primula World https://primulaworld.blogspot.com.

37 'Primula boveana', www.iucnredlist.org, accessed 22 March 2015.

38 Karim Omar, 'Assessing the Conservation Status of the Sinai Primrose (*Primula boveana*)', *Middle-East Journal of Scientific Research*, XXI (2014), pp. 1027–36.

39 Xue Da-Wei et al., 'High Genetic Diversity in a Rare, Narrowly Endemic Primrose Species: *Primula interjacens* by ISSR Analysis', *Acta Botanica Sinica*, LXVI (2004), pp. 1163–9.

40 Richards, *Primula*, p. 85.

41 Stephen Lacey, 'A Blooming Good Chelsea Flower Show', *The Telegraph*, 24 May 2014, www.telegraph.co.uk.

2 Mr Darwin's Primroses

1 Quoted in 'Following the Primrose Path – Why Early Botanists May Have Not Dallied Long Enough to Understand the Secrets of Heterostyly', John Innes Historical Collections Blog, 12 August 2015, www.collections.jic.ac.uk. The passage appeared in text accompanying a plate of *Primula elatior* in William Curtis, *Flora Londinensis. New Edition revised and enlarged by George Graves and W J Hooker*, vol. IV (Henry G. Bohn, London, 1835).

2 Charles Darwin, *On the Origin of Species: The Illustrated Edition* (New York, 2008), pp. 59–63.

3 Quoted in Jim Endersby, *Imperial Nature: Joseph Hooker and the Practices of Victorian Science* (Chicago, IL, 2008), p. 162.

4 See letter addressed to 'Mr. Urban' and signed by 'A Southern Faunist', *The Gentleman's Magazine* (1793), p. 101, www.books.google.com.

5 R. C. Stauffer, ed., 'Charles Darwin's *Natural Selection* (1856–8, transcribed in 1975), p. 128, www.darwin-online.org.uk, accessed 23 November 2015.

6 Ibid., p. 129.

7 'Darwin Correspondence Project, Letter 1708', www.darwinproject. ac.uk/letters.

8 Ibid., Letter 2503.

9 Charles Darwin, *The Different Forms of Flowers on Plants of the Same Species* (London, 1877), p. 60.

10 Ibid., p. 61.

11 David Elliston Allen, *The Naturalist in Britain: A Social History* (Bungay, Suffolk, 1976), p. 79.

12 Ibid.

13 'Darwin Correspondence Project, Letter 2781', www.darwinproject.ac.uk/letters.

14 See Robert Mays, *Henry Doubleday: The Epping Naturalist* (Marlow, Bucks, 1978).

15 Darwin, *Different Forms*, pp. 57–8.

16 Ibid., p. 73.

17 Ibid., p. 71.

18 R. Miller Christy, 'The Origin of the Hybrid *Primula elatior × vulgaris* Demonstrated Experimentally in the Field, with Notes on Other British Primula Hybrids', *New Phytologist* (1922), pp. 293–300.

19 R. Miller Christy, '*Primula elatior* in Britain: Its Distribution, Peculiarities, Hybrids, and Allies', *Botanical Journal of the Linnean Society* (1897), p. 183.

20 Ibid., p. 189.

21 Ibid., p. 191.

22 Ibid., p. 196.

23 Oliver Rackham, 'The Woods 30 Years On: Where Have the Primroses Gone?', *Nature in Cambridgeshire*, no. 41 (1999), pp. 73–87, www.natureincambridgeshire.org.uk.

24 'Oxlip', Essex Biodiversity Project, www.essexbiodiversity.org.uk, accessed 2 July 2015.

25 'Rare Oxlip plant collected from College by Great Bardfield parish children', October 2007, www.writtle.ac.uk, accessed 2 July 2015.

26 'Walk Great Bardfield', www.uttlesford-wildlife.org.uk, accessed 2 July 2015.

27 See Kenneth Taylor and Stanley R. J. Woodell, 'Biological Flora of the British Isles: *Primula elatior* (L.) Hill', *Journal of Ecology* (2008), pp. 1098–116; Hans Jacquemyn et al., 'Biological Flora of the British Isles: *Primula vulgaris* Huds. (P. acaulis (L.) Hill)', *Journal of Ecology* (2009), pp. 812–33; Rein Brys and Hans Jacquemyn, 'Biological Flora of the British Isles: *Primula veris* L.', *Journal of Ecology* (2009), pp. 581–600.

28 John Clare, 'The Primrose Bank', quoted in *John Clare: The Critical Heritage*, ed. Mark Storey (London, 1973), p. 131.

29 'Five Easy Ways to Tell Cowslips from Oxlips', www.uksafari.com; 'Oxlip', www.essexbiodiversity.org.uk, accessed 6 July 2015.

30 Brys and Jacquemyn, 'Primula veris', see section , 'Phenology'.

31 'Hayley Wood: An Ancient Coppiced Woodland with a Fantastic Display of Oxlips in the Spring', www.wildlifebcn.org, accessed 15 July 2015.

32 Oliver Rackham, *Hayley Wood: Its History and Ecology* (Cambridge, 1975), p. 157.

33 Oliver Rackham, *Ancient Woodland: Its History, Vegetation, and Uses in England* (Colvend, Dalbeattie, Kirkcudbrightshire, 2003), p. 51.

34 Charles Darwin, *Autobiographies* (London, 2002), p. 78.

35 P. M. Gilmartin, 'On the Origins of Observations of Heterostyly in *Primula*', *New Phytologist* (2015), pp. 39–51.

36 Quoted in Sam George, *Botany, Sexuality and Women's Writing, 1760–1830: From Modest Shoot to Forward Plant* (Manchester, 2007), p. 47.

37 Darwin, *Different Forms*, p. 14.

38 Ibid.

39 'Heterostyly before Darwin: Tracing Early Observations of Primula Floral Morphs', 14 September 2014, blog.biodiversitylibrary.org.

40 Darwin, *Different Forms*, p. 17.

41 Quoted in Michael Boulter, *Darwin's Garden: Down House and the Origin of Species* (Berkeley, CA, 2009), p. 145.

42 Darwin, *Different Forms*, p. 22.

43 Ibid.

44 Ibid., p. 23.

45 Ibid., p. 45.

46 Arabella B. Buckley, 'The Life of a Primrose', in *The Fairy-land of Science* (London, 1880), www.archive.org, accessed 5 June 2015.

47 Tania Marien, 'Educational Wallcharts Teach Less, Better', 28 October 2011, www.artplantaetoday.com.

48 Katrien Van der Schueren, *The Art of Instruction: Vintage Educational Charts from the 19th and 20th Centuries* (San Francisco, CA, 2011). See also Anna Laurent, *The Botanical Wall Chart: Art from the Golden Age of Scientific Discovery* (London, 2016).

49 Darwin, *Different Forms*, p. 28.

50 James Cohen, 'Special Invited Paper: "A Case to Which No Parallel Exists": The Influence of Darwin's Different Forms of Flowers', *American Journal of Botany* (2010), pp. 701–16.

51 *S* refers to style length. The short style (*S*) is dominant to the long style (*s*).

52 'Biologists Unlock 51.7 m-year-old Genetic Secret to Darwin Theory', University of East Anglia Press Release, 12 February 2016, www.uea. ac.uk.

53 Sonia Mermagen, '1995 Purchase of Primula "Blue Jeans" Leads to Discovery of Supergene', www.thompson-morgan.com.

54 Jinhong Li et al., 'Genetic Architecture and Evolution of the *S* locus Supergene in *Primula vulgaris*', *Nature Plants* (2016).

55 Michael D. Nowak, 'The Draft Genome of *Primula veris* Yields Insight into the Molecular Basis of Heterostyly', *Genome Biology* (2015).

56 Ben Haller, a former member of Elena Conti's primula research team at the University of Zurich and now at Cornell University, describes this work for the general audience in a scientific paper titled 'A Tale of Two Morphs', which appears on the Eco-Evo-Evo-Eco Blog; see also B. C. Haller et al., 'A Tale of Two Morphs: Modeling Pollen Transfer, Magic Traits, and Reproductive Isolation in Parapatry', *PLoS ONE* (2014).

57 B. C. Haller et al., 'Magic Traits: Distinguishing the Important from the Trivial [Letter]'. *Trends in Ecology and Evolution*, (2012), pp. 4–5. This term was originally coined by Sergey Gavrilets; for background see Maria Servedio et al., 'Magic Traits in Speciation: "Magic" but Not Rare?', *Trends in Ecology and Evolution* (2011), pp. 389–97.

58 B. C. Haller et al., 'A Tale of Two Morphs'.

59 Jurriaan M. de Vos et al., 'Heterostyly Accelerates Diversification via Reduced Extinction in Primroses', *Proceedings of the Royal Society B* (2014).

60 'Following the Primrose Path: Why Early Botanists May Have Not Dallied Long Enough to Understand the Secrets of Heterostyly', John Innes Historical Collections blog, 12 August 2015, www.collections.jic.ac.uk.

61 Ibid.

62 Anne Secord, 'Science in the Pub: Artisan Botanists in Early Nineteenth-century Lancashire', *History of Science* (1994).

63 A vasculum is a metal case, usually cylindrical, for carrying specimens collected in the field.

64 F. Douglas, *Gardeners' Chronicle* (29 March 1879), p. 401.

65 Ibid., pp. 401–2.

66 Ibid., p. 402.

67 Gertrude Jekyll, 'The Spring Garden', in *A Gardening Companion: A Selection of Articles and Notes by Gertrude Jekyll*, introduced by Francis Jekyll and G. C. Taylor (Ware, Hertfordshire, 2006), p. 197.

68 James Douglas, 'The Auricula, Show and Alpine', *Memoirs of the Royal Caledonian Society*, vol. 1, Part 2 (1908), p. 151, www.archive.org.

69 'Darwin Photographs', www.aboutDarwin.com; 'Darwin's Sandwalk', www.youtube.com, accessed 14 November 2015.

70 Charles Darwin, 'Letters to the Editor: Flowers of the Primrose Destroyed by Birds', *Nature* (23 April 1874), p. 482, www.nature.com.

71 Ibid.

72 Shirley Hibberd, *Field Flowers: A Handy-book for the Rambling Botanist Suggesting What to Look For and Where to Go in the Out-door Study of British Plants* (London, 1870), p. 25. www.archive.org.

3 The Plant Hunter's Primrose

1 E.H.M. Cox, *Farrer's Last Journey* (London, 1926), p. 153.

2 Thomas Mayne Reid, *The Plant Hunters, or Adventures among the Himalaya Mountains* [1882] (Amsterdam, 2002), p. 1.

3 Ibid., p. 2.

4 E.H.M. Cox, *A History of Plant Hunting in China* (London, 1945), p. 36.

5 Ibid., p. 120.

6 'China: Pai Lang White Wolf Bandit, 1913–1914', www.globalsecurity.org, 7 November 2011; see also 'Bai Lang Rebellion', www.wikipedia.com, accessed 13 June 2018.

7 Brenda McLean, *George Forrest: Plant Hunter* (Woodbridge, Suffolk, 2004). This wonderfully illustrated biography is a superb account of Forrest's life and work.

8 Philip Short, *In Pursuit of Plants: Experiences of Nineteenth Century and Early Twentieth Century Plant Collectors* (Portland, OR, 2004), p. 114.

9 Erik Mueggler, *The Paper Road: Archive and Experience in the Botanical Exploration of West China and Tibet* (Berkeley, CA, 2011), p. 1.

10 Royal Botanic Garden Edinburgh, 'George Forrest's Camera Work', www.stories.rbge.org.uk, accessed 23 March 2016.

11 'George Forrest in China', www.youtube.com, accessed 23 March 2016.

12 Mueggler, *The Paper Road*, p. 82.

13 Ibid.

14 Quoted in McLean, *George Forrest*, p. 102.

15 Quoted ibid., p. 119.

16 Quoted ibid., p. 50.

17 The Joy Creek nursery in Oregon still carries it as *P. anisodora*, but others carry it as *P. wilsonii*; see Kevock Garden Plants, www.kevockgarden.co.uk.

18 McLean, *George Forrest*, p. 206.

19 Ibid., p. 85.

20 Nicola Shulman, *A Rage for Rock Gardening: The Story of Reginald Farrer, Gardener, Writer & Plant Collector* (Boston, MA, 2004), p. 8.

21 Ibid., p. 11.

22 Reginald Farrer, *On the Eaves of the World* (London, 1917), pp. 222–3, available at www.babel.hathitrust.org.

23 Reginald Farrer, *The Rainbow Bridge* (London, 1922), p. 184.

24 Ibid., pp. 182–3.

25 Ibid., pp. 185– 6.

26 Ibid.

27 Ibid., pp. 281–2.

28 Cox, *Farrer's Last Journey*, p. 140.

29 McLean, *George Forrest*, p. 151.

30 'How One Shotgun Explorer Helped Shape the Great British Garden', *Yorkshire Post*, 31 August 2017, www.yorkshirepost.com.

31 Cox, *A History of Plant Hunting in China*, p. 179.

32 Cox, *Farrer's Last Journey*, p. 179.

33 Charles Lyte, *Frank Kingdon-Ward: The Last of the Great Plant Hunters* (London, 1989).

34 Quoted in Tony Schilling, 'Frank Kingdon-Ward: Plant Hunter and Romantic', *Journal of the American Rhododendron Society*, XLV/3 (1991), www.scholar.lib.vt.edu; see also 'Frank Kingdon-Ward: Plant Hunter, Explorer and his Travels in Arunachal Pradesh', www.thenortheasttravelblog.com, 11 January 2016.

35 Frank Kingdon-Ward, *In the Land of the Blue Poppies: The Collected Plant-hunting Writings of Frank Kingdon-Ward*, ed. Tom Christopher (New York, 2003).

36 Ibid., p. 125.

37 Ibid.

38 Ibid., pp. 143, 147.

39 Ibid., pp. 133–4. *P. eucyclia* is now known as *P. vaginata* var. *eucyclia*.

40 Quoted in Lyte, *Frank Kingdon-Ward*, pp. 97–8.

41 Ibid., p. 98.

42 Pete Boardman et al., 'Discovering Primulas of Subsection Agleniana', *The Plantsman*, IX (June 2010), pp. 88–92. Available at www.rhs.org.uk.

43 Ibid., p. 89.

44 Kingdon-Ward, *In the Land of the Blue Poppies*, p. 110.

45 Ibid.

46 Lyte, *Frank Kingdon-Ward*, pp. 96, 137.

47 John Hoyland, 'Perfect Primulas', *Gardens Illustrated*, 223 (July 2015), pp. 56–62.

48 'Plants with Provenance: Emma Tennant at the Fine Art Society', www.flint-pr.com, accessed 11 January 2017.

49 Daniel P. Bebber et al., 'Big Hitting Collectors Make Massive and Disproportionate Contribution to the Discovery of Plant Species', *Proceedings of the Royal Society B*, CCLXXIX/1736 (June 2012), www.rspb.royalsocietypublishing.org.

50 'George Sherriff (1898–1967)', www.plants.jstor.org, accessed 12 January 2016. See also John Richards, *Primula*, 2nd edn (Portland, OR, 2003).

51 Pam Eveleigh, 'Looking for Primulas in Google Earth Pro', www.primulaworld.blogspot.com, April 2015; 'The Best Christmas Puzzle', https://primulaworld.blogspot.com, December 2014.

52 'The Plant Seekers Exhibition at the Garden Museum' (photo gallery), *The Telegraph*, www.telegraph.co.uk, accessed 15 April 2016.

53 See, for example, 'Primula alpicola', www.seedaholic.com, accessed 10 February 2016.
54 Royal Botanic Garden Edinburgh, 'Science and Horticulture Must Combine Forces to Save Nature', 2017, www.rbge.org.uk.
55 Ibid.

4 The Well-bred Primrose

1 Antoine de Saint-Exupéry, *The Little Prince* (Boston, MA, 2000), p. 64.
2 Sacheverell Sitwell, *Old Fashioned Flowers* (London, 1939), p. 49.
3 John Richards, *Primula*, 2nd edn (Portland, OR, 2003), pp. 219–20.
4 M. T. Masters, 'On Some Points in the Morphology of the Primulaceae', *Transactions of the Linnean Society of London*, 2nd series, vol. 1, Botany (August 1880), pp. 285–300.
5 Noel Kingsbury, *Hybrid: The History and Science of Plant Breeding* (Chicago, IL, 2009).
6 George Gessert, *Green Light: Toward an Art of Evolution* (Cambridge, MA, 2010), p. 26.
7 'Mr Geoffrey Yates: Primula and Polyanthus', The Alpine Garden Society, Central Sussex Group, newsletter, October 2006, www.agscentralsussex. plus.com; 'The Enigma of the Green Man', www.greenmanenigma.com, accessed 10 May 2016.
8 Margaret A. Webster, 'Floral Morphogenesis in *Primula*: Inheritance of Mutant Phenotypes, Heteromorphy, and Linkage Analysis', PhD thesis, University of Leeds, 2005. Available at www.etheses.whiterose.ac.uk.
9 Sitwell, *Old Fashioned Flowers*, p. 57.
10 Ibid.
11 Graham Rice, 'Hose in Hose Primula: The You and Me Series', www.transatlanticplantsman.typepad.com, 26 January 2010.
12 'The Oak Leaf Primula', www.heronswood.com, accessed 15 May 2016.
13 Webster, 'Floral Morphogenesis in *Primula*'.
14 John Gerard, *The Herball or Generall Historie of Plantes* (1597).
15 Roy Genders, *Collecting Antique Plants: The History and Culture of the Old Florists' Flowers* (London, 1971).
16 Quoted in Ernest Thomas Cook, *Gardens of England* (London, 1911), p. 139, 141. For background on Gerard, Lyte, Parkinson and Turner, see Charles E. Raven, *English Naturalists from Neckham to Ray: A Study of the Making of the Modern World* (Cambridge, 1947).
17 Charles E. Nelson, *A Heritage of Beauty: The Garden Plants of Ireland* (Dublin, 2000), p. 181.
18 Ibid.
19 'Heritage Irish Plants: An Update', www.igpsblogs.wordpress.com, 30 January 2016.
20 Sitwell, *Old Fashioned Flowers*, pp. 49–50.
21 Jodie Mitchell and Lynne Lawson, *The Plant Lover's Guide to Primulas* (Portland, OR, 2016), p. 87.

22 Karen Rexrode, 'A New Primrose for Spring', www.karenrexrode.
typepad.com, 17 March 2015; Jack Sidders, 'Interview: David Kerley,
Owner, D. W. & P. G. Kerley', www.hortweek.com, 16 July 2010.

23 See www.barnhaven.com.

24 Graham Rice, 'Double Laced Polyanthus: New from Hayloft Plants',
www.mygarden.rhs.org.uk, accessed 30 July 2017.

25 Margery Fish, *An All the Year Garden* (Newton Abbot, Devon, 1958), p. 40.
See also Jim Cable, 'Gardens: The Plot that Packs a Punch', *The Guardian*,
20 June 2015, www.theguardian.com.

26 Quoted in Cook, *Gardens of England*, p. 140.

27 Sitwell, *Old Fashioned Flowers*, p. 53.

28 Val Bourne, 'How to Grow Primula "Francisca"', *The Telegraph*, 3 March
2011, www.telegraph.co.uk.

29 Mark Keenan, 'Tigroney Weaves the History of Avoca and the Wynn [*sic*]
Sisters', *Irish Independent*, 12 June 2015, www.independent.ie.

30 'Julius Caesar, Where Did You Come From?', www.igpsblogs.wordpress.
com, 9 November 2015.

31 Jane Maxwell, 'The Diary of Winifred Frances Wynne for 2016',
Library of Trinity College Dublin, www.tcd.ie; see also Janet Wynne,
'An Edwardian Gardener (Strawberry Mystery)', newsletter of the Irish
Garden Plant Society, January 2006, www.irishgardenplantsociety.com.

32 'Kennedy Irish Primrose Collection', www.fitzgeraldnurseries.blogspot.
com, 3 January 2011; Jane Powers, 'Move Over Shamrocks, Here Come
the Irish Primroses', www.onebeanrow.com, 16 March 2012.

33 'The Gifting of a Kennedy Irish Primrose', www.fitzgeraldnurseries.
blogspot.com, 18 March 2011.

34 Margery Fish, *Gardening in the Shade* (London, 1964), p. 52. See also Rachel
Cooke, 'A Gardener's Revenge: Margery Fish's Popular Gardening Book
Bid Farewell to her Late Husband's Lawn and Launched a Career',
www.slate.com, 18 March 2015.

35 Lys de Bray, *Cottage Garden Year* (London, 1983), p. 30.

36 Timothy Clark, *Mary McMurtrie's Country Garden Flowers* (Frome, Somerset,
2009), p. 10.

37 Quoted ibid., p. 13.

38 'Obituary: Mary McMurtrie', *The Scotsman*, 10 November 2003.

39 Plant Heritage: National Council for the Conservation of Plants and
Gardens, www.nccpg.com, accessed 12 June 2017.

40 Caroline Stone, personal communication, 12 September 2017.

41 'The Impossible Garden: Primroses', www.leagardens.co.uk,
5 July 2011.

42 Noel Kingsbury, 'Polyanthus, Polychrome Princess of the Petrol Pump',
The Telegraph, 2 February 2014, www.telegraph.co.uk. Noel Kingsbury,
'Dialectic of the Polyanthus', www.noels-garden.blogspot.com,
15 March 2012.

43 John S. Harrison, 'The Primrose and the Polyanthus', 1976,
www.harislau.co.uk.

44 Martin Wood and Judith Tankard, *Gertrude Jekyll at Munstead Wood* (Phoenix Mill, Gloucestershire, 1996), p. 15.
45 Barbara Shaw, *The Book of Primroses* (Newton Abbot, Devon, 1991), p. 81.
46 Gertrude Jekyll, *Wood and Garden* [1899] (Woodbridge, Suffolk, 1981), p. 296.
47 Ibid., pp. 299–300.
48 Gertrude Jekyll, 'Epilogue: In a Primrose Wood', in *A Gardening Companion: A Selection of Articles and Notes by Gertrude Jekyll*, introduced by Francis Jekyll and G. C. Taylor (Ware, Hertfordshire, 2006), p. 259.
49 For a full discussion of the modern breeding history of the polyanthus, see Peter Ward, *Primroses & Polyanthus: A Guide to the Species and Hybrids* (London, 1997).
50 Genders, *Collecting Antique Plants*, p. 99.
51 Ibid., p. 100.
52 Florence Bellis guarded her privacy, but see the autobiographical account in Angela Bradford's Barnhaven Catalogue.
53 Florence Bellis, *Gardening and Beyond* (Portland, OR, 1986), p. 143.
54 'Barnhaven 1948 Catalogue', p. 16, Ethel Z. Bailey Horticultural Catalogue Collection, Liberty Hyde Bailey Hortorium, Cornell University.
55 Bellis, *Gardening and Beyond*.
56 Ibid., pp. 144–5.
57 Kim Pokorny, 'At her Fingertips: How a Gresham Woman's Touch Gave Primroses New Life', www.loghouseplants.com, 15 April 2015.
58 Bellis, *Gardening and Beyond*, p. 143.
59 Ibid., p. 149.
60 Florence Bellis, 'Hang Up the Shovel and the Hoe . . .', *Spring Yearbook 1965: Quarterly of the American Primrose Society*, XXIII/2 (1965), pp. 57–62.
61 Ibid., p. 62.
62 Bellis, *Gardening and Beyond*, p. 144.
63 'Barnhaven 1956 Catalogue', p. 3, Ethel Z. Bailey Horticultural Catalogue Collection, Liberty Hyde Bailey Hortorium, Cornell University.
64 'Barnhaven 1950 Catalogue', p. 35, Ethel Z. Bailey Horticultural Catalogue Collection, Liberty Hyde Bailey Hortorium, Cornell University.
65 Val Bourne, 'Plants with a Pedigree', *The Garden*, March 2015, p. 56; see also 'History', www.barnhaven.com, accessed 28 July 2017.
66 Florence Bellis, 'First Steps', *Primroses: Quarterly of the American Primrose Society* (Summer 1976), pp. 2–4.
67 Shaw, *Book of Primroses*, p. 82.
68 Judith Sellers, 'Primula juliae: Tiny, Influential *Primula juliae*', under 'Species and Types', www.americanprimrosesociety.org, accessed 5 June 2016.
69 'Barnhaven 1948 Catalogue', p. 14, Ethel Z. Bailey Horticultural Catalogue Collection, Liberty Hyde Bailey Hortorium, Cornell University.

70 'Barnhaven 1950 Catalogue', p. 11, Ethel Z. Bailey Horticultural Catalogue
   Collection, Liberty Hyde Bailey Hortorium, Cornell University.
71 'The Berry Botanic Garden at Twenty-five', www.pacifichorticulture.org,
   accessed 5 January 2016.
72 Pokorny, 'At her Fingertips'.
73 'Rae Selling Berry Seed Bank and Plant Conservation Program',
   www.pdx.edu, accessed 12 May 2016.
74 Quoted from *Gardening Illustrated*, LXI (29 July 1939), p. 486, in Nelson,
   A Heritage of Beauty, p. viii.
75 Clark, *Mary McMurtrie's Country Garden Flowers*, p. 8.

5 The Reckless Primrose

1 Howard Spring, *These Lovers Fled Away* (New York, 1955), p. 42.
2 Margaret Willes, *The Gardens of the British Working Class* (New Haven, CT,
   2014).
3 David Wheeler, quoted on inside front cover of Patricia Cleveland-Peck,
   Auriculas through the Ages: Bear's Ears, Ricklers and Painted Ladies (Marlborough,
   Wiltshire, 2011).
4 Ibid., p. 28.
5 Brenda Hyatt, *Auriculas: Their Care and Cultivation* (London, 1989).
6 'Them Reckless Plants', www.cardunculus.blogspot.com, 8 March 2016.
7 *Dictionary of the Scots Language* (Dicionar o the Scots Leid), www.dsl.ac.uk,
   accessed 12 March 2016.
8 Patricia Cleveland-Peck, *Auriculas through the Ages*, p. 152.
9 Spring, *These Lovers Fled Away*, p. 46.
10 Online Etymology Dictionary, www.etymonline.com, accessed
   11 November 2015.
11 The Gentle Author of Spitalfields, 'The Auriculas of Spitalfields',
   www.spitalfieldslife.com, 13 May 2012.
12 Quoted in Cleveland-Peck, *Auriculas through the Ages*, p. xx.
13 Richard Roths, 'Primula Auricula', *Horticulture*, XVII (8 March 1913),
   p. 322. Available at www.forgottenbooks.com.
14 'A Primula Conference', *The Garden*, XXVII/701 (1886), p. 359.
15 G. C. Churchill, 'Origin of the Auricula', *The Gardeners' Chronicle*,
   1 May 1886, pp. 563–4. This is a summary of Kerner's 'History
   of the Auricula', which was presented at the first Primula
   Conference, 1886.
16 James Douglas, 'The Auricula, Show and Alpine', *Memoirs of the Royal
   Caledonian Society*, I/2 (1908), p. 148. Available at www.archive.org.
17 The Gentle Author, 'The Auriculas of Spitalfields'.
18 See www.auriculasuite.net, accessed 15 March 2016.
19 Willes, *The Gardens of the British Working Class*, pp. 92–7.
20 Quoted ibid., p. 96.
21 Ibid.
22 Quoted ibid., p. 95.

23 Quoted ibid., p. 94.

24 The Gentle Author, 'The Auriculas of Spitalfields', and 'Thomas Fairchild, Gardener of Hoxton', www.spitalfieldslife.com, 2 July 2011.

25 Rowland H. Biffen, *The Auricula: The Story of a Florist's Flower* (Cambridge, 1951), p. 34.

26 Ibid., pp. 111–12.

27 Ibid., p. 20.

28 Quoted in M. M. Mahood, *The Poet as Botanist* (Cambridge, 2008), p. 19.

29 George Eliot, *The Mill on the Floss* (London, 1985), p. 32.

30 Margery Fish, *Cottage Garden Flowers* (London, 1961), p. 60.

31 Tshering Doma Bhutia, 'Exudate Flavonoids in Primulaceae: Comparative Studies of Chemodiversity Aspects', dissertation, University of Vienna, 2013.

32 'Flavone', www.merriam-webster.com, accessed 7 June 2018.

33 Walter C. Blasdale, 'The Chemistry of the Farina Produced by Certain Primulas', *Primroses: The Quarterly Journal of the American Primrose Society*, 11/4 (April 1945), pp. 54–5.

34 Quoted in 'Primulas in Gardens Open to the Public. iv. Caulke Abbey', *National Auricula and Primula Society (Southern Section) Year Book*, 1991, p. 49.

35 Quoted in Cleveland-Peck, *Auriculas through the Ages*, p. 97.

36 Ibid.

37 John Rea, quoted ibid., p. 76.

38 Donald O'Connell, 'Color in the Auricula', *Primroses: The Quarterly Journal of the American Primrose Society*, 1/4 (April 1944), pp. 105–6.

39 Spring, *These Lovers Fled Away*, p. 58.

40 Gertrude Jekyll, *Wood and Garden* [1899] (Woodbridge, Surrey, 1981), p. 307.

41 William Salmon, *Botanologia* (London, 1710), pp. 911–13.

42 Cleveland-Peck, *Auriculas through the Ages*, p. 87.

43 Biffen, *The Auricula*, p. 21.

44 Quoted ibid., p. 22.

45 'Standards of Perfection: Introduction', www.auriculaandprimula.org.uk, accessed 15 April 2015.

46 Cleveland-Peck, *Auriculas through the Ages*, p. 178.

47 Sacheverell Sitwell, *Old Fashioned Flowers* (London, 1939), p. 22.

48 'Standards of Perfection'.

49 Hyatt, *Auriculas*, p. 9.

50 Jack Wemyss-Cooke, 'The Brompton Experience', National Auricula and Primula Society (Southern Section) yearbook, 1991, pp. 45–8.

51 D. T. Fish, 'Auriculas as Border Plants, and for Cutting', in *The Florist and Pomologist, and Suburban Gardener* (London, 1880), p. 153.

52 Ibid.

53 Ibid.

54 Douglas, 'The Auricula, Show and Alpine', pp. 148–53.

55 See 'The Norman People and their Existing Descendants in the British Dominions and the United States of America' (London, 1874).

56 *The Garden*, 11 June 1881, p. 603.

57 John Laurence, *A New System of Agriculture* (Dublin, 1727), Book V, p. 300.

58 Quoted in Cleveland-Peck, *Auriculas through the Ages*, p. 88.

59 Allan Guest, The Auricula: History, Cultivation and Varieties (Suffolk, 2009), pp. 53–4.

60 Thomas Hogg, *A Practical Treatise on the Culture of the Carnation, Pink, Auricula, Polyanthus . . . and Other Flowers* (London, 1832), p. 95.

61 Ibid., p. 128.

62 Ibid., p. 130.

63 Hyatt, *Auriculas*, p. 12.

64 Thomas Peacock, *The Works of Thomas Love Peacock: Including his Novels, Poems, Fugitive Pieces, Criticisms, Etc.* (London, 1875), p. 8.

65 Sitwell, *Old Fashioned Flowers*, p. 25.

66 C. Oscar Moreton, *The Auricula: Its History and Character* (London, 1964).

67 Ibid.

68 Biffen, *The Auricula*, p. 48.

69 Sitwell quoted in Cleveland-Peck, *Auriculas through the Ages*, p. 8.

70 Elizabeth Kent, *Flora Domestica; or, The Portable Flower-garden: With Directions for the Treatment of Plants in Pots; and Illustrations from the Works of the Poets* (London, 1831).

71 Ibid., p. 47; see also Edward Hone, *The Every-day Book or Everlasting Calendar* (London, 1826), vol. I, pp. 675–6. Available at www.books.google.com.

72 Kent, *Flora Domestica*, p. 46.

73 Ibid., p. 51.

6 Cult Primroses from the East

1 See Ayako Nagase, 'Japanese Floriculture Development in the Edo Period (1603–1868)', *HortResearch*, 65 (2011), pp. 1–5. Epigraph for this chapter taken from p. 3.

2 Noel Kingsbury, *Garden Flora: The Natural and Cultural History of the Plants in your Garden* (Portland, OR, 2016), p. 27.

3 Noel Kingsbury, 'The Lost Plants of the Victorian Golden Age', *The Telegraph*, 16 January 2016.

4 Pam Eveleigh, '*Primula sinensis* . . . or Not', https://primulaworld.blogspot. com, accessed 7 June 2018.

5 E.H.M. Cox, *Plant Hunting in China* (London, 1945), p. 53. In Greek mythology, Nestor, an Argonaut and the king of Pylos, symbolized leadership and wisdom, although those qualities were diminished somewhat by his boastfulness.

6 J. Hutchinson, '*Primula calciphila*: The So-called Wild Form of *Primula Sinensis*', *Bulletin of Miscellaneous Information*, 3 (1923), pp. 98–102.

7 A. W. Sutton, 'Chinese Primulas', *Journal of the Royal Horticultural Society*, XII (1891), pp. 99–114.

8 Ibid., p. III.

9 'Arthur Warwick Sutton (1854–1925): Plant Breeder and Businessman', John Innes Centre, www.jic.ac.uk, accessed 13 May 2016.

10 William Bateson, 'Exhibition of a Series of *Primula sinensis*', *Linnean Society, Report of General Meeting*, 18 February 1904, pp. 2–3.

11 For a discussion of possible wild progenitors, see John Richards, *Primula*, 2nd edn (Portland, OR, 2003), pp. 117–18.

12 For accounts with varying details, see Cox, *Plant Hunting in China*, p. 103; *The Gardeners' Chronicle*, 29 April 1902, p. 269; Hutchinson, '*Primula calciphila*'; and Richards, *Primula*, pp. 117–18.

13 Sutton, 'Chinese Primulas', pp. 99–114.

14 Richards, *Primula*, p. 118.

15 Matt Mattus, 'What I Currently Lust For', www.growingwithplants.com, 9 January 2014.

16 Tong-Jian Liu et al., 'Complete Plastid Genome Sequence of *Primula sinensis* (Primulaceae): Structure Comparison, Sequence Variation, and Evidence for *accD* Transfer to Nucleus', *PeerJ*, IV (2016).

17 'Extract from Barnhaven's 1976 Catalogue', www.barnhaven.com, accessed 7 June 2018.

18 Nagase, 'Japanese Floriculture Development', pp. 1–5.

19 Sacheverell Sitwell, *Old Fashioned Flowers* (London, 1939), p. 25.

20 Barnhaven refers to its varieties as 'seed strains' because it grows them from seed, whereas in Japan varieties are named cultivars propagated by the division of plants.

21 Jodie Mitchell and Lynne Lawson, *The Plant Lover's Guide to Primulas* (Portland, OR, 2016), p. 141.

22 Ibid. Mitchell and Lawson's book has an excellent discussion, with photographs, of the various groups of cultivars.

23 Tomoshige Hirota, 'The Sakurasou, the Mountain, and Me', www.sakurasou.jp, accessed 5 January 2015.

24 Izumi Washitani et al., 'Conservation Ecology of *Primula sieboldii*: Synthesis of Information Toward the Prediction of the Genetic/Demographic Fate of a Population', *Plant Species Biology*, XX (2005), pp. 3–15.

25 Yosuke Yoshioka et al., 'Ability of Bumblebees to Discriminate Differences in the Shape of Artificial Flowers of *Primula sieboldii* (Primulaceae)', *Annals of Botany*, XCIX (2007), pp. 1175–82.

26 Yosuke Yoshioka et al., 'Quantitative Evaluation of the Petal Shape Variation in *P. sieboldii* Caused by the Breeding Process in the Last 300 Years', *Heredity*, XCIV (2005), pp. 657–63.

27 Masato Ohtani et al., 'Conservation of an Endangered Perennial Herb, *Primula kisoana* Miq. var *kisoana* on Mt Narukami', *Japanese Journal of Conservation Biology*, XIV (2009), pp. 91–9.

28 Akiko Minosaki, 'Kiryu's Botanical Treasure: Kakkoso', *Kiryu Times*, www.kiea.jp, accessed 11 November 2016.

7 Writing the Primrose

1 Emily Brontë, *Wuthering Heights* [1847] (New York, 1968), p. 420.
2 Meg Harris Williams 'Reversing Perversion: the Byronic Hero in *Wuthering Heights*', www.artlit.info, p.11; Lyn Pykett, *Emily Bronte* (Lanham, MD, 1989), p. 85.
3 Quoted in M. M. Mahood, *The Poet as Botanist* (Cambridge, 2008), p. 43.
4 Quoted ibid., p. 35.
5 Mary Baker, *Primrose Time: A Cornish Childhood Remembered* (Landfall, Cornwall, 1993), p. 11.
6 Shirley Hibberd, *Field Flowers: A Handy-Book for the Rambling Botanist, Suggesting What to Look For and Where to Go in the Out-door Study of British Plants* (London, 1870), p. 25. Available at www.archive.org.
7 Daphne Du Maurier, *Rebecca* [1938] (New York, 1997), p. 30.
8 George Whicher, trans., *The Goliard Poets: Medieval Latin Songs and Satires* (New York, 1949), p. 177.
9 Du Maurier, *Rebecca*, p. 30.
10 Gilbert White, *Gilbert White's Journals*, ed. Walter Johnson (Newton Abbot, Devon, 1970), pp. 289, 358, 427.
11 Francis Kilvert, *Kilvert's Diary 1870–1879* (New York, 1947), p. 25.
12 H. E. Bates, *Through the Woods: The English Woodland – April to April* [1936] (London, 1995), p. 26.
13 Ibid., p. 128.
14 H. E. Bates, *The Watercress Girl and Other Stories* (Bungay, Suffolk, 1959), pp. 9–10.
15 Most of these writers knew the difference between the common primrose and the cowslip, so it is almost certain that the allusions in the texts cited refer to the former (*P. vulgaris*).
16 John Donne, 'The Primrose, Being at Montgomery Castle upon the Hill, on Which It Is Situate', in *Poems of John Donne*, ed. E. K. Chambers (London, 1896), vol. I, pp. 64–5. Available at www.archive.org.
17 Gary Stringer, 'Donne's The Primrose: Manna and Numerological Dalliance', *Explorations in Renaissance Culture*, I (1974), pp. 23–9.
18 Mahood, *The Poet as Botanist*.
19 II, i, 6–15.
20 William Curtis, 'Primula officinalis', in *Flora Londinensis* (London, 1977), vol. VI, n.p. Available at www.biodiversitylibrary.org.
21 Mahood, *The Poet as Botanist*.
22 Edmund C. Blunden, 'An Annotation', www.poetrynook.com, accessed 1 November 2015.
23 Mahood, *The Poet as Botanist*, p. 14.
24 Henry Vaughan, 'Regeneration', www.poetryfoundation.org, accessed 13 June 2018.
25 Mahood, *The Poet as Botanist*, p. 9.
26 William Wordsworth, 'Peter Bell: A Tale', in *The Complete Poetical Works* (London, 1888).

27 John Ruskin, *Modern Painters* (London, 1843–60), vol. III, ch. 12, quoted in Mahood, *The Poet as Botanist*, p. 7.
28 Mahood, *The Poet as Botanist*, p. 46.
29 Quoted ibid., p. 25.
30 Lucy Newlyn, *William and Dorothy Wordsworth: All in Each Other* (Oxford, 2013), p. 274.
31 William Wordsworth, *The Tuft of Primroses and Other Late Poems for The Recluse*, ed. J. F. Kishel (Ithaca, NY, 1986).
32 Mahood, *The Poet as Botanist*, p. 37.
33 Quoted ibid., p. 25.
34 Ibid.
35 D. H. Lawrence, *Reflections on the Death of a Porcupine and other Essays*, ed. Michael Herbert (Cambridge, 1988), p. 335, quoted in Mahood, *The Poet as Botanist*, p. 47.
36 E. L. Griggs, ed., *Collected Letters of Samuel Taylor Coleridge* (Oxford, 1956–9), vol. II, p. 864, quoted in Mahood, *The Poet as Botanist*, p. 21.
37 John Keats, 'Letter to J. H. Reynolds, 3 February 1818', in *Letters of John Keats*, ed. Robert Gittings (Oxford, 1970), p. 61.
38 Keats, 'Letter to J. H. Reynolds, 17, 18 April 1817', ibid., p. 131.
39 Samuel Taylor Coleridge, 'To a Primrose' (1796), *Delphi Complete Works of Samuel Taylor Coleridge* (2013), www.delphiclassics.com.
40 Guido Giglioni, 'Mastering the Appetites of Matter: Francis Bacon's *Sylva Sylvarum*', *Studies in History and Philosophy of Science*, XXV (2010), pp. 149–67.
41 Quoted in Anne Pratt, *The Flowering Plants and Ferns of Great Britain* (London, 1855–67), vol. III, p. 37. Available at www.archive.org.
42 Quoted ibid.
43 Mahood, *The Poet as Botanist*, p. 14.
44 George Monbiot, 'John Clare: The Poet of Environmental Crisis – 200 Years Ago', *The Guardian*, 9 July 2012, www.theguardian.com.
45 John Clare, 'To a Primrose', www.johnclare.blogspot.com, accessed 23 October 2015.
46 John Clare, 'Primroses', *Delphi Complete Works of John Clare* (2013), www.delphiclassics.com.
47 Robert Burns, 'The Primrose (1793)', in *The Poetry of Robert Burns* (Edinburgh, 1897), vol. IV, pp. 100–102. Available at www.books.google.com.
48 Edward Thomas, 'March', in *The Collected Poems and War Diary, 1917* (London, 2004), p. 8.
49 Quoted in Jacek Wisniewski, *Edward Thomas: A Mirror of England* (Cambridge, 2009), p. 121.
50 Edward Thomas, *In Pursuit of Spring* [1914] (Berkeley, CA, 2013), pp. 166–7; Eric Hilaire, 'Edward Thomas's *In Pursuit of Spring*: Historic Photo Locations Revisited', *The Guardian*, 7 April 2016, www.theguardian.com.
51 Thomas, *In Pursuit of Spring*, p. 166.
52 'Edward Thomas, "The Father of Us All"', www.stdavidsny.org.

53   Mahood, *The Poet as Botanist*, p. 46.
54   'Letters from a Lost Generation: Vera Brittain: Roland Leighton
     (Vera's Fiancé) to Vera', in Michael S. Neiberg, ed., *The World War I Reader*
     (New York, 2007), p. 227.
55   May Sarton, *Conversations with May Sarton*, ed. Earl G. Ingersoll
     (Jackson, MI, 1991), p. 67.
56   May Sarton, *Selected Letters 1916–1954*, ed. Susan Sherman (New York,
     1997), p. 150. See Maria Popova, 'May Sarton on the Artist's Duty to
     Contact the Timeless in Tumultuous Times', www.brainpickings.org,
     6 February 2017.
57   Jeff Lunden, 'In *Freshwater*, a Lighter Side of Virginia Woolf',
     www.npr.org, 25 January 2009; *Freshwater* is available online at
     www.novedadesaltera.com, accessed 5 May 2016.
58   Ted Hughes, 'A Primrose Petal's Edge', in *Gaudete* (London, 1977), p. 185.

8 Picturing the Primrose

 1   Rory McEwen, *The Colours of Reality* (Richmond, Surrey, 2013), p. 116.
 2   Margaret B. Freeman, *The Unicorn Tapestries* (New York, 1976), p. 133.
 3   Brian W. Ogilvie, *The Science of Describing: Natural History in Renaissance Europe*
     (Chicago, IL, 2006), pp. 27, 269.
 4   Brian Ogilvie, 'Image and Text in Natural History', in *The Power of Images in
     Early Modern Science*, ed. Wolfgang Lefevre et al., (Basel, 2003),
     pp. 141–66.
 5   Quoted in Patricia Cleveland-Peck, *Auriculas through the Ages*
     (Marlborough, Wiltshire, 2011), p. 22.
 6   Cynthia J. Brown, *The Queen's Library: Image-making in the Court of Anne of
     Brittany* (Philadelphia, PA, 2011), p. 10.
 7   John Harthan, *Books of Hours* (Golborne, Lancashire, 1977), p. 133. *Les
     Grandes Heures* is now held by the Bibliothèque nationale de France, Paris.
 8   Ogilvie, 'Image and Text in Natural History', pp. 141–66.
 9   Apparently a monk in Greece was still using it for identification in 1934
     (see 'De Materia Medica', www.wikipedia.com, accessed 13 June 2018).
10   Patricia Cleveland-Peck, *Auriculas through the Ages*, p. 21.
11   Lys de Bray, *The Art of Botanical Illustration: The Classic Illustrators and their
     Achievements from 1550 to 1900* (Secaucus, NJ, 1989), p. 20.
12   John Ayrton Paris, *Pharmacologia; Or the History of Medicinal Substances*,
     vol. 1 (London, 1825), p. 67.
13   'Helmingham Herbal and Bestiary, circa 1500', www.collections.
     britishart.yale.edu, accessed 11 June 2018.
14   Ibid.
15   'Otto Brunfels', www.botany.edwardworthlibrary.ie, accessed 11 June
     2018. The cowslip was then called in Latin *Herba paralysis*. The German
     name also appears at the bottom: *Himmelschlüssel* (the keys to Heaven).
16   Holland Cotter, 'Art Review: The Renaissance Followed Him North',
     New York Times, 22 March 2013.

17 Agnes Arber, *Herbals: their Origin and Evolution* (Cambridge, 1912), p. 170.
18 Lucia T. Tomasi, 'Gherardo Cibo: Visions of Landscape and the Botanical Sciences in a Sixteenth-century Artist', *Journal of Garden History*, IX/4 (1989), pp. 199–216.
19 Ibid., p. 202.
20 Ibid.
21 'Gherardo Cibo's 16th Century Watercolor Illustrations of Medicinal Herbs', www.linesandcolors.com, 21 September 2015.
22 Bruce Madge, 'Elizabeth Blackwell: The Forgotten Herbalist?', *Health Information and Libraries Journal*, XXVIII/3 (2001), pp. 144–52; see also British Library, 'A Curious Herbal: Dandelion', www.bl.uk, accessed 3 September 2016.
23 P. M. Gilmartin, 'On the Origins of Observations of Heterostyly in *Primula*', *New Phytologist*, CCVIII (2015), p. 46.
24 Ogilvie, 'Image and Text in Natural History', p. 162.
25 Twigs Way, *The Tudor Garden: 1485–1603* (Oxford, 2013).
26 Alexander Marshal, *Mr Marshal's Flower Book, Being a Compendium of the Flower Portraits of Alexander Marshal Esq. as Created for his Magnificent Florilegium* (New York, 2008), p. 12.
27 Ibid., p. 14.
28 Cleveland-Peck, *Auriculas through the Ages*, p. 112.
29 Maud Goodheart, 'How an 18th-century Duchess Helped Sow the Seeds of Modern Botany', *Financial Times*, 22 May 2015.
30 David Scrase, *Flower Drawings* (Cambridge, 1997).
31 William Curtis, *Flora Londinensis* (London, 1777), vol. VI, n.p. Available at www.biodiversitylibrary.org.
32 Jim Endersby, *Imperial Nature: Joseph Hooker and the Practices of Victorian Science* (Chicago, IL, 2008), p. 132.
33 'Thomas Worsey', British Paintings Since about Victorian Times (Roughly 1837 On) blog, 31 January 2009, www.goldenagepaintings. blogspot.com.
34 Catherine Horwood, *Women and their Gardens* (Chicago, IL, 2010), pp. 244–6.
35 Anne Pratt, *The Flowering Plants and Ferns of Great Britain* (London, 1855–67), vol. III. Available at www.archive.org.
36 Nat Williams, 'The Gentle Stranger: A Primrose from England Downunder', www.nia.gov.au, accessed 8 June 2018.
37 Bronwyn Watson, 'Public Works: Edward Hopley', *The Australian*, 12 November 2011.
38 Elizabeth von Arnim, *Mr Skeffington* (1940). Available at www.gutenberg. net.au.
39 John Witt, *William Henry Hunt (1790–1864): Life and Work with a Catalogue* (London, 1982).
40 'Review of *Shakspere's* [sic] *Garden* by Sidney Beisly', *Journal of Botany: British and Foreign*, ed. Berthold Seemann, III (1865), p. 134. Available at www.biodiversitylibrary.org.

41 'The Primrose', *Gloucestershire Echo*, 19 April 1920. Available at www.britishnewspaperarchive.org.uk.

42 'The Art of Agnes Miller Parker', www.savedfromthepaperdrive. blogspot.com, 12 March 2013.

43 Clare Leighton, *Four Hedges: A Gardener's Chronicle* [1935] (Toronto, 1991), p. 11.

44 Clare Leighton, *Country Matters* [1937] (Dorchester, Dorset, 2017).

45 Ibid., p. 44.

46 'Wild Girl: The Artistic Rebellion of Gertrude Hermes', www.anothermag.com, 18 November 2015.

47 Quoted in Shirley Sherwood, *A New Flowering: 1000 Years of Botanical Art* (Oxford, 2005), p. 175.

48 'Foreword', www.brigidedwards.co.uk, accessed 8 June 2018; 'New Works on Vellum by Brigid Edwards', www.botanicalartandartists.com, 12 February 2016.

49 Barbara Shaw, *The Book of Primroses* (Newton Abbot, Devon, 1991), p. 13.

50 Ibid.

51 Robin Lane Fox, 'Brushed with Genius: The Botanical Art of Rory McEwen', *Financial Times*, 23 August 2013; Rory McEwen, *The Colours of Reality*, ed. Martyn Rix (London, 2013); Mark Hudson, 'Flowers and Rock and Roll: The Botanical Art of Rory McEwen', *The Telegraph*, 9 May 2013.

52 'Lizzie Riches Archives', www.thereddotgallery.com, accessed 13 June 2018; 'Lizzie Riches', www.artodyssey1.blogspot.it, accessed 7 May 2016.

53 Hazel West-Sherring, 'The Auricula Collection', www.hazelwestsherring. co.uk, accessed 2 February 2016.

54 Ibid.

55 'The Making of the Highgrove Florilegium', www.botanicalartandartists. com, 9 April 2016.

56 'Reverend William Keble Martin', www.wildlink.org, 15 November 2015.

57 'Obituary: Roger Banks', *The Scotsman*, 20 March 2008.

58 Roger Banks, *Old Cottage Garden Flowers* (Kingswood, Gloucestershire, 1983), p. 20. Bibbesworth is misspelled as Biblesworth in his text. The lines can be translated as 'The primrose and the cowslip appear early on the earth.'

59 Walter of Bibbesworth, *The Treatise of Walter of Bibbesworth*, trans. Andrew Dalby (Totnes, Devon, 2012), p. 93.

60 'Ole Fogh Kirkeby Talks about Harald Slott-Møller's "Spring"', www.youtube.com, accessed 15 October 2015.

61 In 'All in the Detail', *Country Living*, April 2016, p. 100, Kathy Corrigan quotes the botanical artist Lizzie Harper: 'Cowslip leaves are a nightmare. In order to make a leaf look real, you have to get the shadows right, and that depends on where the light falls. It can take five hours to reproduce one leaf.'

62 Irish Society of Botanical Artists and Irish Garden Plant Society, *Heritage Irish Plants: Plandaí Oidhreachta* (Dublin, 2016).

9 The Beneficial, Versatile, Influential, Positive Primrose

1 Oliver Rackham, *Woodlands* (London, 2012), p. 16.
2 Margaret B. Freeman, *The Unicorn Tapestries* (New York, 1976), p. 133.
3 Konrad von Megenberg, *Book of Nature*, www.wdl.org, p. 412. Megenberg wrote more than 30 books, but in this one he compiled the natural history of the world in just eight chapters; it was not printed until 1475.
4 Pliny the Elder, *The Natural History*, trans. John Bostock and H. T. Riley (London, 1855), book 25, section 9, www.perseus.tufts.edu; for the original Latin see Bill Thayer, 'Pliny the Elder: The Natural History', www.penelope.uchicago.edu.
5 Both roots and flowers were used to cure paralysis. Lizzie Deas, *Flower Favourites: Their Legends, Symbolism, and Significance* (London, 1898), p. 43. Available at www.hathitrust.org. See also H. Essenhigh Corke and G. Clarke Nuttall, *Wild Flowers as They Grow* (London, 1912/13), pp. 38–47.
6 Perhaps the *Mayflower*, which brought the first English Puritans to the New World in 1620, was named after the cowslip, although 'May flower' and 'Mayflower' were also used to refer to several other spring blooms.
7 'Prymerole, Prymerose', The Medieval Garden Enclosed blog, 3 May 2013, www.blog.metmuseum.org.
8 The archbishop may have been inspired by Ralph Waldo Emerson's statement in 1844 that 'language is fossil poetry.' See Robert Macfarlane, *Landmarks* (London, 2015), p. 6.
9 John Ciardi, *Ciardi Himself: Fifteen Essays on Reading, Writing, and Teaching Poetry* (Fayetteville, AK, 1989), p. 40.
10 Marguerite Norrbo, 'Sweden's Cowslips,' *Primroses: Quarterly Journal of the American Primrose Society*, 1 (1943), p. 32.
11 Deas, *Flower Favourites*, p. 47; 'Otto Brunfels', www.botany.edwardworthlibrary.ie, accessed 12 June 2018.
12 Deas, *Flower Favourites*, p. 47; Corke and Nuttall, *Wildflowers as They Grow*, pp. 38–47.
13 James Britten and Robert Holland, *A Dictionary of English Plant-names* (London, 1878), I, p. 123.
14 Macfarlane, *Landmarks*, p. 3.
15 George Rousseau, *The Notorious Sir John Hill: The Man Destroyed by Ambition in the Era of Celebrity* (Bethlehem, PA, 2012).
16 Quoted in Theodore Gill, 'Some Questions of Nomenclature', *Annual Report of the Board of Regents of the Smithsonian Institution Showing the Operations, Expenditures, and Condition of the Institution to July, 1896* (Washington, DC, 1898), p. 466.
17 See Sydney Eddison, 'It's Primrose Time', *Fine Gardening*, 72, www.finegardening.com, accessed 13 June 2018; John and Janet Gyer, 'Abschasica Revisited', *Primroses: Quarterly Journal of the American Primrose Society* (Winter 1999), pp. 29–32; Lee Nelson, 'In Search of Abschasica', *Primroses: Quarterly Journal of the American Primrose Society* (Winter 2010), p. 33.

18 'A Primula Conference', *The Garden*, XXVII (25 April 1886), p. 359.

19 Ibid.

20 'Primula Conference', *The Gardeners' Chronicle*, XVII (1885), p. 530.

21 Deas, *Flower Favourites*, pp. 44–8; Corke and Nuttall, *Wild Flowers as They Grow*, pp. 38–47.

22 Manfred Kyber, 'The Key of Heaven', www.satyagrahafoundation.org, 17 December 2014.

23 William Shakespeare, *The Tempest*, V.I, 89.

24 Terri Windling, 'Myth and Moor: Wildflower Season', www.terriwindling.com, 29 April 2016.

25 Hildegard von Bingen, 'CCIX. Primrose', in *Physica: The Complete English Translation of her Classic Work on Health and Healing*, trans. Priscilla Throop (Rochester, VT, 1998). Available at www.books.google.com.

26 David Attenborough, 'Ortus Sanitatis', http://cudl.lib.cam.ac.uk, accessed 1 June 2017.

27 Maud Grieve, *A Modern Herbal* [1931] (New York, 1971).

28 Ibid.; see also 'Cowslip', *A Modern Herbal*, www.botanical.com, accessed 5 April 2016.

29 Carole Guyett, *Sacred Plant Initiations: Communicating with Plants for Healing and Higher Consciousness* (Rochester, VT, 2015), p. 19.

30 Quoted ibid.

31 Quoted ibid.

32 W. T. Fernie, *Herbal Simples Approved for Modern Uses of Cure* [1895] (Bristol, 1995). Available at www.books.google.com.

33 'Local History: The Victorian "Water Cure" Doctors of Great Malvern', www.123-mcc.com, 8 June 2017.

34 See Matthew Wood, *The Earthwise Herbal*, vol. I: *A Complete Guide to Old World Medicinal Plants* (Berkeley, CA, 2008), pp. 400–401.

35 Guyett, *Sacred Plant Initiations*, p. 75.

36 Ibid., p. 74.

37 Ibid., p. 19.

38 James L. Bardsley, 'The Retrospective Address', *The Transactions of the Provincial Medical and Surgical Association*, VI/I (1838), p. 83.

39 European Medicines Agency Committee on Herbal Medicinal Products, 'Assessment Report on *Primula veris* L. and/or *Primula elatior* (L.) Hill, radix', www.ema.europa.eu, 19 September 2012.

40 See Lysanne Apel et al., 'Comparative Metabolite Profiling of Triterpenoid Saponins and Flavonoids in Flower Color Mutations of *Primula veris* L.', *International Journal of Molecular Sciences*, XVIII/I (2017), p. 153.

41 '*Primula verticillata* Forssk.', http://powo.science.kew.org, accessed 3 February 2015.

42 Ibid.

43 Most recipes that mention primulas, intend the common primrose.

44 Leonardo da Vinci, *Leonardo's Kitchen Note Books: Leonardo da Vinci's Notes on Cookery and Table Etiquette*, ed. Shelagh Routh and Jonathan Routh (London, 1987), p. 139.

45 *A Noble Boke* and *The Compleat Angler* both quoted in Grieve, 'Cowslip', in *A Modern Herbal*, www.botanical.com, accessed 3 November 2015.

46 'Simnel Cake', www.bbc.co.uk, accessed 13 June 2018; Lara Cory, 'The Debated History of the Simnel Cake', www.foodepedia.co.uk, 19 March 2012; Glyn Hughes, 'Simnel Cake: What It Is and What's the Story Behind It?', www.lovefood.com, 28 March 2017.

47 A photograph of her cake was released on Instagram (@whispering_earth).

48 Susan Clark, 'Cooking with Primroses', www.theecologist.org, 10 March 2013.

49 Quoted in Bascove, ed., *Sustenance and Desire: A Food Lover's Anthology of Sensuality and Humor* (Philadelphia, PA, 2004), p. 93.

50 Alison Uttley, *Recipes from an Old Farmhouse* (London, 1966), pp. 85–7.

51 Quoted in Grieve, 'Cowslip'.

52 Laurie Lee, *Cider with Rosie* [1959] (London, 2014), p. 72.

53 'Tissty-tossties', Plant-Lore blog, 3 March 2015, www.plant-lore.com.

54 Allan Jenkins, 'Primroses for Mother's Day', 11 March 2018, www.theguardian.com

55 Quoted in John Aplin, *Memory and Legacy: A Thackeray Family Biography, 1876–1919* (Cambridge, 2011), p. 220.

56 'Primroses from Devon', www.ivybridge-heritage.org, accessed 19 May 2015.

57 T. Hull et al., 'Primrose Picking in South Devon: The Social, Environmental and Biological Background', *Nature in Devon*, III (1984), pp. 44–54.

58 'Primrose', Devon Biodiversity and Geodiversity Action Plan, Devon BAP, Version: May 2009, www.devon.gov.uk.

59 Some suggest that 'his' referred to Prince Albert, Queen Victoria's consort, rather than Disraeli, but there is no evidence for that.

60 Tom Crewe, 'Disraeli's Flowery History', www.history.blog.gov.uk, 29 April 2013.

61 Quoted ibid.

62 'Custom Demised: Primrose Day', www.raditionalcustomsandceremonies. wordpress.com, 30 April 2013.

63 A. E. Dangerfield, 'The Primrose', *Gloucestershire Echo*, 19 April 1920. Available at www.britishnewspaperarchive.co.uk.

64 See, for example, George W. Bush's 'primrose path of fancy financial footwork' from his remarks at the Economic Recovery and Job Creation Session of the President's Economic Forum in Waco, www.presidency. ucsb.edu, 13 August 2002; for other examples, see 'Primrose Path' at www.vocabulary.com.

65 Bram Stoker, '*The Primrose Path*', p. 365.

66 'Primrose Path (1940)', www.imdb.com, accessed 13 June 2018.

67 Albert Olaus Barton, *The Story of Primrose, 1831–1895* (Madison, WI, 1895). Available at www.archive.org.

68 See the home page of the Primrose Foundation, www.primrosefoundation.org, accessed 4 April 2016.

69 Mary Russell Mitford, *Our Village* [1824] (New York, 1986), p. 41.

70 Francine Raymond, 'Auriculas: Primulas with Personality', *The Telegraph*, 16 April 2013.

71 Graham Rice, 'A New Red-hot Poker Primula that's Cool as Ice', www.rhs.org.uk, 28 June 2016.

72 'Page Frights! – Black Flowers', www.biodivlibrary.tumblr.com, 25 October 2016.

73 Nancy R. Hugo, *Earth Works: Readings for Backyard Gardeners* (Charlottesville, VA, 1970), p. 44.

74 'On Growing Primroses', *The Selborne Magazine for Lovers and Students of Living Nature*, December 1888, p. 177. Available at www.books.google.com.

75 Ibid., pp. 178–9.

76 Michael D. Nowak et al., 'The Draft Genome of *Primula veris* Yields Insights into the Molecular Basis of Heterostyly', *Genome Biology*, XVI/12 (2015), n.p. See 'Background' section for this personal communication from John Richards to the authors of the study.

77 'The Nation's Favourite Wildflower Vote', www.plantlife.org.uk, accessed 15 October 2015.

78 Deborah Stone, 'Top Five Wildflowers in England, Wales, Scotland and Northern Ireland Revealed', *The Express*, 7 April 2015.

79 For a list of specialist societies, see Associations and Websites, pp. 275–6.

80 'The Country Garden', *Lakeview Journal*, XII/12 (January 2003), pp. 3–4.

81 Josephine Nuese, *The Country Garden* (New York, 1970), p. 76.

82 Two books that explore co-evolution and co-domestication are Jonathan B. Losos's *Improbable Destinies: Fate, Chance, and the Future of Evolution* (New York, 2017) and Alice Roberts's *Tamed* (London, 2017).

83 See Miroslav Dvorský, 'Vascular Plants at Extreme Elevations in Eastern Ladakh, Northwest Himalayas', *Plant Ecology and Diversity*, VIII (2015); and 'Nejkrasnejsi rostliny Ladakhu', www.butbn.cas.cz, accessed 12 June 2018, for a slideshow.

Further Reading

Biffen, Rowland H., *The Auricula: The Story of a Florist's Flower* (Cambridge, 1951)

Buchmann, Stephen, *The Reason for Flowers: Their History, Culture, Biology, and How They Change our Lives* (New York, 2015)

Cleveland-Peck, Patricia, *Auriculas through the Ages: Bear's Ears, Ricklers and Painted Ladies* (Marlborough, Wiltshire, 2011)

Darwin, Charles, *The Different Forms of Flowers Found on Plants of the Same Species* (London, 1877)

Farrer, Reginald, *On the Eaves of the World* (London, 1917)

—, *The Rainbow Bridge* (London, 1921)

Fenderson, Kris, *A Synoptic Guide to the Genus Primula* (Lawrence, KA, 1986)

Gardner, Christopher, and Basak Gardner, *Flora of the Silk Road: An Illustrated Guide* (London, 2014)

Gessert, George, *Green Light: Toward an Art of Evolution* (Cambridge, MA, 2010)

Guest, Allan, *The Auricula: History, Cultivation, and Varieties* (London, 2009)

Irish Society of Botanical Artists and Irish Garden Plant Society, *Heritage Irish Plants: Plandaí Oidhreachta* (Dublin, 2016)

Kilpatrick, Jane, *Fathers of Botany: The Discovery of Chinese Plants by European Missionaries* (London, 2014)

Kingdon-Ward, Frank, *In the Land of the Blue Poppies: The Collected Plant-hunting Writings of Frank Kingdon-Ward*, ed. Tom Christopher (New York, 2003)

Kingdon-Ward, Jean, *My Hill so Strong* (London, 1952)

Kingsbury, Noel, *Garden Flora: The Natural and Cultural History of the Plants in your Garden* (Portland, OR, 2016)

Laird, Mark, *The Flowering of the Landscape Garden: English Pleasure Grounds, 1720–1800* (Philadelphia, PA, 1999)

—, *A Natural History of English Gardening* (New Haven, CT, 2015)

Lancaster, Roy, *Travels in China: A Plantsman's Paradise* (Woodbridge, Suffolk, 1989)

—, *A Plantsman in Nepal* (Woodbridge, Suffolk, 1995)

Losos, Jonathan B., *Improbable Destinies: Fate, Chance, and the Future of Evolution* (New York, 2017)

Mabey, Richard, *Flora Britannica* (London, 1996)

—, and Tony Evans, *The Flowering of Britain* (London, 1980)

McLean, Brenda, *A Pioneering Plantsman: A. K. Bulley and the Great Plant Hunters* (London, 1997)
—, *George Forrest: Plant Hunter* (Woodbridge, Suffolk, 2004)
Mitchell, Jodie, and Lynne Lawson, *The Plant Lover's Guide to Primulas* (Portland, OR, 2016)
Moreton, C. Oscar, *The Auricula: Its History and Character* (London, 1964)
Nelson, Charles E., *A Heritage of Beauty: The Garden Plants of Ireland* (Dublin, 2000)
Rackham, Oliver, *Ancient Woodland: Its History, Vegetation and Uses in England* (Colvend, Kirkcudbrightshire, 2003)
—, *Woodlands* (London, 2006)
Raven, Charles E., *English Naturalists from Neckham to Ray: A Study of the Making of the Modern World* (Cambridge, 1947)
Richards, John, *Primula*, 2nd edn (Portland, OR, 2003)
Shaw, Barbara, *The Book of Primroses* (Newton Abbot, Devon, 1991)
Ward, Peter, *Primroses & Polyanthus: A Guide to the Species and Hybrids* (London, 1997)
Willes, Margaret, *The Making of the English Gardener: Plants, Books, and Inspiration, 1560–1660* (New Haven, CT, 2013)
—, *The Gardens of the British Working Class* (New Haven, CT, 2015)

Associations and Websites

ALPINE GARDEN SOCIETY
www.alpinegardensociety.net

AMERICAN PRIMROSE SOCIETY
www.americanprimrosesociety.org

BARNHAVEN PRIMROSES
www.barnhaven.com

HIMALAYAN PLANT ASSOCIATION (CHRIS CHADWELL)
www.shpa.org.uk

IRISH GARDEN PLANT SOCIETY
www.irishgardenplantsociety.com

KEVOCK GARDEN PLANTS
www.kevockgarden.co.uk

NATIONAL AURICULA AND PRIMULA SOCIETY (MIDLAND AND WEST SECTION)
www.auriculaandprimula.org.uk

NATIONAL AURICULA AND PRIMULA SOCIETY (NORTHERN SECTION)
www.auriculas.org.uk

NORTH AMERICAN ROCK GARDEN SOCIETY
www.nargs.org

PLANT EXPLORERS
www.plantexplorers.com

PLANT HERITAGE
www.plantheritage.com

Associations and Websites

PRIMULA WORLD (PAM EVELEIGH)
https://primulaworld.blogspot.com

ROYAL BOTANIC GARDEN EDINBURGH
www.rbge.org.uk

SCOTTISH AURICULA AND PRIMULA SOCIETY
www.thescottishauriculaandprimulasociety.com

SCOTTISH ROCK GARDEN CLUB
www.srgc.org.uk

Acknowledgements

A work of nonfiction that includes historical research, fact checking, citations and illustrations draws upon the assistance of many people. Emails wing their way around the world, and eventually, voilà, a beautiful book is born! I acknowledge all responsibility for errors of interpretation, phrasing and notation. Reaktion's staff has been relentless in working towards a flawless presentation: I thank Alexandru Ciobanu, Phoebe Colley, Michael Leaman, Howard Trent, Matt Milton, Rebecca Ratnayake and the designers and copy-editors whose names I never learned for their dedication to the process.

Philip Gilmartin, Jodie Mitchell, Caroline Stone, Susan Schnare, Judith Sellars and Margaret Webster. Other readers included writer Sarah Jefferis and non-primrose-expert family members on whom I tested the Introduction: Douglas Fernandez, David Fernandez, Betsy Hillman, Rob Hillman and Jack Whalen. I would like to thank Jane Bain, who scanned images and worked wonders with Photoshop, and Kate Bloodgood, who expertly suggested cuts for a manuscript that was way over the word limit. There is so much to say about primroses . . ..

I thank members of a large, diverse group that includes artists, friends, gallery staff, librarians, permission givers, photographers and others: Alison Alcorn at Crowood Press; Pete Boardman; Paul Buck; Paola Busonera, naturalist and photographer; Chris Caldwell, Himalayan plant expert; Danielle Castronovo, Project Archivist at Harvard University Libraries; Flaminia Cervesi, friend and translator; Xiao Pei Chu, Image Licensing Assistant at Kew Publishing; Lynda Clark, Image Library Manager at the Fitzwilliam Museum, Cambridge; Patricia Cleveland-Peck; Deborah Cooper, Collections Specialist at Cornell University; Paul Curtis, of paulcurtisart.com; Stephen Dast at the University of Wisconsin Digital Collections; Jane Dorfman, retired Exhibitions Librarian at the New York Botanical Garden; Miroslav Dvorský at the Institute of Botany of the Czech Academy of Sciences; Caroline Edwards; David Esslemont, of solmentes.com; Rob Farrow; Kris Fenderson at the American Primrose Society; Peter Fraissinet at the Bailey Hortorium of Cornell University; Tony Frates; Heather Gent; Lorne Gill; Jack Whalen and Heather Hillman; William Gray; Paul Held; Katie Herbert at the Penlee House Gallery and Museum, Penzance; Nancy Hillegas (Roger Banks); Alice Howard, Picture Library Assistant at the Ashmolean Museum of Art and

Archaeology, University of Oxford; Esther Jackson, Librarian at the New York Botanical Garden; Harry Jans; Melvyn Jones, of pennysprimulas.co.uk; David Kerley, of kerley.co.uk; Karen Lawson, Picture Library Manager at the Royal Collection Trust; David Leighton; Susan Lesser ('Wanda'); Dominic Maciocia (Robert Burns); Ewan Mathers; Matt Mattus, of growingwithplants.com; Christabel McEwen; Melissa Minty, Licensing Co-ordinator at Penguin Ventures; Jodie Mitchell, Barnhaven; Lorna Mitchell at the Royal Botanic Garden Edinburgh; Ray Molin-Wilkinson; Pam Moncur, Picture Librarian at the Scottish Natural Heritage (SNH); Milt Moody, webmaster at utahbirds.org; Peter and Renate Nahum; Lee Nelson (*Primula abschasica*); Carol Norton, who mentioned Howard Spring's *These Lovers Fled Away* in the 'Auricula-itis' post on dovegrey-reader.typepad.com; Fiona Owen, of weedsintheheart.co.uk; Irene Palmer; Leonie Patterson at the Royal Botanic Garden Edinburgh; Michael Plumb, website manager at the American Primrose Society; David and Sheila Rankin at Kevock Garden Plants; Wendy Robertson (cowslip fairy); Abigail Rorer, of theloneoakpress.com; Andrew and Michael Shaw, sons of 'Primrose Lady' Barbara Shaw; Randy Smith, Missouri Botanic Garden; Stacy Snyder (taciturnity); David Stuart, of davidcstuart.wordpress.com; Emma Sykes, Picture Specialist at Bonhams; Sharon Sutton, Digital Resources and Imaging Services at the Library of Trinity College Dublin, University of Dublin; Judith Tankard, of judithtankard.com; Martin Walsh, garden designer; Lucinda Warner, of whisperingearth.co.uk; Joy Wheeler at the Royal Geographical Society; Charlotte Whalen; John van Wyhe, of darwin-online.org.uk; Jenny Wildgrass, of RomanySoupArt; Terri Windling, of terriwindling.com; Sarah Wilmot at John Innes Historical Collections; Kotomi Yamamura; 'Zuzu', of garden.org; and those whose names should be here.

And finally, I thank the lovely staff at the Ithaca Coffee Company on Triphammer Road, Ithaca, NY, for nurturing their 'in-house' writer in the early morning – and sometimes in the late afternoon as well – as I followed the primrose path!

Photo Acknowledgements

The author and publishers wish to express their thanks to the below sources of illustrative material and/or permission to reproduce it:

Image © Ashmolean Museum, University of Oxford (Accession number WA.RS. RUD.289): p. 180; from Cicely Mary Barker, *Flower Fairies of the Spring* (London, 1923) – © The Estate of Cicely Mary Barker, 1923, 1990: p. 54; © Barnhaven (www. barnhaven.com): pp. 102, 160; image from the Biodiversity Heritage Library, digitized by Archives of the Gray Herbarium, Harvard University Botany Libraries: p. 65; The Board of Trinity College Dublin: p. 106; © The Board of Trustees of the Royal Botanic Gardens, Kew: p. 177; © Pete Boardman: p. 92; © Pete Boardman (collage created by Pam Eveleigh): p. 27; from Jean Bourdichon, *Horae ad usum Romanum, dites Grandes Heures d'Anne de Bretagne* (Paris, 1505–10): p. 189; Bridgeman Images: p. 206; British Library / Science Photo Library: p. 193; Dr Jeremy Burgess / Science Photo Library: p. 135; Paola Busonera: pp. 40, 42; © Patricia Cleveland-Peck: p. 138; courtesy of Patricia Cleveland-Peck and Crowood Press: p. 132; from Walter Crane, *Flowers from Shakespeare's Garden* (London, 1906): p. 62; courtesy of Crowood Press: pp. 139, 149; courtesy of Paul Curtis: p. 243; from Charles Darwin, *The Different Forms of Flowers on Plants of the Same Species* (London, 1877): p. 66; © Miroslav Dvorský: p. 39; © David Esslemont: p. 212; permission granted by the Estate of Tony Evans: p. 239; © Pam Eveleigh: pp. 90–91, 94; © Rob Farrow: p. 236; Paul Fearn / Alamy Stock Photo: p. 207; © The Fitzwilliam Museum, Cambridge: p. 199; Florilegius / Alamy Stock Photo: p. 96; © Tony Frates: p. 29; © Lorne Gill / SNH (Scottish Natural Heritage Image Library): p. 32; courtesy of Philip Gilmartin: pp. 68, 195; © William Gray: p. 30; courtesy of the Hawk Conservancy Trust: p. 9; from Shirley Hibberd, *The Floral World and Garden Guide*, vol. XI (London, 1876), courtesy of the LuEsther T. Mertz Library of the New York Botanical Garden (via Biodiversity Heritage Library): p. 14; from Joseph Dalton Hooker, *The Botany of the Antarctic Voyage of H. M. Discovery Ships Erebus and Terror in the Years 1839–1843* (London, 1844), via Biodiversity Heritage Library: p. 203; from Nathaniel Hughes and Fiona Owen, *Weeds in the Heart: A Five Valleys Herbal* (Nailsworth, Gloucestershire, 2016) – © Fiona Owen (weedsintheheart. org.uk): p. 226; © Harry Jans: p. 24; © Melvyn Jones: pp. 162–3; © David Kerley:

pp. 12, 13; from Anton Kerner von Marilaun, *Pflanzenleben*, vol. III (Leipzig, 1916): p. 129; used by permission, L. H. Bailey Hortorium, Department of Plant Biology, Cornell University (all rights reserved): p. 117; from Elizabeth Lawson: pp. 6, 18, 23, 51, 59, 60–61, 101, 222; from Clare Leighton, *Country Matters* (London, 1937), reproduced courtesy of the artist's estate: p. 209; Library of Congress, Washington, DC, Prints and Photographs Division: p. 159; from Jean Linden, *L' Illustration horticole*, XXXV/45 (1888), via www.plantillustrations.org: p. 155; permission granted by Christabel McEwen (the Estate of Rory McEwen): p. 211; © Ewan Mathers, *The Cloisters of Iona Abbey* (Glasgow, 2001), sculpture by Chris Hall: p. 223; © Matt Mattus (www.growingwithplants.com): p. 118; from Robert Mays, *Henry Doubleday: The Epping Naturalist* (Marlow, Buckinghamshire, 1978): p. 48; © Medici / Mary Evans: pp. 231–2; © Ray Molin-Wilkinson: pp. 136, 145; © Peter & Renate Nahum: p. 19; National Gallery of Art, Washington, DC: p. 202; © National Portrait Gallery, London: p. 36; The Natural History Museum / Alamy Stock Photo: p. 56; Naturalis Biodiversity Center / Wikimedia Commons: p. 158; stamp design illustrated by Peter Newcombe © Royal Mail Group Limited: p. 185; Newlyn Art Gallery, on loan to Penlee House Gallery & Museum, Penzance: p. 235; © Susumu Nishinaga / Science Photo Library: p. 64; from *Order of the proceedings at the Darwin celebrations held at Cambridge June 22–June 24, 1909* (Cambridge, 1909) – reproduced with permission from John van Wyhe ed. 2002 – *The Complete Work of Charles Darwin Online* (http://darwin-online.org.uk): p. 72; John Palmer (permission granted by his widow): p. 67; courtesy of Peter H. Raven Library / Missouri Botanical Garden: p. 127; courtesy of David and Sheila Rankin (Kevock Garden Plants): p. 25; RM Floral / Alamy Stock Photo: p. 107; © RomanySoupArt: p. 150; © 2011 Abigail Rorer of The Lone Oak Press (www.theloneoakpress.com): p. 81; Royal Botanic Garden Edinburgh: pp. 77, 82, 83, 84; Royal Collection Trust / © Her Majesty Queen Elizabeth II 2018: p. 198; © Royal Geographical Society (with IBG): p. 74; permission granted by Andrew and Michael Shaw: p. 110; illustrations by J. Sowerby, J. W. Salter or J. W. Sowerby for *English Botany* (VII/1129–1130, 1867), via Biodiversity Heritage Library: p. 55; David C. Stuart, 2015: p. 10; photo by Professor John Harshberger, image courtesy of Judith B. Tankard: p. 112; © The Trustees of the Natural History Museum, London: p. 35; University of Wisconsin Digital Collections: p. 133; UPI / Landov / Barcroft Media: p. 143; from Louis Benoît van Houtte, *Flore des serres et des jardins de l'Europe*, vol. IV (Ghent, 1848), via Biodiversity Heritage Library: p. 240; © Martin Walsh: p. 26; © Lucinda Warner (www.whisperingearth.co.uk): p. 229; © Margaret Webster: p. 104; Tim Wright / Alamy Stock Photo: p. 142; Yale Center for British Art, Helmingham Herbal and Bestiary (www.collections.yale.edu): p. 190; Yale Center for British Art, Paul Mellon Collection: p. 170; © Kotomi Yamamura: p. 16.

the work in the manner specified by the author or licensor (but not in any way that suggests that they endorse you or your use of the work), and if they alter, transform or build upon this work, they may distribute the resulting work(s) only under the same or similar license to this one.

Index

Page numbers in *italics* refer to illustrations